INTRODUCING THE OLD TESTAMENT

Student Text
Second Edition

Rev. Anne Robertson

Copyright © 2013 by the Massachusetts Bible Society

Copyright © 2nd Edition 2014

All rights reserved. No part of this book may be reproduced, stored in a retrieval system, or transmitted in any form or by any means, electronic, mechanical, including photocopying, recording, or otherwise, without the written permission of the publisher.

Unless otherwise indicated, Bible quotations in this book are from the New Revised Standard Version Bible, copyright © 1989 by the National Council of Churches of Christ in the U.S.A. Used by permission. All rights reserved.

Massachusetts Bible Society
199 Herrick Road
Newton Centre, MA 02459

Book design by Thomas Bergeron
www.thomasbergeron.com
Typeface: Jenson Pro, Gill Sans

ISBN-13: 978-0-9907212-2-2

SECOND EDITION

Photography Credits

Image #1 (p. 12) Session 1, The Sons of God Saw the Daughters of Man That They Were Fair by Daniel Chester, 1923, image from www.sandstead.com; Image #2 (p. 36) Session 2, Joseph in Dreamcoat, image courtesy of Costumeworld Theatrical, Deerfield, Florida; Image #3 (p. 48) Session 2, God's Covenant with Abraham, Jan Goeree and A. de Blois, used with permission of the Pitts Theological Library, Emory University; Image #4 (p. 64) Session 2, Chorus from Joseph and the Amazing Technicolor Dreamcoat, image courtesy of Costumeworld Theatrical, Deerfield, Florida; Image #5 (p. 81) Session 3, Sabbath Cartoon by Baloo, purchased from Cartoonstock at www.cartoonstock.com; Image #6 (p. 87) Session 3, purchased from Cartoonstock at www.cartoonstock.com; Image #7 (p. 110) Session 4, Virupaksha Temple at Hampi, India, photo by Adam Jones, adamjones.freeservers.com; Image #8 (pg. 191) Session 5, Bleak, Mark Goldstein, www.photographyblog.com/forums/lofiversion/index.php/t1224

This course is dedicated to Emily Barrett, Maybritt Muller, and all other Sunday School teachers and religious educators who have ever brought the stories of the Old Testament to life for a child.

You allowed us to stand with Daniel and experience a faith that made hungry lions lie down at our feet. You showed us that we could go against the mighty Goliaths of our lives and win. You made sure that we knew we could wrestle with God, as Jacob did, and still receive a blessing. You warned us not to be deceived by snakes in fruit trees but then assured us that our God still wanted to be with us, even when we fell for it and sinned.

Especially to Emily, Maybritt, and the Sunday School teachers of the North Scituate Baptist Church where I grew up, but also to all of you who let the great stories of an ancient faith live and breathe—thank you.

TABLE OF CONTENTS

Acknowledgments i
Welcome iii
   Beware the Chronology of this Course v
   Old Testament vs. Hebrew Bible vii
   Introducing <u>Exploring the Bible: The Dickinson Series</u> viii
      The Exploring the Bible Program viii
      The Exploring the Bible Students ix
      The Exploring the Bible Sponsors x
   Our Theological Point of View xiii
   Course Administration xiii
To the Student xv

Session 1: Older than Dirt 1
Session 2: Who's Your Daddy? 31
Session 3: Laying Down the Law 69
Session 4: United We Stand 103
Session 5: Divided We Fall 147
Session 6: Age of Empires 195

continued on next page

TABLE OF **CONTENTS Cont.**

What Now? 240

Appendices

1. <u>What Is the Bible?</u> Session 3 — 243
2. Student Evaluation — 263
3. Massachusetts Bible Society Statement on Scripture — 269
4. A Covenant for Bible Study — 270
5. Help! I Have Questions! — 271
6. Dealing with Difficult Texts — 272
7. Glossary — 273

Acknowledgments

As with the first course in Exploring the Bible: The Dickinson Series, I have to first acknowledge Dr. Charles Dickinson, whose gifts of time, expertise, and treasure have made this entire series possible. You can read more about him on p. x-xi and can watch a brief video about his hopes for this series on the website.

Given the potential minefields of approaching a text that is sacred to multiple faiths, I want to give special thanks to Dr. Marc Zvi Brettler, the Dora Professor of Biblical Studies at Brandeis University, who read through the Student Text with a particular eye toward interfaith sensitivities as well as for the accuracy of the information presented. Those interested in the Exploring the Bible series would probably also be interested in the book Dr. Brettler wrote with Dr. Peter Enns and Dr. Dan Harrington entitled The Bible and the Believer: How to Read the Bible Critically and Religiously (Oxford University Press; September 2012).

I also continue to be indebted to the following congregations and group facilitators who have served as pilot groups to test the effectiveness of both the Student Text and the class sessions outlined in the Leader's Guide: Dr. Ellen Porter Honnet and Jacqui James at the First Unitarian Society of Newton (West Newton, MA); Derek Kotze and Lynne Osborn at St. Matthew's United Methodist Church (Acton, MA); Aurelio Ramirez at the Lutheran Church of the Newtons (Newton, MA); Frances Taylor, Director of Faith Formation at Sacred Heart Parish (Lynn, MA); and Rev. Dr. Thomas D. Wintle at First Parish Church (Weston, MA). They had to deal with this material in its raw, unedited form, and their feedback has been critical to shaping the final product.

Our production team continues their awesome work, from editor Nancy Fitzgerald, copyeditor Jennifer Hackett, proofreader Maria Boyer, designer Thomas Bergeron, to the amazing staff I am privileged to work with at the Massachusetts Bible Society: Jocelyn Bergeron, Michael Colyott, and Frank Stevens. The MBS Trustees are also to be commended for their work in offering feedback on the materials and reaching out to find appropriate places to offer these courses.

In Gratitude,
Anne Robertson

Welcome

I have run into so many people, including some of my clergy colleagues, who say they don't like the Old Testament. Some clergy actually refuse to preach from it and many Christians seem to think that the Old Testament plays second fiddle to the New Testament, or that the New Testament has rendered the Old obsolete. By the time you're finished with this course, I hope you will be able to join me in responding, "Are you kidding me?"

I love the Old Testament. I love the glimpses of an ancient world and the peek into the origins of all things. I love the stories—stories that give us insights into human nature in both its glory and its shadow. I love the eternal themes of relationship through thick and thin, sin and forgiveness, wilderness and promised land, exile and return. I love the poetry, the images, and the characters that spring to life in its pages.

Once I learned to read the Bible seriously but not literally; once I learned that myth and story can often teach "truth" much more effectively than a mere presentation of facts, I found that the Old Testament was as alive and vivid as any of the Hollywood presentations of its contents. Although these primitive texts can sometimes be as baffling as they are beautiful, the more I read, the more I find that my own Christian faith is only a shallow (and often misinformed) shell without them.

So, stop fretting. Come on in. The primordial water's fine. A new world is about to emerge from the chaos.

<u>Introducing the Old Testament</u> is the second course in <u>Exploring the Bible: The Dickinson Series</u>. If you took the first course in the series (<u>What Is the Bible?</u>), then the lesson format should be familiar to you and you can skip over much of the introductory and supplemental material. **Be aware that this course covers a lot more material than the first and you will need more time to do the readings in between classes than you did the first time around.**

If this is the first Exploring the Bible course you're taking, I strongly recommend that you turn to Appendix 1 on page 243 and read the chapter from the first course related to the Old Testament before you begin. That material will give you some helpful perspective on how the Old Testament is organized, how it came to be in its current form, and why different Christian traditions either add or subtract material from it.

Even though this entire course is focused on the Old Testament, remember that this is still only an introduction. When we get to the end of the six sessions, you'll probably know more than you do now about these ancient texts. I've been reading and studying the Bible my entire life and I still discovered new things as I did the research to write this course. But the chances are good that you'll end the course with more questions than when you started. In fact, that is my goal in writing it. Jonas Salk, the medical doctor who invented the polio vaccine, once said, "What people think of as the moment of discovery is really the discovery of the question." You'll learn more about the Bible by uncovering "good questions" than by hearing the "right" answers.

Note that the Bible reference numbers used in this course (i.e., the chapter and verse numbers) reflect the numbering of the New Revised

Standard Version of the Bible unless otherwise noted. As we discussed in the first course, the chapter and verse numbers were added to the text much later and occasionally there are differences, especially between Protestant and Catholic translations and between translations based on the Hebrew Bible and those based on the Septuagint. If you turn to a reference in your study Bible and don't find the right verse, first consult your study Bible notes (which may tell you where variant verses appear) and if that fails ask your group leader.

Beware the Chronology of this Course

Unlike the Old Testament itself, which is arranged categorically, this course takes a chronological approach. Each session will advance across the earliest years of human history, dealing with the biblical texts that represent that historical epoch. At the beginning of each chapter is a timeline, marking important developments, events, and people associated with that era. The dates listed at the beginning of each session are the historical dates covered by the chapter, which encompass, but are not limited to, the biblical books and persons discussed in that session.

Placing biblical stories and events on a timeline is a treacherous process. For every date I pick, six people think it's wrong. What I have attempted to do is to indicate both the approximate time period in which a story is set and also the time period in which the story was written in the form we now have in our Bibles. When scholars of sufficient number disagree about dating, I have tried to indicate that.

Dating biblical stories and events on a timeline is not meant to indicate any particular interpretation of those things. For example, dating the stories of Adam and Eve, Cain and Able, Noah, and the like is not a statement for or against their accuracy as historical accounts. It is simply an indication of the time period in which the stories were set. For example, we are told that Cain presented a grain offering to God. The setting of the story, therefore, had to be after the development of agriculture. Noah is said to have planted a vineyard—that dates the story sometime after the first cultivation of grapes, and so on.

The nice, neat layout of a timeline seems to imply that we know these things—that they are indisputable, easily verified facts. They are not. They aren't pulled out of a hat—they do represent a good amount of research and what credible scholars on each side of the theological spectrum think—but you should know going in that there are competing claims about the dates for almost every stop along the timeline as well as scholars who think that many biblical characters are not historical figures at all.

Then why include dates? Because the stories and texts that came to comprise the Old Testament were not created in a vacuum. We have no way of knowing who the first person was to tell the story of Adam and Eve. But we have it now because someone told it very early in human history and those who came later thought it was important enough to write it down and preserve it for us. The stories give us clues to where those early storytellers lived—they tell of rivers and mountains and locations that we can identify on today's maps (as well as those we can't). And they hint to us of their faith and their motivations in passing the stories on to others.

Whether you approach these texts as sacred Scripture or as historical artifacts, they are the product of particular people in actual places reporting the beliefs and worldviews of both the storytellers and their neighbors. They are a window into a time that we can access in no other way. As St. Paul says in 1 Corinthians 13:12, we see through that glass only with difficulty. The window is not crystal clear. But at least locating the biblical narratives within various periods of known history gives us some sense of the world that is only dimly seen through the biblical glass.

Old Testament vs. Hebrew Bible

One of the first things Christians have to acknowledge about the first portion of our holy book is that the Jews know what we call the Old Testament as the Hebrew Bible. As Jews and Christians dialogue about this set of texts, one of the points of discussion surrounds how Christians should refer to this group of writings. Are we diminishing its importance to Judaism by calling it the Old Testament? Should we use the term "Hebrew Bible" instead?

I have opted to use the term "Old Testament" for the following reasons:

- I once heard a rabbi weigh in on this issue. His comment was that when Christians read the Hebrew Bible, they bring a fundamentally different kind of reading and interpretation to the text than Jews do. In his eyes, the term "Hebrew Bible" should be reserved for those reading the text specifically as a Jewish book. The term "Old Testament," he argued, accurately represented the fundamentally different reading that Christians brought to the text. This rang true for me. Although this course is hopefully accessible to people of all faiths or no faith, the course is part of a three-part series that deals with the Christian Bible. The term "Old Testament" seemed the better choice for our purposes.

- There are also differences in the order and sometimes even the content of the Hebrew Bible and the Old Testament as it is printed in Christian Bibles. Having different terminology allows for those distinctions to be made more clearly.

The issues can be complex, but I hope this makes clear why I adopted the terminology that I did. It doesn't mean this is the only right way to do it—others make different choices for equally good reasons. I was just swayed by these particular arguments and circumstances.

If this is your first course with Exploring the Bible: The Dickinson Series, then continue on to the Introduction to the series that follows and the To the Student section on page xvii. If you took the first course, you've read that material before and you can just turn to page 1 and start thinking about how little any of us really knows about the early Stone Age.

Introducing Exploring the Bible: The Dickinson Series:

Exploring the Bible: The Dickinson Series is a series of three, six-week courses that leads to a Certificate in Biblical Literacy from the historic Massachusetts Bible Society.

Each of the three courses is designed to fit six ninety-minute sessions with a group of eight to fifteen people. The Massachusetts Bible Society provides training, materials, and ongoing support for those who would like to run the program in their local churches or communities. Those leading the courses are not expected to be biblical experts or pastors. They are those gifted and trained to facilitate a warm, welcoming, and open group environment where the material can be presented and discussed with respect for all participants.

The Exploring the Bible Program

Three Courses: A Bird's-Eye View

I. **What Is the Bible?** A broad overview of the Bible, including chapters on how to select a Bible suitable for your needs, how the Bible is organized, how the collection of books that comprise the Bible were chosen, different ways that people approach the text, and what archaeology has to tell us about the text and its stories.

II. **Introducing the Old Testament.** A look at the best-known stories, most influential passages, and unforgettable characters that comprise the Old Testament. What are the primary themes and narratives? What are the characteristics of ancient Hebrew literature and the mindset of people in the ancient Near East? Explore both the writings themselves and the historical contexts that gave them birth.

III. **Introducing the New Testament.** Learn about Jesus as a man, as a Jewish rabbi, and as the Christ of Christian faith. Explore first-century Nazareth, what ancient letter-writing practices can tell us about Paul's letters, and the wild apocalypse of Revelation.

Online Resources

Join us for discussion on the Exploring the Bible Facebook page and follow us on Twitter @ExploreBible and swap questions and experiences with others across the country and across the world who are doing the courses in their local communities. Many of you are asking for the opportunity to take the courses online and we hope to be able to offer that down the road. And you can always check out our website at exploringthebible.org for other news, recommended reading, and to find a course near you.

Exploring the Bible Students

The series is designed for two distinct types of students:

The Casual or Informal Students. The first group is made up of those who might know something about the Bible but have gaps in their knowledge or those who just want to test the waters of biblical studies. These students might want simply to take one of the three courses without doing all that is necessary to complete the certificate program. While it's expected that this group will still actively participate in whatever course(s) they select, there is less work expected of them outside the group setting.

The Intentional or "Extra Mile" Students. The second group represents those who have determined that they really want to do some work to build a strong foundation for Bible study. They might be Christians considering seminary, people of faith who don't know their own Scriptures very well, people of other faiths who want a clearer understanding of the Christian text, or even people of no faith who recognize the cultural and geopolitical influence of the Bible and want to understand it better. The common denominator among this group is that they want to do the whole program, including the "Extra Mile" assignments required to earn the Certificate of Biblical Literacy or Continuing Education Units (CEUs).

We hope each study group will consist of both casual and more intentional learners, and our design includes opportunities in class sessions for those engaging the material more deeply to share what they've learned with the others.

Exploring the Bible Sponsors

The Benefactor

Exploring the Bible: The Dickinson Series is named in honor of its chief benefactor, Dr. Charles C. Dickinson III, a biblical scholar and long-time trustee of the Massachusetts Bible Society. Dr. Charles Dickinson was born in Charleston, West Virginia, on May 13, 1936; was educated there and at Phillips Academy, Andover, Massachusetts; and graduated cum laude in religion and philosophy from Dartmouth College, Hanover, New Hampshire. After serving three and a half years with the US Marine Corps in the USA and Far East, he studied theology and philosophy in Chicago, Pittsburgh, West and East Germany, at Yale University, and at Union Theological Seminary in New York. He received his B.D. (Bachelor of Divinity) and Ph.D. degrees in Pittsburgh in 1965 and 1973 respectively and did post-doctoral study at Oxford University and Harvard Divinity School. Dr. Dickinson has taught in Richmond, Virginia; Kinshasa, Zaire, Congo; Charleston, West Virginia; Rome, Italy; the People's Republic of China; Andover Newton Theological School; and Beacon Hill Seminars in Boston. He lives with his wife, JoAnne, and their son, John, in Boston.

The Author

This series was conceived and designed by Rev. Anne Robertson, executive director of the Massachusetts Bible Society, who also developed and wrote the three student texts and leader's guides. She is the author of three additional books: Blowing the Lid Off the God-Box: Opening Up to a Limitless Faith (Morehouse, 2005); God's Top 10: Blowing the Lid Off the Commandments (Morehouse, 2006); and God with Skin On: Finding God's Love in Human Relationships (Morehouse, 2009). Rev. Robertson is an elder in the New England Conference of the United Methodist Church, is a winner of the Wilbur C. Ziegler Award for Excellence in Preaching, and is a sought-after speaker and workshop leader. She can be found on the web at www.annerobertson.org.

The Massachusetts Bible Society

Founded on July 6, 1809, the Massachusetts Bible Society is an ecumenical, Christian organization that has historically been a place where those across the theological spectrum of belief could unite for a common purpose. At the beginning of its history, that purpose was simply getting a copy of the

Bible into the hands of anyone who wanted one, especially those without the means or opportunity to obtain one themselves. In more recent times, that work has been supplemented by the development of a variety of educational programs highlighting the importance of the Bible for faith, culture, history, and politics, as well as providing a forum for the many different voices of biblical interpretation. Exploring the Bible is a significant addition to those efforts and attempts to continue the historic tradition of being a place where those of many different faith traditions can unite for a common purpose—in this case, biblical literacy. You can find out more about the Massachusetts Bible Society at www.massbible.org.

You

Exploring the Bible: The Dickinson Series is made possible because you have elected to be a part of it. While we believe the course materials are useful in and of themselves, it is the community of students and group leaders who bring those materials to life as you engage with one another in your classes and online. Just by participating, you are helping to raise the level of biblical literacy in our world. You can ensure that this ministry continues by completing the leader and student evaluations for each course, by purchasing the materials, and by telling others about Exploring the Bible. There are also opportunities for you to provide scholarship assistance for future students, to attend training to become a group leader, or simply to offer moral or financial support to the mission of the Massachusetts Bible Society. Our most important sponsor is you. Find out how you can help at exploringthebible.org.

Our Theological Point of View

In the creation of this series there are several obvious biases:

- The Bible is a book that can and should be read by individuals both inside and outside the church.
- Understanding of the Bible is enhanced and deepened in conversation with others.
- The tools of scholarship are not incompatible with a faithful reading of Scripture.
- Diversity of opinion is both a welcome and a necessary part of any education—especially biblical education.

Beyond those points we have tried to give an unbiased theological perspective, describing differences of opinion and scholarship in neutral terms. Although named for and written by Christians, <u>Exploring the Bible: The Dickinson Series</u> is designed to be an educational tool, not an evangelistic tool. The Massachusetts Bible Society affirms that the making of Christian disciples is the job of the local church. These materials are designed either to fit into the overall disciple-making effort of a local church or into a secular environment where people of other faiths or of no faith can gain a deeper understanding of the nature and content of the Bible.

Course Administration

Obtaining Credit for Certification or CEUs

Those wishing to enroll in the certificate program or obtain CEUs for their work must fill out an application and do the work in an approved small-group setting. Those who simply work their way through the materials on their own are not eligible for credit or certification. To find out more or to obtain an application, go to exploringthebible.org/getting-credit.

The Cost

Costs will vary depending on whether you are a casual student (which has no cost apart from the books) or are taking the course either for CEUs or certification (for which there is a fee). Please check our website at exploringthebible.org/getting-credit for more information, current rates, and information on discounts and scholarships.

Keeping in Touch

Go to exploringthebible.org to learn more or contact the Massachusetts Bible Society at 199 Herrick Road, Newton Centre, MA 02459 or dsadmin@massbible.org. You may also call us at 617-969-9404.

To the Student

Welcome to the second of three courses in <u>Exploring the Bible: The Dickinson Series</u>. Most people who decide to study the Bible attempt to do so by just diving in. They get a Bible and start reading on page one, often expecting that it will flow in some kind of orderly succession to the end.

While it's not impossible to study the Bible that way, it may not be the most helpful strategy, because the Bible is a different sort of book. In fact, it isn't even really accurate to call the Bible a "book"; it's more like an anthology of texts, collected in one bound volume, that have become sacred to a variety of religious traditions. Without some understanding of what the Bible is and isn't, conflicts about its contents can easily escalate.

Most of the arguments and conflicts over the Bible aren't really about **what** the Bible says, but about how to **interpret** what it says. At their root, the conflicts represent different ways that people approach the book as a whole and which biblical texts are most important or authoritative, as well as what sort of book they believe the Bible to be. We'll examine a number of those differences in these courses.

For example, the debates about creationism versus evolution aren't about what the Bible says per se. They're about whether what the Bible says should be read as religious truth (and therefore full of metaphor and symbol), as scientific fact (and therefore if the text says "seven days," it means precisely seven twenty-four-hour periods), or as a historical document that describes what an ancient people once believed about the creation of the world.

These courses will allow you to dip your toes into some of the more famous stories and passages of the Bible as you read and discuss parts of the text itself. The broader purpose, however, is to take you up to the balcony that overlooks several thousand years of history and to help you to understand how we got this particular collection of ancient texts into a bound volume called the Bible.

Questions, Please!

You'll probably finish any one of these courses with more questions than you had at the beginning—or at least with a different set of questions. So it's important to see yourself less as a typical student in a classroom and more as an explorer or investigative reporter. Learning to ask good, incisive questions is more important to the learning process than memorizing answers that have been handed to you.

Don't be afraid of your questions and try not to be frustrated if there doesn't appear to be an easy answer. When dealing in the realm of religion (whether that religion represents your faith or not), people often spend entire lifetimes seeking answers and sometimes the only "answer" available will be a variety of opinions. Even on matters that seem like they should have verifiable, factual answers, like "Who wrote this text?" or "When did this happen?" the response, "No one really knows but there are several schools of thought" is more common than you might expect.

As questions arise for you, write them down. Especially if you plan to go on to other courses in the Exploring the Bible series or even other Bible studies in other places, keeping a journal of your questions and thoughts can be very helpful. You may find that some of your early issues are settled later on. At the very least, be sure your question is raised either in your group or in the online forums. If you have the question, you can bet someone else does also, and if it turns out that a lot of people are asking the very same question, we can revise this text to address it for others down the road.

From the second session onward, there will be an opportunity for each person to ask a question about the material at the very beginning of each class, and there is a section at the end of each session in this text to encourage you to think about your questions ahead of that "check-in" time. These "check-in" questions will be noted by your group leader but not immediately addressed, as many of them may be dealt with during the ensuing class(es). You'll also be learning about the various Bible study tools and resources available to you, so that you can seek out your own answers. See Appendix 5 (p. 271) for a list of tools and resources to help you find answers to your questions.

Diversity Helps You Learn

Exploring the Bible isn't designed solely for people of Christian faith. It is our hope that people of other faiths, or even of no faith, who wish to better understand the Christian Scriptures can engage with this series to learn more about the book that has shaped so much of the world's culture, politics, and even geography. We hope that many groups will have a mix of people with many different perspectives learning about the Bible for a variety of reasons.

We learn very little when we're only exposed to thinking that mirrors our own, and we encourage every person using this book for study to find a way to engage others in dialogue. Ideally that's your small group of eight to fifteen people who get to know one another over the six-week period. But if you're doing the study on your own, try to visit the Exploring the Bible Facebook page, @ExploreBible on Twitter, and exploringthebible.org to see what others who are studying the same text are asking and talking about. This will enhance your learning experience.

Pick Your Level of Engagement

Exploring the Bible: The Dickinson Series has two different levels of engagement and you may well have both represented in your group. In fact, class sessions have been designed with the assumption that most groups will have both kinds of students in the same group.

As explained in the Introduction, the series of three courses is designed to culminate in a Certificate of Biblical Literacy and each of the three courses can be taken for Continuing Education Units (CEUs), which might be required by various professional organizations. Students seeking either certification or CEUs are asked to do extra work to earn that recognition. We have called this group the Extra Mile students and at the end of each session in the Student Text, you'll see an additional homework assignment just for them.

We expect, however, that other students will simply engage the course from a sense of general interest. Some may feel that only one or two of the three courses would be helpful to them or that their current circumstances would not allow for doing the extra work. These "informal" students also have homework, but to a much lesser degree. Of course, any informal student is welcome to do the Extra Mile exercises simply to delve deeper into a topic of interest. Several class sessions have time set aside for those who have done the Extra Mile work (no matter to which category of student they belong) to share what they've learned with others in the group.

Whichever group you're in, try not to leave the homework until the last minute. Extra Mile students can always count on several hours per session for their homework, but the informal student homework ramps up from about an hour per session for the first course to almost three hours in some sessions of courses two and three. Plan ahead.

As with most everything in life, you'll get out of this course what you put into it or, as the Bible so aptly puts it, "You reap whatever you sow." (Galatians 6:7) If you're an Extra Mile student, not doing the work will waste your money and cost you your certificate or CEUs. If you're an informal student, you simply won't learn as much and the others in the group will be deprived of the insights, questions, and opinions that you might have otherwise contributed. You came here to learn, so don't shortchange yourself. Do the work.

For the Christian Student

If you're coming to this class as a Christian seeking to enrich your faith by engaging your own sacred text, you'll almost certainly have different kinds of questions than those who want to learn about the Bible for other reasons. Information in this course and others may challenge some of your basic faith assumptions. Be assured that there are literally millions of Christians with a deep, Spirit-filled, Christ-centered faith who have found their faith grounded and strengthened by some of the very questions that once felt strange or threatening to them.

Hang with it. Keep a journal to record your feelings and your questions. Bring them to your specific faith community, raise them on the Facebook page or in your denominational gatherings. Pray about the issues that arise for you. Christian faith is never static. It is a journey during which we change and grow along the way. Sometimes we take a wrong path and have to cut through the brambles to get back on track, and other times we come out of a hard climb to suddenly see the most splendid view.

The questions you have will be your own and you will be the one sorting through the variety of responses to see what resonates in your spirit. The Bible itself is full of people having their faith challenged by the circumstances they face or the information they obtain, and none of them are struck by lightning for their honest searching. If you find yourself in such a place, remember the words from Joshua 1:9: "Be strong and courageous. Do not be afraid; do not be discouraged, for the LORD your God will be with you wherever you go."

Be sure to recognize, however, that the goal of this series is to make the Bible more understandable and accessible to all people, regardless of their faith perspective. If you have people of other faiths or of no faith in your group, recognize and respect those differences in your questions and discussions. Trust the Bible to speak in its own way to those who choose to study it for their own reasons.

For Students Outside the Christian Tradition

While the Bible contains texts that are sacred to other faiths, Exploring the Bible: The Dickinson Series examines the text as it is used in Christian communities. It is more than likely that there will be some in your group taking this class for reasons related to their Christian faith, and their questions and comments will often be quite different from yours.

It is difficult to truly understand the Bible apart from hearing the perspectives of those who turn to this set of texts as part of their faith. At the Massachusetts Bible Society, we recognize that the use of the Bible by Christians has at times been harmful, oppressive, and counter to the very faith Christians claim to represent. We also believe, however, that such uses are not the inevitable result of a Bible-based faith.

We have tried in this book and in the class exercises to present the sacred text of Christians in a way that is welcoming of those who want to know more about it for other reasons. Our goal in Exploring the Bible is educational rather than evangelical. This doesn't mean you won't hear a variety of Christian perspectives and/or debates, but it does mean that you should not feel pressured to adopt the Christian faith or engage those debates on any basis other than their own merits.

Give Us Feedback!

If the Bible is taught in public schools, it excludes the faith perspective. If it is taught in a religious setting, it often either ignores or attempts to discredit secular issues and perspectives. Exploring the Bible: The Dickinson Series seeks to include both perspectives and all kinds of students in mixed groups and with the same study—and that is perhaps our greatest challenge with this material. We welcome your feedback regarding the success of our efforts and encourage you to complete the evaluation at the end of this text. If you don't want to cut it out of your book and didn't receive one in class, you can also download a copy at exploringthebible.org/forms.

R-E-S-P-E-C-T

You are about to engage with others in reading, talking, and learning about the Bible. For some, the Bible is the text that led them to encounter God and so it can have deep and powerful resonance. For some, what seems like a simple question about the Bible can be heard as an attack on everything they know to be true and believe. Others may have experienced the Bible as an instrument of great harm in their personal relationships, or they may have learned about its negative effects in history and politics. For still others, the Bible is a curiosity—a foreign object about which they have no strong feelings.

The conflicts between faith traditions and the conflicts in our culture can easily become evident in your group. You have the chance in this study to model something our culture desperately needs—civil and respectful dialogue about important and meaningful differences.

Don't be a hater. Don't flame the Facebook page or Twitter feed. Don't rant in your group or condemn the perspectives of others. If you find a discussion is raising strong feelings and you don't know how to express them with respect, you can always say, "I'm having a very strong reaction to this and don't know how to express it well." Your group leader can then help move the group forward.

Defining the Era: Notating the Date

When it comes to measuring time, Western culture has often adopted the calendar of Christianity, which puts the birth of Jesus at the center of history. In the Christian calendar everything that happened before that time is notated as B.C. (before Christ) and everything afterwards as A.D. (Anno Domini in Latin, meaning "the year of the Lord"). According to Merriam-Webster, the first known use of A.D. in a system of dating was in 1512.

It is no surprise that other faiths and other cultures have retained their own methods of dating the years, which then becomes problematic in a global culture trying to figure out a common way to measure time. This problem has been addressed by an academic compromise of keeping the year zero as it has been on the Christian calendar, but adopting a more neutral system of describing the years before and after. In that compromise system what Christians refer to as Before Christ (B.C.) becomes Before the Christian (or Common) Era (B.C.E.) and what Christians refer to as Anno Domini (A.D.) becomes simply the Christian (or Common) Era (C.E.).

Because we want this course to be a resource for all who want to know about the Bible—regardless of their religious beliefs—we have adopted the more neutral B.C.E. and C.E. system of annotating time.

Old Testament vs. Hebrew Bible

One of the first things Christians have to acknowledge about the first portion of our holy book is that the Jews know what we call the Old Testament as the Hebrew Bible. As Jews and Christians dialogue about this set of texts, one of the points of discussion is about how Christians should refer to this group of writings. Are we diminishing its importance to Judaism by calling it the Old Testament? Should we use the term "Hebrew Bible" instead?

I have opted to use the term "Old Testament" for the following reasons:

- I once heard a rabbi weigh in on this issue. His comment was that when Christians read the Hebrew Bible, they bring a fundamentally different kind of reading and interpretation to the text than Jews do. In his eyes, the term "Hebrew Bible" should be reserved for those reading the text specifically as a Jewish book. The term "Old Testament," he argued, accurately represents the fundamentally different reading that Christians bring to the text. This rang true for me. Although I hope this course is accessible to people of all faiths or no faith, it is part of a three-part series that deals with the Christian Bible, and so the term "Old Testament" seems the better choice for our purposes.

- There are also differences in the order—and sometimes even the content—of the Hebrew Bible and the Old Testament as it is presented in Christian Bibles. Having different terminology allows for those distinctions to be made more clearly.

The issues can be complex, but I hope this explains why I adopted the terminology that I did. It doesn't mean this is the only right way to do it—others make different choices for equally good reasons. I was just swayed by these particular arguments and circumstances.

OLDER THAN DIRT

Materials you will need for your first class session:

This student text

A study Bible (a Bible with notes, maps, and supplemental information that helps you understand the biblical text and context)

Materials for taking notes

An open mind

Historical Era: Beginning–3000 B.C.E.
Portions of the Bible covered: Genesis 1–11

Timeline for **Session One**

☐ **World Events (Outside the Bible)**

8500 B.C.E.	**Domestication of sheep and goats in the Middle East**
8000 B.C.E.	**First known dugout canoe (Africa)**
7500 B.C.E.	Walls of Jericho built
7000 B.C.E.	Cultivation of foods in the Middle East *Since in the story of Cain and Abel (Genesis 4:1-8), Abel brought gifts from his flocks and herds and Cain brought gifts of agriculture, the story could not precede this date.*
6500 B.C.E.	**First known calendar (marking months on bone)**
5000 B.C.E.	Possible date of Great Flood from geologic evidence
4000 B.C.E.	Grapes and olives are cultivated in the Middle East *Since the story of Noah (Genesis, chapters 6-9) mentions that Noah planted a vineyard, the story could not precede this date.*
3900 B.C.E.	**Climate change creates the Sahara Desert, driving people toward river valleys, especially the Nile**
3600 B.C.E.	**Transition from the Stone Age to the Early Bronze Age**
3500 B.C.E.	**First time-telling device (the gnomon)** **Invention of the wheel**

3000 B.C.E.	**Invention of writing (cuneiform)**
	Invention of sailboats
	First schools (boys only)
3000 B.C.E.	The Ziggurat of Etemenanki built *(Possibly the reference for the Tower of Babel story)*

In the Beginning

Any number of bad essays begin with the words, "Since the dawn of man…." That does not, however, negate the fact that there actually was a dawn for humankind a very, very long time ago. If God had been kind enough to put a time stamp on that moment, we would've been spared a lot of school board debates and challenges about who made what, when, and whether evolutionary processes had anything to do with it. But, alas, we're left with nothing so precise and can only assume that God must either love watching the wild Reality TV we humans have provided on the subject—or that God thought those details didn't matter.

Most of the first eleven chapters of the first book of the Bible (Genesis) belong to a time period that was still figuring out how to measure time periods. The first calendar that we know of comes from Zaire, in Africa, and was merely the marking of the phases of the moon on bone. It dates to about 6500 B.C.E. The earliest actual time-telling device was the gnomon, dating to about 3500 B.C.E., an upright pillar or stick with which people determined the time by measuring the length of its shadow.

The latest story from this period in the Bible (in terms of the events it represents, not in terms of its writing) is the Tower of Babel in Genesis 11. Many scholars think this story remembers the building of the seven-story brick ziggurat of Etemenanki, which was built along the banks of the Euphrates in Babylon somewhere around 3000 B.C.E.—that's about the same time writing was developed. If the students learning cuneiform in the first, boys-only schools (opened in Sumer and Egypt) had wanted to time-stamp their essays, they'd have had to go out and measure the shadow on a nearby gnomon to do it. Tough, since the first very primitive numerical systems were just being developed. It would be another six hundred years before anybody got actual math.

Ziggurat of Ur in present-day Dhi Qar Province, Iraq, Photo by Michael Lubinski

And yet, without even rudimentary mathematics, towers were being built. They must have been as fascinating to ancient peoples as the first skyscrapers were to us, and it isn't surprising that one of the stories recorded about that period in the Bible is about just such a tower.

> **Read Genesis 11:1–9.**
> The story of the Tower of Babel.

The story describes the origins of language—just one story of origins woven throughout these early biblical narratives. In addition to language, we learn the origins of the world itself and how order took control over chaos. We see ancient Israel's depiction of the origins of sin, of different races and cultures, and of the way God started to relate to and make covenant agreements with human beings. Even the genealogies give us the origins of all the important biblical figures that will come later.

What our own scientists and historians tell us about technological origins are the only kind of clues we have to plot these stories on a historical timeline and to discern how early the stories might have been orally transmitted. Noah planted a vineyard. Genesis 9:20 claims that he was the first ever to do so.

Ziggurat

A ziggurat is a stepped platform built in ancient Mesopotamia as part of a temple complex. The place of worship, however, was not at the top, but at the bottom. The top was typically described (as it is in the Genesis account) as having "its head in the heavens." The ziggurat was a divine stairway, built to reach into heaven so that the gods could get down, receive the worship of human beings, and confer any blessings they might be moved to bestow. People did not go any further than the place of worship at the base, which was often a complex of gardens and sacred spaces.

In fact, ancient cities began as large temple complexes, not as places where people lived and conducted anything other than divine business. That's why in Genesis 11 the people build both a city and a tower. The tower is the stairway and the city is the temple where people come to worship whatever gods have descended the stairs.

This is, in fact, exactly what God uses it for in Genesis 11. The people build the city/temple with its tower/stairway and God says, "Oh look! Stairs!" God goes down, apparently disapproves of the entire project, and confuses their speech so they won't do it again.

We know that grapes and olives were first cultivated in the Middle East around 4000 B.C.E., so that gives us a rough placement for the story of Noah, who was, according to Genesis 9:21, also the first drunk.

If we go further back to the story of the first murder in Genesis 4, when Cain kills his brother Abel because God likes Abel's meat offering better than Cain's harvest, we can say only that the domestication of sheep and goats happened in what are now Iran and Afghanistan somewhere around 8500 B.C.E. and the earliest known cultivation of foods was in the Middle East around 7000 B.C.E. There is a debate among food historians about whether the development of bread preceded beer or the other way around. My thinking is that if beer had come first, nobody would have ever gotten around to bread, but that's just me. In any case, they both came very early on.

Cain is the first (mentioned) child of Adam and Eve, so you can see why young-earth creationists are so ADAMant (groan…sorry) that the earth is no more than 10,000 years old. While the weight of all the scientific and historical research says unequivocally that they are wrong, you do have to grant them that things really started to get cranking, civilization-wise, between 10,000 and 3,000 B.C.E.

During this period, human beings had finally figured out how to band together enough that they wouldn't starve or get eaten by whatever leviathans and behemoths were eyeing them from a wary distance. With that new security, people could turn their attention to improving their quality of life, and they invented new technologies that made their lives easier. They began to learn more about the world around them and devise systems to teach that learning to others. They began to take a little time to actually enjoy one another and form the foundations of culture. And they began to pass it all along to the next generation through stories.

Once Upon a Story

It's a busy day in 3000 B.C.E. You invent the wheel while your neighbor is trying to explain how some guy in Egypt cured the king's nostril problem without magic. You're a bit nervous about those folks over in Sumer who have just invented something called a helmet, and are putting this new metal (bronze) on things that seem kind of dangerous. The kids are delighted with the donkey that the next village over just figured out how to tame and now it's a challenge to get them to do their homework, even though school has only existed for a week. You'd like to sow your oats, but that's another two thousand years down the road.

So what do you do? The sun is set, the fire is lit, and you join the others in the light and warmth that keeps the hyenas and lions at bay. Someone pulls out the world's first drum, beginning a slow beat; and the song that joins the beat is a story. There are the stories of the day, of course, but better still are the old stories—the ones you learned from your father and your grandmother, who in turn learned them from their own elders, whose memories still dance in your fires. They were songs about how things came to be, stories about the god who favors your village and people and how that god's story is different than the stories of other gods sung that very night around other fires.

Someday someone will record those stories with this new writing. But not tonight. Not for a long time. Because, when the stories are written, the stories will be preserved, but it will be hard for them to live. Once they are written, some might forget what it means to be a story—that truth is also conveyed in tone and gesture and the context of the telling. They will read the words but forget the music that gave them life.

Of course eventually the stories told around those early fires were written down, perhaps by Moses as tradition claims, or perhaps by a variety of people over time. The stories (or at least some of them) were preserved and now they sit in our laps, trying to live and breathe and dance again if we'll let them.

What We Don't Know

All that historical context highlights two things. First, these stories are old. They define old. Even the writing of them is over two thousand years removed from our day and the stories themselves predate us by some five to seven thousand years. We're talking the period from the late Stone Age to the earliest phases of the Bronze Age.

Second, they're not American stories, not even Western stories. They are from ancient Mesopotamia in the Middle East. Western thought and custom are very different from Eastern thought and custom, and we are not good at comprehending the differences among our cultures even today, let alone the differences that existed seven thousand years ago. If your business takes you to Asia, you'll find that out quickly.

> **Read Genesis 4:1–26.**
> The story of Cain and Abel.

Cain's Wife

A common mistake that people make in reading the Bible—especially the portions that refer to this pre-historic era—is to assume that the Bible is giving us a full, literal, and comprehensive account of everything that happened. This assumption leads to one of the most common questions I get about the beginning chapters of Genesis. Where did Cain get his wife?

Continued on next page

The First Mourning by William, Adolphe Bouguereau

OLDER THAN DIRT

Cain's Wife (Continued)

I am not one to take this early story literally, but I do want students of this course to realize that the setting of these stories is placed in a real geographic area in the context of a specific historical epoch. With that in mind, let's look at the issue of Cain's wife.

From Genesis 1 through Genesis 4:16, the only human beings mentioned are Adam, Eve, and their two sons, Cain and Abel. Because Cain kills Abel, he gets sent packing to the land of Nod and all of a sudden in Genesis 4:17 it says, "Cain knew his wife, and she conceived and bore Enoch…" So apparently the land of Nod (we only know that the Bible says it was "east of Eden") was not uninhabited and other things had been going on while Cain and Abel were duking it out on their side of the Tigris and Euphrates Rivers.

Archaeology tells us that some pretty major things were going on, some of which intersect later with the biblical story. In a couple of chapters we'll look at Joshua's famous battle at Jericho, immortalized in the African American spiritual in which "the walls came a-tumblin' down." Well, guess what? Archaeologists have documented that those fabled walls were built about 7500 B.C.E. The wall around the city of Jericho was fourteen feet high, ten feet thick, and eight hundred yards in circumference. To top it off, it included a cylindrical tower that was twenty-five feet high. That wasn't Adam and Eve playing Legos. That feat of engineering took a whole pile of people, who managed to build a wall and tower a whopping 3,500 years before even the most primitive numerical systems, before writing, before the wheel, and before anybody had devised any means of telling time at all. No wonder it was such a big deal when those ancient walls came a-tumblin' down!

Continued on next page

> **Cain's** Wife (Continued)
>
> I'm not saying the text implies that Cain went to Jericho—Jericho is west and not east of where the Bible describes Eden. The point is, if this monumental construction was going on in Jericho that early in time, those who first heard these early stories knew that there were more than four people on the earth when Farmer Cain killed his brother. Lots more. So many more that Cain's marriage probably didn't even count as incest. These early storytellers were not thinking of us when they told about human beginnings. They were thinking of their listeners, who knew things and thought about things in ways that are now largely lost to us.

These stories are as old as stories get, from a culture about as far removed from our own as is possible, and written in languages that no one speaks anymore. Put this book down right now, go stand in front of a mirror and tell yourself, "Self, you do not have any idea how people thought or lived or understood either God or the world in the Middle East during the Stone Age." Repeat that exercise every time you find yourself pontificating about what is "true" in Genesis 1–11. Hang on; I'm going to go do that myself right now.

Of course there are experts who study these things, and they're generally the first to tell you how little even they know for sure. The reconstruction of an ancient worldview is like a giant puzzle for which we only have some of the pieces. We think we know what we're looking at and then some archaeologist unearths a new piece and we say, "What on earth is that thing? That doesn't belong here!" But of course it does. We just have to rethink what we thought we were seeing.

Almost everyone has that **what-on-earth-is-that-thing** reaction when they read,

> The Nephilim were on the earth in those days—and also afterward—when the sons of God went in to the daughters of humans, who bore children to them. Those were the heroes that were of old, warriors of renown. (Genesis 6:4)

Ummmmm…what?

The Sons of God Saw the Daughters of Man That They Were Fair, Daniel Chester (1923)

This odd little set of verses is a fragment of an ancient Near Eastern myth. Why is a fragment of an old myth sitting here right before Noah reads the weather forecast? Well, why not? There's not the first shred of evidence in the text itself, in literary criticism, in historical or cultural inquiry, or in any other place that indicates these stories are to be read as history textbooks that contain facts and nothing more. The Old Testament has some history in it, to be sure, but no ancient fact-checkers went through and graded the stories for historical accuracy. "But God wrote it!" you say. Well, don't you think God enjoys a good story? Haven't you read fiction to your children that you hoped would teach them something true?

Jesus made most of his points by telling fictional stories called parables. In doing that, he was following good Hebrew tradition that has for millennia taught religious truth through the telling of stories. Those stories may or may not have a basis in real people, places, or events, and the storytellers felt completely free to rework any historical details—and even add their own—in order to enhance the larger "truth" of the story. To do so wasn't making the story false, because they weren't trying to preserve history. They were trying to convey what they understood as the truth about the nature of God and God's relationship with humanity. To Kill a Mockingbird isn't a false picture of racial inequality in 1930s America just because there was never a real man named Atticus Finch. It's one of the truest stories ever told. It just didn't happen—at least not in the exact way that Harper Lee put it down on paper.

We have got to get beyond the mindset that truth equals facts and only facts—and the corollary error that claims that admitting the presence of myth in the Bible is the same as saying that the Bible isn't "true" or that God is some kind of bumbler who couldn't get the facts straight. Myth (defined in its classical sense as a timeless story, steeped in a particular tradition, that presents a particular worldview, belief, or practice) was a primary means of truth-telling for millennia. Poems and songs and stories were the ways that values, morals, and beliefs about the world were shaped and transmitted from generation to generation. To look to them for facts, either in history or science, is to demean them and make them incomprehensible. To try to make the epic poetry of Genesis 1 into science is to insult the poet. Is it true? Of course it's true. But it's true in the way that poetry is true, not in the way that science is true.

And did all those folks in Genesis 5 really live to be eight hundred to nine hundred years old or more? Well, if you want to date the Noah's Ark story to the first cultivation of grapes in 4000 B.C.E., then the oldest man in the Bible, good old Methuselah, could have only recorded his age with that bone calendar to mark the phases of the moon that an observant person in Zaire invented in 6500 B.C.E. That's a lot of bones, is all I'm saying.

These early stories are a treasure-trove, even if some of the treasure is a bit mystifying. They are beautiful and fun and often cut like a skilled surgeon's scalpel to expose the truth about our own human nature. They tell us that God is a creator God who looks at the world and says, "Wow—that's really good!" and that even when we are disobedient— even when we murder our own flesh and blood—God reaches out to protect us from ourselves.

> **For Reflection**
>
> Did you have a favorite story growing up? When and how was it told? In a book? A movie? A relative's tale around the kitchen table?
>
> What is the earliest story you can remember sharing with someone else? Why did you share it?
>
> Did you learn anything "true" from the stories you heard or told?
>
> Has a fictional story ever helped you with a real-life situation?

These stories give us tiny little windows into an ancient world that we can only vaguely imagine; puzzle pieces to be placed in the beautiful and baffling mosaic of the world's beginnings and the origins of kinship, love, pride, and faith. Don't box them into a twenty-first century worldview of facts and science and historical accuracy. They can't breathe there. Look at them in their natural habitat—in the world of the ancient Near East, where myths were truer than facts and stories taught the ways of God to those who knew how to listen.

What We Do Know

While no person alive today can claim to know beyond all doubt the mind of a Middle Eastern Stone Age person, a few people have worked long and hard with archaeology, ancient history, sociology, anthropology, and literature to try to give us some direction. We'll be looking at some of their findings throughout these sessions.

The **Experts**

If you're interested in delving deeper into the minds of the ancients, the material I present here (and in the rest of this course) came chiefly from three sources. The first is a very accessible book called <u>Ancient Near Eastern Thought and the Old Testament: Introducing the Conceptual World of the Hebrew Bible</u> by John H. Walton (Baker Academic, 2006). Walton is a professor of Old Testament at Wheaton College.

The second is much more academic in its presentation but is written by one of the premier voices in biblical scholarship and archaeology of our age, the late Frank Moore Cross. Its title is <u>From Epic to Canon: History and Literature in Ancient Israel</u> (Johns Hopkins University Press, 1998).

The last is one of my all-time favorite books: <u>The New York Public Library Book of Chronologies</u>, put together by Bruce Wetterau. It was first published back in 1990 and I believe it is now out of print, but it's a fascinating listing of what happened—and when—across history and across the world. Mentions of what was invented/built/founded when throughout this course are drawn from this surprisingly fun reference. If you have connections to the NYPL, ask them to publish a new edition, please.

Other helpful sources are listed on the massbible.org website.

The first thing I'd like us to look at from a slightly different angle is… well…the actual first thing: the stories of creation. As you discovered if you took the first course in this series, there are not one but two creation stories in the book of Genesis. The first is the epic poem of Genesis 1 and the second is the more folksy tale of Adam and Eve, which begins in Genesis 2:4. The details of creation differ in these two stories, but if you've been hanging with me through the first part of this chapter, that shouldn't either surprise or trouble you.

But what did those creation stories mean to the actual people of the Stone Age who first heard and told them? What did they think they were saying? What did they see as the lessons to be learned?

> **Read Genesis 1–3.**
> The stories of creation.

God Is a Given

The first thing to bear in mind is that nobody in the ancient Near East was debating the existence of God or distinguishing between the sacred and the secular. There wasn't even a word for "religion" in any of the ancient Near Eastern languages because the existence of a God or gods was simply assumed. The question was not "Does God exist?" but "What does God want?"

The question of what God wanted drove everything from family roles and values to (later) the most complex decisions of kings and nations. If they had had T-shirts in those days, the most popular one would have read, "If God ain't happy, ain't nobody happy." To the mind of the ancients, figuring out what God wanted was the key to human survival. So there are no non-religious stories or people in this period. God(s) and a sacred origin and structure to the cosmos are assumed in Israelite culture and everywhere else. While we will see that in many cases the stories of Israel's God were meant to make a distinction between the God of Israel and the gods of surrounding cultures, there are zero stories trying to convince anyone of the existence of God. It simply wasn't questioned, and we should look elsewhere for answers to our own issues around the matter.

Existence: It's Complicated

One of the overarching themes of the stories in Genesis 1–11 is the theme of origins, and the creation stories kick us off with the origin of the earth itself.

To be, or not to be

One of the things that always baffled me about the story of creation in Genesis 1 was the conflict between what I was taught—that God created the universe out of nothing—and the words of the actual text. "Wait," I thought, "God's not starting from scratch. There's **stuff** there. There's this formless, voidy, primordial soup (Genesis 1:2). Well, where did **that** come from? Who made **that**?"

The reason I had that question was that I am a child of the modern age. To me, physical existence is about matter. If I can see it, touch it, and stub my toe on it, then it exists. I give some ground to make room for the existence of a spiritual realm, where the rules might be a bit different, but in the world of physical matter, to exist is to occupy space.

What I learned, however, was that the ancient Near East had a very different notion of what it meant to "exist." For them, the primordial soup that so troubled me did not exist, even if you could have drowned in it. For them, three criteria had to be met before anything could be said to "exist":

1. It must be separated out as a distinct entity;
2. It must be given a function;
3. It must be given a name.

Let's say I'm an ancient woodcarver staring at a big, long log. I begin to carve out the middle of it just to see what's in there. In a few days I'm looking at the world's first dugout canoe (the earliest one known is from Africa in 8000 B.C.E.). Have I created the canoe? Does it exist? Nope.

It doesn't exist because it has only met the first of the three criteria for existence. It has been separated out from the log as a distinct entity. But I still don't know what it's for and when I try to explain it to my kids I just call it "my log." The kids come down to see what I'm up to and all of a sudden there's a downpour. It rains so hard and so fast that the low-lying area around my log floods. The water is rising and the kids are scared, so I scoop them out of the knee-high water and put them in my log, getting in with them to calm their fears.

The rain continues and in short order my log, with us in it, actually begins to float. I'm fascinated and, clever soul that I am, I begin to see how I might get further out into the river to fish with my log. By golly, there's a purpose for this thing! Ding. Criteria number two is met. By now the kids have forgotten that it's pouring and are filled with the wonder of sitting inside a floating log. My daughter says, "Wow! This isn't a log. This is a cut-out-log-that-rides-on-water!" Bingo. There's a name, however crude, and my canoe now actually exists. Then my son leans too far to the right and we all very quickly learn to swim.

That three-fold understanding of existence—separation, function, and name—can be seen very clearly in the epic creation poem of Genesis 1. Let's look at it more closely:

> In the beginning when God created the heavens and the earth, the earth was a formless void and darkness covered the face of the deep, while a wind from God swept over the face of the waters. (Genesis 1:1–2)

By modern standards we have plenty of existing things in those first two verses. Apart from God, we have wind, we have water, and whatever else might be lurking under the "face of the deep." But the words "formless void" are key. To the ancients those words were the signal that nothing exists. Nothing has been differentiated from anything else.

> ### The Start of the Day
>
> Ever wonder why the day for both Jews and Muslims begins at sundown instead of in the morning? The recurring phrase "And there was evening and there was morning…" at the end of each day of creation in the Genesis 1 account is the reason. I really wish the rest of the world would adopt this. I hate starting the day with getting up. I would rather start it with a leisurely dinner, a cozy fire, and bed.

> Then God said, "Let there be light"; and there was light. And God saw that the light was good; and God separated the light from the darkness. God called the light Day, and the darkness he called Night. And there was evening and there was morning, the first day. (Genesis 1:3–5)

Now we're talking. Or rather, God is talking. God doesn't just create photons here. God separates the light from the darkness that covered the deep we learned about back in verse 2. So now both light and dark are on their way to existence and, indeed, God continues that process by giving them names.

Notice those names, however. The names are not "light" and "dark." The names are "Day" and "Night." The names describe a function and that function is further described in the phrase that echoes through each day of creation, "and there was evening and there was morning." God has not created matter here. God has created time, and as day follows day with the same refrain, God has created days and then put them together to form an entire week. Each day of creation in Genesis 1 has those same three "existence" elements.

The Adam and Eve story in Genesis 2 doesn't have everything so obviously aligned, but the elements can be found there as well. In this story it isn't the mysterious waters that need some differentiation but rather the dust of the ground. Everything that is created in Genesis 2 comes from the ground instead of the water, beginning with the first human being in Genesis 2:7.

We call him Adam, because that's the Hebrew word used in the passage, but the word isn't a name. The word **adam** in Hebrew simply means "human" (there's a different Hebrew word, **ish**, that indicates a male human). But remember that we are at the beginning of language as well as the beginning of time. The reason the word **adam** came to mean human is because it was already the word for soil—for red earth—and in the ancient Hebrew story of the creation of human beings, the human is made from that red dirt. Every time someone speaking Hebrew mentions a human being, the memory of a body formed from the dust of the ground is evoked.

The Creation of Adam, Michelangelo

Remembering that the ground in Genesis 2 is the equivalent of the deep waters of Genesis 1, look at this passage from Genesis 2:9 as this second creation story continues: "Out of the ground the Lord God made to grow every tree that is pleasant to the sight and good for food…" The trees are first separated from the ground and then given functions—beauty and food. Because this is a story focused on characters and events rather than a poem focused on creation itself, there is not the same precision and structure in describing each element that we saw in Genesis 1. But look ahead to Genesis 2:18–20:

> Then the Lord God said, "It is not good that the man should be alone; I will make him a helper as his partner." So out of the ground the Lord God formed every animal of the field and every bird of the air, and brought them to the man to see what he would call them; and whatever the man called every living creature, that was its name. The man gave names to all cattle, and to the birds of the air, and to every animal of the field; but for the man there was not found a helper as his partner.

I love this little section of the story for the things it implies about the nature of God and the creative process. The God of the epic narrative in Genesis 1 speaks and things come to be. Very God-like. Here, however, God is apparently still trying to figure out the details of this new world. God is realizing that the work of the garden is pretty big and poor Adam is going to need some help. Here in Genesis 2, the creation of the animals isn't just the result of God's spoken command. Here it is God's experiment in trying to find a helper for the man.

Moreover, Adam gets to participate in the creation process. God does the differentiation—out of the ground, God forms every animal and bird. But if you remember, that's only part of the creation process. God has a function in mind—God is trying to find a helper for Adam, but they don't have the final element yet. They don't have a name.

How do they get their names? God brings them all to Adam and lets him give them names. This is not Dad letting the kids name the new puppy. This is God allowing human beings to help in the creation of the world. The final step of creation in the Genesis 2 account is handed over to Adam. And Adam does it.

Creation of the Animals, Tintoretto

But there's still a problem. Maybe it was the lack of opposable thumbs, but with all the diversity of animals and birds, nothing in that grand parade of bird and beast produced anything that could help Adam with his garden responsibilities. (Those responsibilities were given in v. 15: "The LORD God took the man and put him in the garden of Eden to till it and keep it." You could argue that Adam is not actually created until he gets that function.)

Since the animal-as-partner thing didn't quite work out, God has another idea. Using some divine anesthesia, God puts Adam into a deep sleep for a bit of surgery. Remember now that in this story the "formless void" from which things are differentiated and created is not the waters but the ground. And the word **adam** means just that—dirt.

The dust of the earth was first differentiated and shaped into the human that we have named from that red soil—Adam. But the creation of humanity wasn't quite complete. The differentiation needed a bit more… refinement. From the dust of the ground we get Adam. From the red soil of Adam we get the one Adam names (and therefore helps create)

> ## For **Reflection**
>
> Think about a time when you created something—maybe a sandcastle, a drawing, clothing, a baby—and think about the following:
>
> What were the steps to your creation?
>
> Were others involved? To what degree?
>
> What had to be in place before you were ready to say it was "finished?"
>
> How did you feel about your creation?
>
> What was the response of others?
>
> How do you think the world was created? Do you see similarities and/or differences to your own creative process?

as "Woman." The Hebrew word for woman is **adamah**—same root and meaning as **adam**, just with a feminine ending to the word.

But what has really been created with the woman? Well, look at the function. She's to join Adam in his garden-tending responsibilities back in v. 15. Her specific function is exactly the same as Adam's. No differing gender roles here. The word for "helper" in v. 18 is not a subservient function. In fact, in many other places in the Bible it is a function that God fills for human beings. Psalm 70:5 is just one of many examples where the psalmist says, "But I am poor and needy; hasten to me, O God! You are my help and my deliverer." That word for help (**ezer**) is the same Hebrew word that is used in Genesis 2:18.

But the assigning of a function isn't quite finished. That happens in Genesis 2:24—"Therefore a man leaves his father and his mother and clings to his wife, and they become one flesh." What has been created here, when all is said and done? A family.

It's My Party and I'll Share if I Want To

Of course Israel's story of creation is not the only one out there and we can make some educated guesses about what the story is trying to convey by looking at how it is different from some of the others. Some people look at stories that are similar across ancient cultures and conclude that when one group met another group they just copied the story or legal code or whatever of the other and put their own name on it. I think that is too simplistic. The books and stories of the Bible were not told in a vacuum.

Imagine that you're with a bunch of friends at a summer barbeque. The host is chatting with several of you and explains that she loves to host barbeques because of the wonderful times she had at her grandmother's barbeques growing up. She tells about how fabulous a cook her grandmother was and laughs at how frustrated her grandfather was because he could never manage to light the charcoal properly.

Someone else responds, "Yeah, I was always envious of my friends who were always grilling out back, but my parents had a bad experience with a fire once and they never would let me go. So now I go to every barbeque I can." A third person responds, "I just love the way food tastes when it's been cooked over an open fire. Reminds me of my old camping days."

You heard three stories about barbeques, but they did not spring up on their own. They were told in the context of the stories of others, each person showing what made their own story, background, and personality unique by comparison. Their own family stories existed before they met each other—everyone had independent experiences with barbeques, but hearing the stories of others shaped the particular way each one told about those experiences.

Ancient stories are like that. Everybody is at the barbeque. Everybody is in this wide, wonderful world and trying to make sense of where it came from, why people can't fly like birds and birds can't run like cheetahs, and why any of it is here in the first place. Ideas grow and those ideas are told as stories both so that people will remember them and because life is, at its heart, the story of who we are. And then we meet others. We tell our story of how things came to be and this new person responds with a twist. We adjust our story to highlight our differences, and life's grand barbeque is on.

The surrounding cultures in the ancient Near East—the Sumerians, the Egyptians, the Hittites, the Akkadians, and others—all had their own stories to tell. And when the ancient Israelites heard them, they responded with their own versions—"Well, in my family, this is how it happened..." We learn from these stories that the ancient Hebrews shared a common worldview with their neighbors (as we saw in the question of what it means to exist) and how they set themselves and their God apart.

My God's Cooler than Your God

When comparing Israel's creation stories to those of others in the region, one element stands out right away. In Israel's story, God has no origin. God simply is, and the ensuing creation of the world is a calm, relatively ordered process. That is not the case anywhere else.

The creation stories from surrounding cultures begin with an ancient battle with great monsters. Somebody wins and somebody loses and the losers are killed, dismembered, disenfranchised, eventually becoming a variety of gods and other elements of the cosmos. It is gods in the plural for the surrounding cultures, and a kind of divine council ends up being established in order for all those deities to try to keep the chaos of those divine battles from returning. That's the primary function of the gods—to maintain order and keep the world from un-creating itself, from slipping back into that undifferentiated chaos where nothing really exists.

One of the best-known stories of this type comes from Akkadia (Babylon) and is called **Enuma Elish** from the first two words of the text. It dates to the second millennium B.C.E. and was written on seven clay tablets. It was most likely a ritual story, used at the celebration of the Babylonian new year.

The first tablet begins this way:

> When heaven above was not yet named
> Nor earth below pronounced by name,
> Apsu, the first one, their begetter
> And maker Tiamat, who bore them all,
> Had mixed their waters together,
> But had not formed pastures, nor discovered reed-beds;
> When yet no gods were manifest,
> Nor names pronounced, nor destinies decreed,
> Then gods were born within them.[1]

Cuneiform Tablet of the Enuma Elish

---

[1] Translation by Stephanie Dalley in "Myth from Mesopotamia," in the World's Classics series, Oxford University Press, 1991.

You have primordial waters as in Genesis, but here they are personified. Apsu represents the fresh water and Tiamat the salt water. It is clear they are not deities from the last line. In Genesis there is simply water and God is already there, ready to work with it.

In the Babylonian poem we can see some of the same Genesis worldview about what it means to exist. The **Enuma Elish** points out that things had no name and there was no distinction in the waters—they were mingled together. But we also hear the distinctive statement from Israel's story that God is not a created being. God was before anything else. For Israel, God has no origin—God simply is.

As the Babylonian epic moves along, gods begin to appear in the belly of Tiamat. Those gods cause trouble, a cosmic battle ensues, Apsu is killed, and Tiamat creates eleven monsters to help her take revenge. Despite the monsters, Tiamat loses the battle and is cut in half. Those halves become the earth and sky, and the gods who won the battle take over. Marduk is chief of the divine council now and he kills Tiamat's husband, using his blood to create humanity. Of course, to exist those humans need a function. In Babylon's story, that function is to serve the gods. This kind of divine chaos is nowhere to be found in Genesis.

We also see a distinction in the function of human beings. The Babylonian story stresses that human beings were created to serve the gods. That's especially handy if you're a nation with a divine king (as Babylon was) who would like to keep his subjects in line. The yearly recital of the **Enuma Elish** reminded the people that to serve the king of ancient Babylon was to serve the gods, which was the reason you were created.

Tiamat (left) Battling Marduk (right) in Enuma Elish

But when nomadic Israel (which rejected any form of kingship in its early history) heard the Babylonian story at the barbeque, they made their own story quite plain. In their family story, human beings were created to till and keep the garden of earth. **Their** ancestors actually **help** God with the creative process, and their purpose on earth is to enjoy one another—to be fruitful and multiply—in kinship groups.

Genesis 3 makes clear that God has some expectations of these new humans—there isn't the sense that humans are somehow on par with God's divinity. But the God of Israel isn't a tyrant. This is a relational God who joins creation in the cool of the day for a garden walk (Genesis 3:8).

This is a God who sits back and says, "Hmmm…what sort of partner would be best for this man I made? How about this, ummm—what did you call it, Adam? An elephant? No? A duck? Oh, I know—here, Adam, how about you take a little nap."

Israel's story is vastly different from the bloody battles, the winners and losers, that we hear about in other stories of the same period. This is the story of a secure God with no competition who can merely speak a world into being. In the stories of other cultures, the gods consult with one another in a divine council. In the stories of Israel, God consults with human beings—a theme that will continue throughout the Old Testament, especially with God's new best friend, Abraham.

Homework (All Students)

The Old Testament is long and covers a period of several thousand years. Relative to that time frame, the reading doesn't take long at all. But this course has significantly more reading in between sessions than the first course did. Plan your time accordingly.

☐ Read through all of the Session 1 Student Text, including the Bible passage assignments in the clear boxes.

☐ Read through all of the Session 2 Student Text, including the Bible passage assignments in the clear boxes.

☐ Answer the questions in the Preparation for Check-In on page 66.

Extra Mile (CEU and Certificate Students)

☐ Read the story of Jacob's reconciliation with Esau in Genesis 32:3–33:17.

☐ Read the parable of the Prodigal Son in Luke 15:11–32.

☐ In an essay of five hundred to seven hundred words, reflect on the following questions:

- What are the similarities in these stories?
- What are the differences?
- Do you think Jesus might have been thinking about Jacob and Esau when he told this parable?
- What does each story teach about the nature of God and reconciliation?

WHO'S YOUR DADDY?

Materials you will need for your second class session:

This student text

Your study Bible

Materials for taking notes

Your responses to the check-in questions on p. 66

Historical Era: 2999–1800 B.C.E.
Portions of the Bible covered: Genesis 2–50

Timeline for **Session Two**

Note: Every one of these dates is approximate and, in most cases, disputed. A new archaeological discovery could change any one of them, and dating of the finds we do have is usually not exact. Use these dates to get a general sense of what is happening in the time frame.

☐ **World Events (Outside the Bible)**	
2950 B.C.E.	**Work on the first dam begins in Egypt**
2900 B.C.E.	**Invention of glass** **First use of papyrus**
2874 B.C.E.	**Development of the first 365-day calendar**
2750 B.C.E.	City of Tyre founded. The city of Tyre features prominently in many biblical accounts and its founding is indicative of the time that Phoenicians settled along what is now the Syrian coast. These peoples are the ancestors of those who became known in the Bible as the Philistines.
2737 B.C.E.	**Invention of tea as a beverage (China)**
2700 B.C.E.	**Construction of Stonehenge begins and continues for several centuries**
2613 B.C.E.	**The Sphinx is built**
2600 B.C.E.	**Domestication of camels and horses**
2550 B.C.E.	**Great Pyramid of Giza completed**
2474 B.C.E.	Golden Age of the city of Ur begins. Ur is the city that eventually gave birth to Abraham. It was located at the mouth of the Euphrates on the Persian Gulf in today's Iraq.

2400 B.C.E.	**Invention of mathematics in Sumer**
2300 B.C.E.	**First organized courier service developed in Egypt**
2240 B.C.E.	The city of Akkad displaces Memphis as the world's largest city. Located somewhere along the Tigris River, its exact location remains unknown. For many years the only known mention of this city was in Genesis 10:10. Later discoveries of Sumerian cuneiform texts revealed its importance in the ancient world.
2150 B.C.E.	Gilgamesh epic written. This epic, named for an ancient king of Sumer, contains a narrative of a great flood with a man who escaped in a boat.
2104 B.C.E.	Dating of the Great Flood according to the Hebrew Calendar
2000 B.C.E.	Setting for the life of Abraham, Isaac, and Jacob
1877 B.C.E.	Destruction of the Cities of the Plain. This would have included the biblical cities of Sodom and Gomorrah. Others have suggested a much earlier date with two scholars claiming it occurred at 4:30 am on June 29, 3123 B.C.E.
1800 B.C.E.	**Invention of the Alphabet**

Fast Forward

Once we're done with the Tower of Babel story in Genesis 11:9, the biblical text fast-forwards about a thousand years by means of a long genealogy. It begins with Noah's son Shem and moves with a single purpose—to get us to the prime mover of Judaism, Christianity, and Islam: Abraham.

With just a listing of names, you'd think not much was going on in the world during that thousand years. But, of course, there was. During the years between Babel and Abraham, the Britons built Stonehenge, the Sumerians invented math, and metalworkers in Mesopotamia discovered glass.

All of that was peanuts, however, compared to what was happening in Egypt. This was the period that saw the building of the pyramids at Giza, the carving of the Sphinx, the construction of the earliest known dam (Sadd el-Kafara on the Nile), the first use of papyrus, the development of the first 365-day calendar, and the first surgical procedures. The Egyptians did it all, and as the pièce de résistance, in 2600 B.C.E. they also invented pancakes. Go, Egypt!

I mention all of the activity in Egypt because Egypt has a significant role in the narratives of the rest of Genesis and beyond. Abraham and his wife, Sarah, go to Egypt during a famine. They have an Egyptian slave named Hagar, who becomes the mother of Abraham's first-born son, Ishmael, whom Muslims look to as the ancestor of Muhammad.

The Great Sphinx of Giza, Giza, Egypt

Abraham's great-grandsons get mad at their little brother, Joseph, tear up his amazing technicolor dreamcoat, and sell him to a slave trader who sells Joseph to an Egyptian household. A great story and a great musical ensue. Then a famine hits Canaan again, and all of Joseph's family heads back to Egypt, the only place around with any food. The family settles there until they become so numerous that the Egyptians are afraid of them and enslave them. Four hundred years go by and then the biblical story is ready for Moses to come to the rescue and lead them out of Egypt and back home. Egypt matters and will continue to play a role in Israelite history throughout the Old Testament.

You'd think a relatively precise date for these stories could be established, since they're filled with the names of places and kings and events. But since those who wrote these stories down lived long after the events described, the accounts are full of anachronisms. The writers described peoples and places as they were at the time of the writing, not as they were at the time of the events being discussed. Not one of the kings mentioned is known to historians.

About That **Dreamcoat**

Don't tell the Broadway cast of <u>Joseph and the Amazing Technicolor Dreamcoat</u>, but the special robe that Jacob had made for his favorite son, Joseph, may not have been a "coat of many colours" as the King James Version of the Bible describes it (Genesis 37:3). The translation of the original Hebrew (**kethoneth passim**) is disputed. It might have been many-colored, but the phrase could also be translated "a full-sleeved robe," "a coat reaching to his feet," "an ornamental tunic," a "silk robe," or "a fine, woolen cloak."

Whatever it was, it set Joseph apart as dad's favorite son—which didn't endear him to his older brothers.

Joseph in Dreamcoat

The dates of two events can be roughly guessed at from findings in archaeology—the destruction of Sodom and Gomorrah, and Joseph's rise to power in Egypt—but both require some unproven leaps and circumstantial evidence. The best we can do is go with the flow of tradition, which puts the Abraham narratives somewhere toward the beginning of the second millennium B.C.E.

What we can say with certainty is that these narratives form the core of Jewish (and, by extension, Christian) faith, identity, and practice. The stories related in Genesis 12–50 are the stories of the patriarchs—the ancestors who established a faith, a people, and a nation. When Americans seek to understand themselves as a nation, we look back to our "founding fathers." Ford Motor Company looks back to Henry Ford, Apple ran with the vision from Steve Jobs. Cities and towns, churches, corporations, movements all root their identity somehow in the person or people who first had the vision, the guts, the persistence, the genius, or whatever else was needed to get things off the ground.

The stories of the Patriarchs—of Abraham, Isaac, Jacob, and their families—give that identity to Jews and Christians alike, and both the Old and New Testaments rely on an understanding of that identity. That is a main reason that we're spending a third of this course on just one of the thirty-nine books of the Old Testament (twenty-four books according to the Hebrew Bible). In both the Old and New Testaments, God is referred to as "the God of Abraham, Isaac, and Jacob," establishing a reference for God's nature, for God's purposes for humanity, and for God's willingness to enter into covenant relationship with those willing to set themselves apart in faith and obedience.

> **For Reflection**
>
> Who are the patriarchs and matriarchs of your own family?
>
> Has anyone delved into genealogy to explore your family roots? What did they find?
>
> What is your particular role in your larger, extended family?

A what relationship? A covenant relationship. It's not an unknown term in the contemporary world, but it is a main theme in the Bible and deserves some close examination.

Covenant

A covenant is a witnessed agreement between two parties that establishes both the relationship between them and the behaviors required of each party toward the other to keep the relationship intact. A covenant is accompanied by a physical sign of some kind that serves both as a reminder to the parties and as a witness to others of the relationship. The best contemporary example we have of a covenant is a marriage. A spousal relationship is established before witnesses, and certain behaviors and conditions are promised in a set of vows. This relationship is then signified, usually by exchanging rings, although I do remember one couple that had butterflies tattooed on their ring fingers.

Wedding Rings,
Photograph by Jeff Belmonte

The marriage covenant in America is also a legal contract, but covenant and contract are two different things and one need not imply the other. We'll talk more about that in a minute. In covenant, the focus is on the relationship and the mutual care and fidelity of the parties it establishes. A contract is focused on the legal rights and benefits of the parties, which may well stay in place even (or sometimes especially) if the relationship between the parties has dissolved. I have seen far too many marriages where the legal contract is still firmly in place but the covenant was broken long, long ago. For those who look to the Bible for direction in faith and life, it is worth noting that God is much more concerned with covenants than with contracts.

The Origins of Covenant

But let's back up. Where did covenant originate? Why did relationships have to be witnessed and signified before others? What purpose did they serve in society? Understanding the roots of covenant-making helps us wrap our brains around this key theme of the Bible and what claims about God, humanity, and the relationship between the two that the practice is making. So let's take another look at ancient culture, remembering our mirror conversation from Session 1 and recognizing that what we "know," we know (as Paul says in 1 Corinthians 13:12) "only in part."

The special kind of agreement known as covenant arose as the solution to a problem, and to understand that problem we need to have a basic understanding of primitive societies.

Anthropologists tell us that, like Adam and Eve and Noah and his brood, the earliest people were organized in family units and the rules of society were based on kinship. Remember in Genesis 4:9 when God questions Cain about Abel, Cain replies, "Am I my brother's keeper?" The unspoken answer to that question was "Yes, you are, because Abel is your kin—a member of your family." The fundamental building block of the earliest societies was the family unit. Your safety, security, care, and provision came from your own flesh and blood—or, as they said in Near Eastern society, your "bone and flesh."

The late Frank Moore Cross, Hancock Professor of Hebrew and Other Oriental Languages at Harvard, said it well:

> "The social organization of West Semitic tribal groups was grounded in kinship. Kinship relations defined the rights and obligations, the duties, status, and privileges of tribal members, and kinship terminology provided the only language for expressing legal, political,

and religious institutions. Kinship was conceived in terms of one blood flowing through the veins of the kinship group. If the blood of a kinsman was spilled, the blood of the kinship group, of each member, was spilled. Kindred were of one flesh, one bone."[2]

Adam is using the language of kinship at the creation of Eve when he says in Genesis 2:23, "This at last is [not in] bone of my bones and flesh of my flesh." In many other instances throughout the Old Testament, some version of being of the "bone and flesh" of another recalls the ties of kinship that require a certain kind of treatment or the fulfillment of a duty.

To understand the origins of covenant, we need to recognize that kinship was the name of the game for millennia. As the population grew, however, the kinfolk became more and more difficult to manage, as anyone with in-laws can tell you. The first way a kinship group grows is through a marriage. Suddenly there is a new question: Is that new spouse kin to his or her in-laws or only to the spouse and ensuing children?

In early societies there was always the possibility that the new spouse might already be established kin. Like Abraham and Sarah, families did intermarry. Prohibitions about family members marrying had more to do with not taking a woman who was the property of another (like your mother, who belonged to your father, or your sister, who also belonged to your father) than with the family relationship per se.

But when a child, like Cain, moved out of the family unit to find a spouse, is that new mate kin? No. But if that new spouse could not enjoy the protections and provision of kinship, the entire family unit would be vulnerable, including any children who **would** be kin by blood. So there was a very basic need to have some way to extend the benefits and obligations of

---

[2] Frank Moore Cross, From Epic to Canon: History and Literature in Ancient Israel. Johns Hopkins University Press, 1998. p. 3.

Household **Gods**

Fresco of Rachel Sitting on the Idols, Giovanni Battista Tiepolo

With society revolving around kinship groups and all of ancient society taking for granted the existence of a god or gods, it was natural that each family unit looked to a special, divine kinsman who looked out for the family. It was as much as people today often think of some form of guardian angel, saint, or other God-appointed caretaker for a specific individual or group. They became the "household gods" of a given family, village, or kindred tribe. These family-based gods were represented by crude statues that were kept in the home, statues that came to be known as idols.

People were aware that the idols themselves were not the gods, but when a statue was first bought or carved and brought into the home, a ritual was performed to invite the family god to be present in the idol so that the family would have a tangible means to interact with a divine being.

The structure of kinship and the notion of household gods come together when Abraham's grandson, Jacob, encounters his uncle, Laban. When they first meet in Genesis 29:14, Laban welcomes Jacob

Continued on next page

> **Household Gods** (Continued)
>
> with phrases associated with kinship: "Surely you are my bone and my flesh!" After marrying two of Laban's daughters and having a host of children with them (and, by extension, their maidservants), the relationship between Jacob and Laban is strained and Jacob flees with his entourage. On the way out the door, however, Jacob's wife (and Laban's daughter), Rachel, steals the household gods (Genesis 31:19).
>
> The practice of household gods is here with Israel's founding family and was almost universal in the region. Even 1500 years later, with monotheism well established in Israel, we'll see that the prophets are still complaining about the people turning to idols.

kinship to this new, non-kin, person. The answer? Covenant: an agreement to extend kinship protections and duties beyond the blood family. This is done with a new, named relationship that is witnessed by others, spells out the kinship promises, and is signified by some external sign so that other family members can tell to and for whom they are responsible.

The main point is that all relationships—personal, political, and religious—were (and still often are) rooted first and foremost in some notion of family and the privileges and obligations that family relationships entail.

Covenants and Contracts

This core need grew more complex as kinship groups turned into tribes and even nations. As very large kinship groups (now including those who became kin through covenant as well as those who are kin by blood) began to expand and meet one another either in peace or in war, it became even more difficult to figure out who was really kin to whom and who should be added to the family.

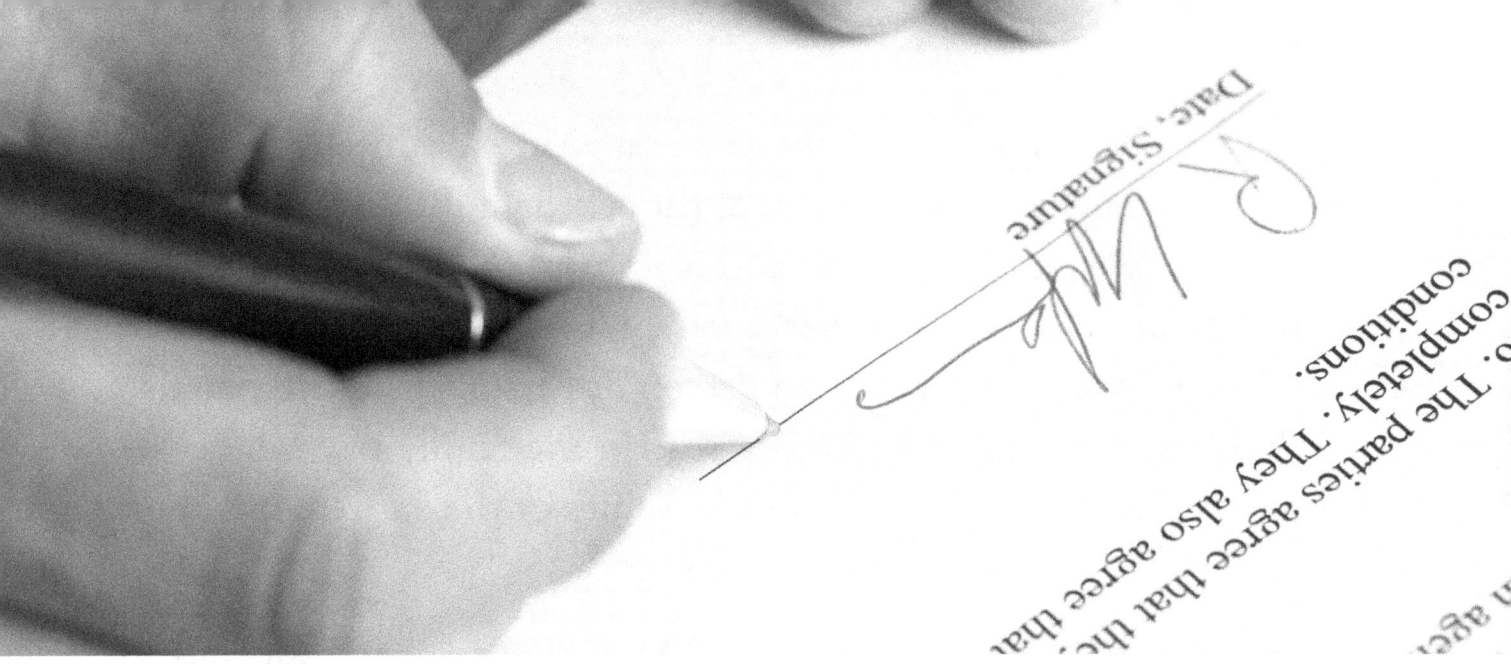

If our tribe signs a peace treaty with another tribe, does that mean they get the benefits and have the obligations of kinship—or is it something less? Is it a covenant or a contract? Do we have a new, special relationship that makes us one family, one body? Or do we have a contract that says we can't just up and kill them if they dig a well right where we always meant to dig one? Can one of our daughters marry one of their sons? It all had to be figured out.

Covenants are freely chosen ways of bringing outsiders into the family, of establishing a special and close relationship with certain parameters. Contracts are agreements about behavior that might include some of the same provisions that exist in a covenant agreement but without the understanding of any special relationship. Contracts and their provisions end when they end. Somebody doesn't keep up their side and the contract is broken and done. There might be anger—even a full-blown war if the particular contract is a peace treaty—but the breaking of a contract doesn't hit you in the gut or affect your basic sense of identity because establishing a contract has not made you a family.

Covenants, on the other hand, are intended for life—a person or persons are grafted into the family and become an organic part of the family identity. They might turn out to be unfaithful or unreliable family members. They might break the vows of the covenant. But it is as difficult and gut-wrenching to remove the covenant relation as it is to actually cast someone out of a family. When a person or group leaves a covenant relationship, it speaks not just to the person or persons who left, but also to the family that remains. There is a scar in the family tree where the member was cut off and the identity and values of the entire family unit have to be reimagined in light of the experience.

This is why church splits are so much more painful and angst-ridden than corporate splits. Corporations operate within contracts. Churches operate within covenants. Corporations see themselves as business partners. Churches see themselves as families, a relationship that is extended to others through the covenant of baptism.

With that larger understanding of the relationship between kinship and covenant, we're ready to move forward with a deeper understanding of what everyone is saying and doing in establishing covenants in the Bible.

You and Me, Together Forever

> ### For Reflection
>
> Who are the people in your family who are not blood relatives?
>
> Are there people who aren't even relatives by marriage that you consider as close as family members?
>
> What sorts of covenants or other rituals mark their importance to you?
>
> Think about the formal agreements you have made with others. Which were covenants and which were contracts?

The very first covenant in the Bible is back in Genesis 9:8–17, and it is notable for two reasons.

First, it is notable for what it says about this very, very early understanding of the God of Israel. This is a god who is willing to make covenants with human beings. Now that you know what a covenant is actually doing, think about what that means. This is not a tyrant god who views human beings as subjects, toys, or pawns (a common narrative of the gods in other surrounding cultures). As we saw from the creation narratives onward, Israel's God enjoys being in relationship with human beings, thinks about their welfare, and is constantly thinking about how to adjust, improve, and nourish that relationship. Unlike the gods of Babylon or Egypt, Israel's story presents a God who invites human beings to become family.

The second thing that's notable in the covenant of Genesis 9 is that it's not just a covenant with human beings.

> Then God said to Noah and to his sons with him, "As for me, I am establishing my covenant with you and your descendants after you, and with every living creature that is with you, the birds, the domestic animals, and every animal of the earth with you, as many as came out of the ark. I establish my covenant with you, that never again shall all flesh be cut off by the waters of a flood, and never again shall there be a flood to destroy the earth." (Genesis 9:8–11)

This first covenant establishes God's care and protection not just with Noah and his descendants but also with all living creatures, signifying that covenant with the rainbow.

Since, in the biblical narrative, everyone else on the earth has been destroyed except Noah and his family, this covenant establishes not only that God is willing to make covenants, but also that God sees all living things as part of the same family unit. The God of Israel welcomes all of

Rainbow, Photograph by Eloine Chapman

creation as family and, by putting all living things in covenant together, calls on all parties within the covenant to mutual care and accountability. All the covenants to come are subtle subsets of this first covenant with the "family" of the earth.

Enter Abraham. Actually, when we first meet this ancestor of the Jewish, Christian, and Muslim faiths, his name is Abram. He's married to a woman named Sarai, and we learned in the genealogy at the end of Genesis 11 that she is actually Abram's niece (marriage within the extended family was a common practice) and that she is unable to have children. His story begins in the twelfth chapter of Genesis, when God calls Abram to leave home and go to a new land. God promises Abram:

> I will make of you a great nation, and I will bless you, and make your name great, so that you will be a blessing. I will bless those who bless you, and the one who curses you I will curse; and in you all the families of the earth shall be blessed. (Genesis 12:2–3)

Why Abraham

"Why Abraham?" people always ask me. Why did God pick Abraham out of all the people available? And if he was so incredible, why couldn't he just stay where he was in Chaldea and carry out God's work at home? There are several ways to look at it.

Jewish tradition has found meaning in a passage about Abraham's family (Joshua 24:2–3) that claims Abraham's father and other ancestors worshipped other gods. From that the tradition grew that Abraham was different and that God selected Abraham because he did not worship other gods. God then preferred Abraham because he recognized that God was one and not many.

This tradition then expands to wonder whether taking the position that there was only one god in a culture that believed in many was getting him in trouble. That would be a reason for God to bring him out of his Chaldean home to a new land.

There has also been speculation that Abraham may have been an astronomer, since astronomy and astrology were the things for which ancient Chaldea was best known. Some think that studying the heavens led Abraham to renounce the belief in many gods.[3]

I've always thought that perhaps God approached a whole bunch of people but only Abraham accepted. My personal take is that God picked Abraham because Abraham said yes and took the leap of faith

Continued on next page

---

[3] There is a full discussion of these strains of Jewish tradition in The Bible As It Was by James L. Kugel (Belknap Press: Cambridge, MA, 1997).

Why **Abraham** (Continued)

that God asked of him. It wasn't a choice based on genetics; it was an offer awarded to the person who had the faith to respond.

We should also remember that we're reading the sacred texts of Israel, which naturally describe the relationship of God with Israel's ancestor. Other cultures have different stories about different faith heroes and different divine agreements.

To ask "Why Abraham?" is natural, but it also misses the point. From the minute God first approaches Abraham in Genesis 12, God makes it perfectly clear that Abraham is being called to a mission, articulated in Genesis 12:3, that "in you all the families of the earth shall be blessed." The person who gets the ball rolling is critically important, but that's because the mission is so huge.

Abraham is chosen for special service—he is called to a job. Through Abraham and his descendants the universal covenant expressed to Noah is to be made a reality.

These promises evoke covenant in that they are based in both kinship language (blessing those who bless you and cursing those who curse you would have been familial duties) and recall the universal language of the covenant with Noah. There are a number of promises made to Abram in the next few chapters, and it's understandable that by chapter fifteen, Abram would like some kind of sign that God intends to follow through with those promises.

God's Covenant with Abraham,
Jan Goeree and A. de Blois

In response to Abram's request, we get a picture of an ancient covenant-making ritual and vision. Abram is instructed to take a heifer, a female goat, a ram, a turtledove, and a young pigeon, slaughter them and cut the larger animals in two. Abram is then engulfed in sleep "and terrifying darkness descended upon him" (Genesis 15:12). In that darkness the captivity of the Israelites in Egypt and their eventual emancipation under Moses are foretold. Then, "when the sun had gone down and it was dark, a smoking fire pot and a flaming torch passed between these pieces" (Genesis 15:17), referring back to the animal parts. There follows the first use of the word "covenant" with Abram, as God promises to give Abram the land and defines those boundaries.

It is still two more chapters, however, before we see the covenant relationship between Abram and God in full bloom. The Genesis 17 covenant signified by circumcision establishes and seals all the promises we've heard from Genesis 12 onward: blessing, entire nations of descendants, land, and the offer of a kinship-based relation with the God offering it all. The covenant is offered to Abram, to his wife, Sarai, to their eventual son, Isaac (who has yet to be conceived, let alone born), and to all those multitudes of nations that follow from that family tree.

Name **Changes**

When new people join a family, they receive their names. For new babies, it might be their first-ever name. If the person is joined through the covenant of marriage it might be a change of name or an additional name taken by one or both parties.

Continued on next page

Name **Changes** (Continued)

In ancient times, and still in many cultures today, a name matters in ways that are hard for the typical American to understand. In the cultures of the Bible—both the Old and New Testaments—your name identified not only to what kinship group you belonged, but it was the marker of what you were expected to become. Remember the lessons from the first session. Naming was part of creation. Nothing fully existed until it had a name. To speak a name was to call something into being and the name a child was given at birth was a way that parents created either a blessing or a curse for that child.

Throughout the Bible we see instances where God changes a person's name. When God formalizes a covenant with Abram in Genesis 17, God changes his name from Abram to Abraham (v. 5) and his wife's name from Sarai to Sarah (v. 15).

In Genesis 32:28, Jacob's name is changed to Israel when a wrestling match with an angel results in a fundamental change to Jacob's character. Even into New Testament times we see Jesus change Simon's name to Peter and Saul's to Paul. Names matter in the Bible and even a close analysis of all those boring genealogies can give you information about the character and faith of the people who are named.

God signifies all this by conferring new names on Abram and Sarai. They are now Abraham and Sarah. For Abraham's part, the sign of the covenant will be visible in Abraham's flesh and in the flesh of all males who enter into this covenant relationship.

> "You shall circumcise the flesh of your foreskins, and it shall be a sign of the covenant between me and you. Throughout your generations every male among you shall be circumcised when he is eight days old, including the slave born in your house and the one bought with

your money from any foreigner who is not of your offspring. Both the slave born in your house and the one bought with your money must be circumcised. So shall my covenant be in your flesh an everlasting covenant. Any uncircumcised male who is not circumcised in the flesh of his foreskin shall be cut off from his people; he has broken my covenant." (Genesis 17:11–14)

Just as the covenant with Noah was notable for going beyond human beings to include all the creatures of the earth, the covenant with Abraham is notable for extending family protections to those who would normally be considered property rather than family—the household slaves. Whether born into the family or bought, slaves were to be included in covenant relation. The benefits of kinship are extended to them, something reflected in the eventual laws surrounding slavery in Leviticus, which sits in the background of any discussion of slavery in the New Testament.

While our modern sensibilities might wish that God had forbidden slavery altogether, we need to remember that these stories are the ways that people in the early Bronze Age distinguished themselves and their God from the peoples around them. Whether the genre is a narrative, a legal code, a name, a covenant, or even a genealogy, all of it serves a single purpose: to witness to the distinct identity and nature of the God and people of Israel.

In that witness Israel also proclaims that God acts within (and not outside of or above) history and culture. God makes covenants with individuals, nations, and creatures in very particular ways in particular cultures at particular points in history. The technology of the period was primitive, and we accept that easily, knowing that learning and development will come as the millennia progress. The same is true of the primitive social structures, legal codes, and value systems. They were a work in progress. They still are.

What we see consistently throughout the Bible is that, **relative to other cultures that would be known to the readers/hearers of the story,** the God of Israel moves the needle away from cruelty and tyranny and toward more egalitarian forms of mercy and justice.

These early covenants with Noah and Abraham underlie all later covenants, inform all legal structures, and form the basis for the development of religious ritual and expectation in Israel. By describing the covenants in detail, Israel continues to distinguish the nature of her God from the detached, violent, and capricious gods described in the literature of the surrounding nations. Israel's God welcomes human and animal, slave and free, male and female into the family.

> ### The **Help**
>
> When our contemporary North American ears hear the words "hired hand" and "slave," we tend to think that the former would be the more desirable position. The hired hand gets paid and can walk away, while the slave has neither option.
>
> But in the mindset of the ancient Israelite (and on into New Testament times), the hired hand was a contract worker and the slave was a part of the covenant. The slave could claim the same privileges of provision and protection that were due to other family/tribal members, while the hired hand had no such guarantee. In a generous family, both would fare well, but if conditions and character were less than ideal, the hired hand actually had the less enviable status.

Christians Take Note

The fundamental notion in these earliest narratives that God enters human history in specific ways and works to bless the world through human agency is the foundational assumption behind the incarnation of

God in Jesus. Christians who limit their biblical grounding to the New Testament are like those who attempt algebra without any understanding of basic mathematics. Sure, these days you can solve algebra problems with a calculator, but without some grounding in simple math, you'll never really "get it."

The New Testament isn't a replacement for the Old. It's one natural outgrowth of fundamental ideas, principles, and values established from the very beginnings of the Jewish faith. Obviously it's not the only way those principles can be applied. Three major (and different) faiths of the world have their origins in these same stories. But Jesus was a Jew from the day he was born to the day he died to the day he arose from the dead and showed himself to his Jewish followers. All the twelve disciples in the Gospels were Jews. Paul was a Jew. Christianity began as a branch of Judaism. To think that we can understand what the New Testament is saying without a fundamental understanding of the Old Testament is folly.

By the Numbers

While the Old Testament was not divided into chapters until the Middle Ages, it's notable that each of the three arcs—the stories of Abraham, the stories of Jacob, and the stories of Joseph—take twelve chapters apiece with just a stray chapter here and there for a genealogy or supplemental story.

Numbers in the Bible are rarely just a head count. They are frequently symbolic and there are entire books devoted to the subject of biblical numerology. This idea is enhanced by the fact that ancient Hebrew did not have distinct characters for numbers. Numbers were represented by their corresponding letters—the first letter of the alphabet representing the number one, and so on. So to read biblical Hebrew is very literally to read numbers and letters at the same time.

Continued on next page

> **By the Numbers** (Continued)
>
> Three, seven, twelve, forty, and their multiples are just some of the numbers you will encounter again and again in both the Old and New Testaments. In this part of Genesis we begin to see the number twelve as Jacob's twelve sons appear on the scene as the ancestors of Israel's twelve tribes. Several numbers represent various aspects of perfection, and the number twelve is one of them. To biblical numerologists, twelve is the number of organizational and governmental perfection and completion.

The Rest of the Story

We've spent a lot of time looking underneath the foundational bed of Genesis but not much time at all examining the fabulous stories luxuriating on the top. You would be well-served (and I think not at all bored) to just read all fifty chapters of Genesis, but that's a bit much to ask for a week's homework. Two key stories will be examined in the exercises in the class session (if you're studying this book on your own, you may want to get a copy of the leader's guide to benefit from those lessons), but I'll try to give a broad overview of the rest of Genesis in what follows.

There are three main narrative arcs in Genesis 12–50, all of which are designed to set the stage for the main event in the book of Exodus: the giving of the Law on Mt. Sinai and the transformation of a ragtag group of Hebrew slaves into the nation of Israel. We will look at each of the arcs in that light. While the various arcs intersect and overlap and some stories are even repeated with different characters, it can be difficult for those not familiar with all the characters to sort out who's who. For that reason, we'll look at them one by one. The family tree on page 56 may also help you keep everyone and their relations straight.

The Arc of Abraham (Genesis 12–24)

We've examined part of the first arc as we looked at the call of Abraham in Genesis 12 and the establishment of a covenant between God and Abraham. Unlike the covenant with Noah, which was universal in scope, the covenant with Abraham singles out a particular man and his descendants. They are, however, singled out to be agents for God's universal blessing of all nations. Covenants with particular individuals, families, and groups—in both the Old and New Testaments—are all building toward that ultimate, all-inclusive goal.

Re-read Genesis 12:2–3. God is clear that the promise is **not** just to bless Abraham and his descendants and let the rest of the world go to hell in a handbasket. The blessings God gives to Abraham and Company are given in order to enable them to be agents of blessing to all nations, presumably by introducing them to the very particular God established in the stories we've seen thus far. It's a privilege, yes. But it's a privilege that comes with a major responsibility.

Abraham and Isaac

The rest of the first narrative arc in these chapters addresses the issue that Abraham himself raises to God when he hears all this business about becoming the father of a "multitude of nations." Remember that Abraham's wife, Sarah, is barren. By chapter 15 Abraham is living comfortably in the land he was promised, but he complains to God that his only heir is a slave that happened to be born in his house. He's not even the father.

The Genealogy of Abraham

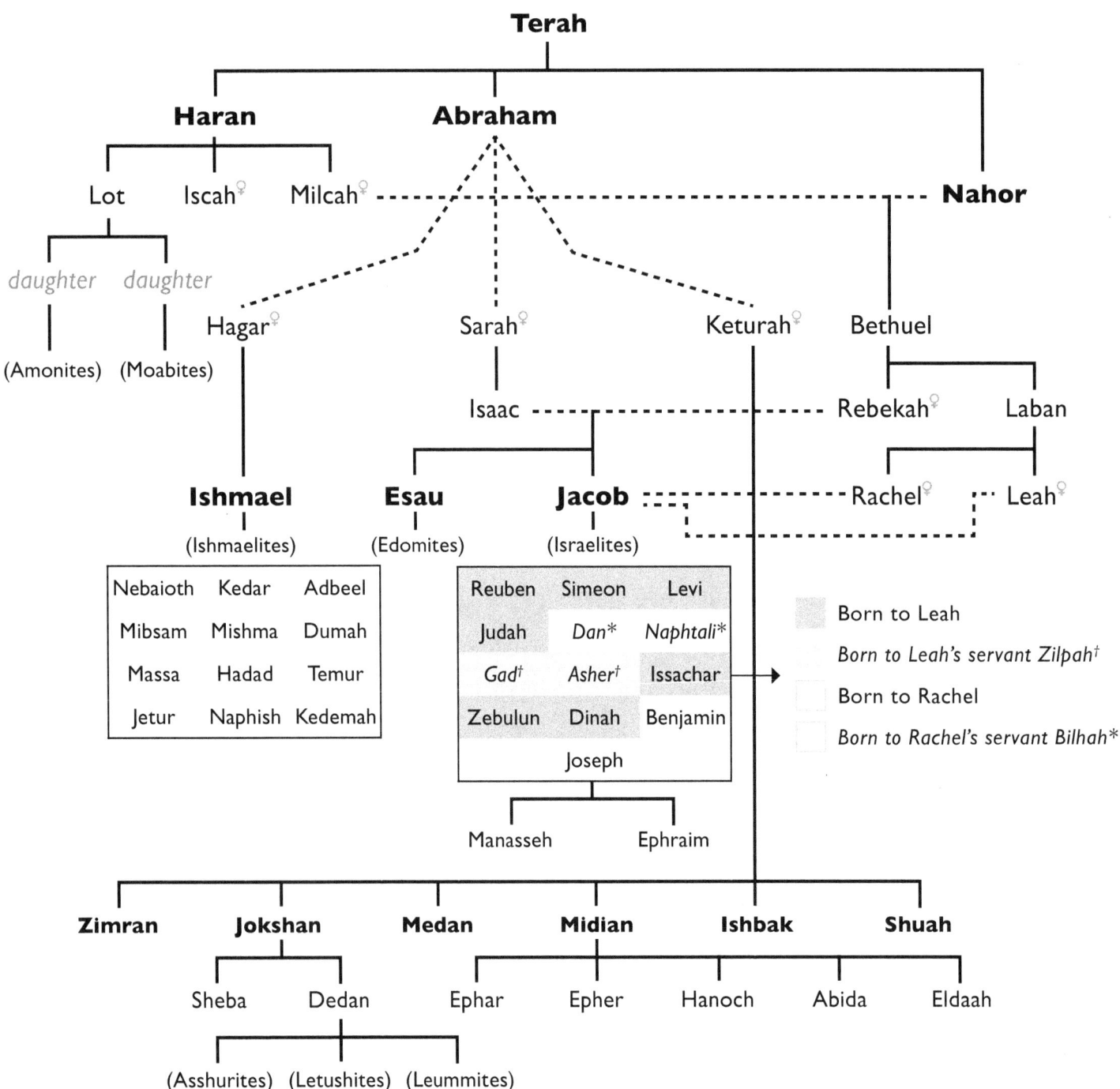

Abraham seeks to rectify the situation by fathering a child with Sarah's slave, Hagar. In the culture of the time, this was perfectly acceptable, and we'll see it happen many times over with Jacob and his wives and their slaves a bit later on. The child of such a union was considered to be the child of the wife, not the child of the slave, and would inherit accordingly.

Hagar conceives and bears Ishmael. The significance of that union cannot be overestimated in terms of its importance to the Muslim faith. God assures Abraham in Genesis 21:13 that Ishmael will get his own blessing and nation, and he does.

For purposes of Jewish history, however, God steps in and says to Abraham, in essence, "No, my covenant with you will be passed along through a different child that you will have with Sarah, not with Hagar." Abraham and Sarah have a good laugh over that, since Sarah is now not only barren but almost a hundred years old. Nevertheless, Sarah conceives and bears Isaac in chapter 21. The name Isaac means "laughter."

Chapter 22 will be examined more closely in the group exercise associated with this chapter, but it's one of the best-known stories of the Bible. Referred to as "The Binding of Isaac," it relates how God tested the faith of Abraham by asking him to sacrifice Isaac.

> **Read Genesis 21-22.**
> Isaac, Ishmael, and Mt. Moriah.

Abraham is about to go through with the deed when an angel stops him and provides a ram as a substitute, making it clear that what God wanted was not child sacrifice, but to be sure that Abraham put God above all else in his life—even the child of the covenant promise.

This story presents major problems for many, many contemporary readers. That Abraham could even consider God's request to sacrifice his son puts him in the realm of monster rather than hero for a large number of people. But the New Testament turns back to this story in Hebrews

11:17–19, using it as an example of Abraham's faith—a faith that the writer of Hebrews is inviting us to replicate. How can we swallow this story?

This is when we need to go back to the mirror and remind ourselves that when we read this story, we are placing ourselves in the early Bronze Age in the Middle East. We go back to the barbeque and remember that stories are told in response to other stories in order to show how we are both the same as and different from the other guests. Surrounding religions practiced child sacrifice. Like the stories we have seen thus far, the story of Isaac's close call is grounded in common cultural practice but then twists to distinguish the God of Israel from the gods of surrounding nations.

The God of Israel is like other gods in that Israel's God wants to be the top priority. That will later be spelled out at Mt. Sinai in the first of the Ten Commandments: "Thou shalt have no other gods before me." Isaac isn't just a beloved son to Abraham. Isaac represents the greatness and blessing that God has promised. Isaac is the key to producing that "multitude of nations" that was promised when God changed Abram's name to Abraham and established the covenant. This is a God who doesn't want to be the sugar daddy in a relationship. God doesn't want Abraham's devotion only as a means to the end of great rewards—and the only way to be sure of that is to test it.

Sacrifice of Isaac, Rembrandt, 1635

58 INTRODUCING THE OLD TESTAMENT

In that way, the God of Israel is like other gods and the first part of the story could have come from any of the surrounding cultures. But it is in the end of the story that we see the distinctiveness of Israel's God. Other gods would have watched Isaac slaughtered and burned as an offering, smacked their lips and said, "Thank you very much." But the God of Israel does not want such sacrifice. This God wants your devotion, not your child, and Abraham and Isaac both live to tell the tale.

(Note: See page 272 for some aids in dealing with difficult texts.)

Sodom and Gomorrah

There is just one other major story of note in the arc of Abraham stories: the destruction of the cities of Sodom and Gomorrah.

As Abraham leaves home and settles into this new land, his nephew, Lot, comes along with him. Abraham needs room for his flocks and chooses to live in the hills, while Lot settles down in the plains near the Dead Sea. Presumably it wasn't dead then, as archaeologists have found evidence of five ancient cities near its banks at the base of the Jordan River. Tradition has it that two of these "Cities of the Plain" were Sodom and Gomorrah, cities whose names have become synonymous with sin.

> **Read Genesis 18–19.**
> The destruction of Sodom and Gomorrah.

The Bible relates that just after God makes Abraham and Sarah laugh by announcing the conception of Isaac, God (in the form of three angels) delivers a more somber message. The cities of Sodom and Gomorrah have become so corrupt that they've got to go. Abraham and God are now family through the covenant, and Abraham's nephew lives in Sodom, so God decides to share the plans to wipe out the cities with Abraham in Genesis 18:16–21.

What follows is a bargaining ritual between Abraham and God. This is just the first of many times throughout the Bible that one of God's people challenges God's justice, and in every single case, the person doing the challenging has a real dialogue with God. This would not be the case if someone were to challenge the justice of the gods of Ugarit or Babylon or Egypt. In fact, it wouldn't be likely that worshippers of those gods would even bring up the matter. They didn't expect their gods to be just in the first place, so why bring it up?

I'll let you read the story, but the end result is that Abraham's request to spare the cities if ten righteous people can be found within them can't be granted, because there aren't that many. Abraham's nephew, Lot, and his family are in the city and therefore in harm's way. God sends in angels to get Lot and his family out, and then rains down fire on the cities. Lot and company are told to leave and not look back. Lot's wife famously does look back and the Bible tells us that she was turned into a pillar of salt. To this day, salt formations around the Dead Sea are called "Lot's wives," with one in particular (shown here) standing out.

"Lot's Wife" Pillar, Mt. Sodom, Israel

This story is referenced a number of times throughout the Bible, usually in a formulation that condemns a sinful person or group while noting that the rain of sulfur that destroyed Sodom and Gomorrah will look like a cakewalk compared to what will happen to this new sinner. Indeed archaeologists say that it does look like the ancient Cities of the Plain came to a fiery and permanent end.

The Sin of **Sodom**

Because of the sordid tale of what happens to the angels who are sent to warn Lot of the coming destruction, it is often assumed that the great sin provoking the destruction of Sodom was of a sexual nature. It is from the town of Sodom that we get our English word, sodomy. Clearly there were sexual cads in Sodom, and if you ask me, Lot was at the top of that list for offering his virgin daughters to a sex-hungry mob. But were sexual issues the reason God decided to destroy Sodom and Gomorrah? The prophet Ezekiel didn't think so:

"This was the guilt of your sister Sodom: she and her daughters had pride, excess of food, and prosperous ease, but did not aid the poor and needy." (Ezekiel 16:49)

The Arc of Jacob (Genesis 25–37)

Once Isaac is safely grown and Abraham's faith confirmed, the story can move on. In chapter 24, the narrative shifts to Isaac as he comes of age and finds a wife from among his uncle's kin. Isaac and Rebekah are wed and, in chapter 25, she gives birth to twins, Esau and Jacob, and the next major arc begins.

Even though they are twins, somebody has to be born first, and in this case the firstborn was Esau (pronounced EE-saw). The name Jacob actually means "heel-grabber," referring to his position relative to Esau as they exited the birth canal. The stories of Jacob and Esau go from chapter 25 through chapter 36. They are engaging, dramatic, and well worth the time it takes to read them.

> **Read Genesis 27-28, 32-33.**
> Jacob and Esau.

This narrative arc moves us from a covenant that thus far has gone from father to one particular son—from Abraham to Isaac and now to Jacob—to a covenant that will extend to an entire kinship group. In chapter 32 (the other story we'll examine in depth during this next class session), God changes Jacob's name to Israel. Jacob/Israel then goes on to have twelve sons. The nation of Israel is the nation of Jacob, those twelve sons, and their descendants. The twelve tribes of Israel we hear about from here on out are named for those twelve sons.

As the stories of Jacob begin, we have to wonder whether God was having second thoughts about passing the covenant on through Jacob rather than Esau. Jacob is an ambitious schemer who (with his equally conniving mother, Rebekah) takes advantage of his father's blindness to steal his brother's inheritance. He then tricks his uncle out of a wealth of livestock, and wrestles with God at the Jabbok River as Esau and four hundred armed men close in on the other side of the river to even the score.

This cycle of stories offers a glimpse into the lives and customs of the day. Jacob takes his uncle's two daughters as wives. Jacob falls for Rachel first and serves his uncle Laban for seven years in order to marry her. The wedding takes place and the next morning Jacob wakes up to discover that he has married Rachel's older sister, Leah, instead. (I'm still trying to figure out why it took him until the next morning to realize the error.)

Jacob's Dream, William Blake

It turns out that conniving runs in the family and it was Laban who made the switch, believing it wasn't proper for the younger daughter to be married before the elder. Jacob does marry Rachel next, but Laban also gets another seven years' labor out of Jacob in return for marrying the second daughter.

Leah is envious of Rachel because Jacob loves Rachel most, and Rachel is envious of Leah because Rachel is having trouble conceiving, while Leah is a baby factory. In the battle to become Jacob's favorite wife, they each give their maids, Bilhah and Zilpah, to Jacob for childbearing. We saw the same practice when Sarah gave Hagar to Abraham. And so Jacob's children start appearing on the scene—twelve sons and at least one daughter, Dinah. Two of those sons at last are born to Rachel: Joseph and Benjamin. Rachel dies giving birth to Benjamin and the stage is set for the story of Joseph, Jacob's favorite son.

The Arc of Joseph (Genesis 37, 39–50)

With the exception of chapter 38, which tells a sidebar story to give us the rather salacious beginnings of King David's ancestry, the rest of Genesis is devoted to the story of Joseph. Hollywood, Broadway, and Disney have all recognized the fabulous tales that comprise this portion of the Bible. The story goes like this:

Jacob loves Joseph best and gives him that special coat or robe (or whatever it was), and his brothers resent the favoritism. Worse, Joseph is into dream interpretation and has the rather poor idea of telling his brothers about a dream he had where they all bowed down before him. Some of his brothers want to kill him, but they settle for selling him to slave traders on their way to Egypt, smearing his famous robe in blood, and telling their father that Joseph was torn apart by wild beasts.

Chorus from *Joseph and the Amazing Technicolor Dreamcoat*

Once in Egypt, Joseph is bought by Potiphar, an officer of Pharaoh. Joseph gains Potiphar's trust and becomes the overseer of the man's household. Potiphar has a wife who would like to see some action from Joseph, but Joseph keeps refusing her advances. She retaliates by telling her husband that Joseph tried to take advantage of her, which gets Joseph thrown in prison.

Joseph is apparently a likeable guy and easily makes friends in prison, using his gifts in dream interpretation with the other inmates. When Pharaoh himself has a troubling dream, he hears about Joseph's talents and calls for him. Joseph correctly interprets Pharaoh's dream as predicting a great famine. Moreover, he tells Pharaoh that a time of plenty will precede the years of famine, advising him to store up food from the bumper crop to hold them over in the looming lean times. Pharaoh likes what he hears and puts Joseph in charge of the project. Before you know it, Joseph is a prince in the land, second in power only to Pharaoh himself.

At the beginning of chapter 42, the famine hits the entire region and the camera pans to Jacob and the remaining family back in Canaan. The famine there is bad and they've heard there's food in Egypt, so Jacob dispatches ten of his sons to go to Egypt and buy grain. The only son who stays behind is young Benjamin—the only connection to his beloved Rachel that remains to Jacob. Or so he thinks.

The next few chapters are storytelling genius. The brothers, of course, have to get their grain from Joseph. Though they don't recognize him, Joseph knows at once who they are and, like a cat with a mouse, toys with them. You can read the grand plot for yourself.

Finally the whole clan arrives in Egypt and is given the rich land of Goshen to settle. The last chapters of Genesis describe the final days of Jacob, the sons of Joseph, and Joseph's own deathbed wish:

> **Read Genesis 42-45.**
> Joseph and his brothers in Egypt.

> "Then Joseph said to his brothers, 'I am about to die; but God will surely come to you, and bring you up out of this land to the land that he swore to Abraham, to Isaac, and to Jacob.' So Joseph made the Israelites swear, saying, 'When God comes to you, you shall carry up my bones from here.' And Joseph died, being one hundred ten years old; he was embalmed and placed in a coffin in Egypt." (Genesis 50:24–26)

And God surely did come. It just took about four hundred years and a man named Moses.

Preparation for Check-In

(Starting with the second class session, each group meeting will begin with a ten-minute check-in during which you will each be asked to give a brief response to the following two questions. Please think about and write your responses here.)

What is one thing that was new to me in this material?

What is one question that this week's topic raises for me?

Homework (All students)

- ☐ Read through all of the Session 3 Student Text, including the Bible passage assignments in the clear boxes.

- ☐ Think about the reflection questions in the text.

- ☐ Answer the questions in the Preparation for Check-In above.

Extra Mile (CEU and Certificate Students)

- ☐ Leviticus 25 describes laws by which debts were forgiven, slaves freed, and land returned to ancestral owners every fifty years. This became known as the Year of Jubilee. Research the practice of Jubilee in both ancient and modern times and write a report of approximately five hundred words describing your findings.

- ☐ Be prepared to share your findings briefly with the group during the next class session.

LAYING DOWN THE LAW

Materials you will need for your third class session:

This student text

Your study Bible

Materials for taking notes

Your responses to the check-in questions on p. 100

Extra Mile Students: Your findings about the Jubilee

Historical Era: 1799–1019 B.C.E.

Parts of the Bible covered: Exodus, Leviticus, Numbers, Deuteronomy, Joshua, Judges, Ruth

Timeline for **Session Three**

Note: As we move into periods with better documentation, the margin of error for a given date gets smaller. Still, however, these events are from a period long gone by. Most dates are still approximate and many are disputed. See the full text for this session for a discussion of the differences in dating the Exodus.

☐ World Events (Outside the Bible)

1750 B.C.E.	**Code of Hammurabi composed in Babylon**
1686 B.C.E.	Possible date for Israelites' entrance into Egypt. This date is adopted by those who would equate the Israelites with the Hyksos, a Semitic people who entered and then came to rule Egypt for a time.
1674 B.C.E.	Hyksos rule Egypt
1650 B.C.E.	**Last species of mammoth becomes extinct (Russia)**
1600 B.C.E.	**Development of the windmill in Persia**
1567 B.C.E.	Hyksos driven out of Egypt Early date for the Exodus
1400 B.C.E.	Golden age of the Canaanite city of Ugarit. This city and its culture, religion, and politics have a huge impact on our understanding of the Old Testament.
1390 B.C.E.	**Assyrians emerge as independent power**
1380 B.C.E.	Early date for the start of the Conquest of Canaan and the period of the Judges
1332 B.C.E.	**King Tut begins his reign in Egypt**

1304 B.C.E.	Reign of Ramses II (The Great) in Egypt begins Late date for the Exodus is sometime during the reign of Ramses II, which ended in 1237 B.C.E.
1274 B.C.E.	**Egyptians and Hittites sign first known peace treaty**
1232 B.C.E.	First mention of the Israelites outside of the Bible. It occurs in a listing of vanquished peoples in Egyptian war records.
1203 B.C.E.	**Trojan War begins**
1200 B.C.E.	End of the Bronze Age as iron is first used in making weapons Late date for the start of the Conquest of Canaan and the period of the Judges
1184 B.C.E.	**The fall of Troy**
1150 B.C.E.	End of Egyptian rule in Canaan

The View from the Balcony

Hold onto your hats. For the first two sessions we've been taking a leisurely stroll through Genesis to get our bearings in an ancient world. But some of you may have noticed that there are thirty-nine books in the Old Testament and only four sessions left to go. In this session we pick up speed, even as human civilization does the same.

This next era moves us from the Bronze Age at the beginning to the early Iron Age at the close, with iron first used for making weapons in 1200 B.C.E. As technology advances, Phoenician trading ships are sailing the Mediterranean, eventually depositing the people who will become known as the Philistines on the shores of Canaan. King Tut's tomb is built (and occupied) and King Hammurabi in Babylon unveils one of the first known written legal codes, putting it on eight-foot-tall stone tablets. Finally, not to be outdone by Egyptian pancakes, the Babylonians invent sausage and the world has breakfast.

In terms of the broad sweep of biblical events, the books we'll look at in this session show us the formation of Israel as a nation sometimes in excruciating detail. The core narrative begins with Moses leading the Hebrew slaves out of Egypt and continues with the forty years they spent in the desert wilderness. During

Charlton Heston as Moses Parting the Red Sea in the 1956 film *The Ten Commandments*

those forty years the Israelites received the Law on Mt. Sinai, renewed the covenant with the God of Abraham, Isaac, and Jacob, built a tabernacle to establish a pattern of worship, and complained so constantly about so much that God sent in some poisonous snakes to shut them up.

Those core stories are told with variations in both Exodus and Deuteronomy, with the laws detailed in Leviticus and a closer look taken at the wilderness period in Numbers. (The book of Numbers is named for the various censuses taken in the book, but the name of the book in the Hebrew Bible is "In the Wilderness.")

Finally the wilderness wanderings come to a close and the baby nation of Israel approaches the land of their ancestors—the land promised to Abraham back in Genesis. By the time of Moses, no Israelite living had seen this land or crossed its border. The land is now known as the Promised Land, and its fertile potential is evident in its frequent description as a land "flowing with milk and honey."

Forty

Forty is another number that crops up with regularity in the Bible. We have seen it already in the story of Noah, as it rains for forty days and forty nights. In this session we see the Israelites wander the wilderness for forty years.

We'll see it in the Gospels of the New Testament, when Jesus launches his ministry by spending forty days fasting and praying in the wilderness, where he is tempted by the devil. What do those things have in common? They are long, difficult struggles out of which something new is born. Whenever you see the number forty, that's the implication. It may or may not have been exactly forty—days, years, or whatever. Forty is used symbolically as a kind of code to say the time was both hard and formative in some way.

LAYING DOWN THE LAW

Unfortunately, the Israelites can't just stroll right in, even though their ancestors are buried there and generally had good relations with their neighbors. That was then, but this is now. Four hundred years have passed since the Hebrews left for Egypt, things have changed back home, and the Canaanites who live there now aren't eager to share the space. The Israelites aren't ready for protracted negotiations, and things get ugly. Things get ugly. Broadly, the march of the Israelites into Canaan is known as the Conquest, and it's detailed in the book of Joshua, named for the successor to Moses who led the effort.

Once in the land, the book of Judges recounts a succession of charismatic military leaders who rose up to unite the twelve scattered tribes whenever an outside threat presented itself. These leaders were known as judges (although their function was more military than legal) and the book of the Bible with that name tells their stories. At this time Israel had no king. It was a loose federation of tribes that joined together to defend against a common foe, but otherwise had no centralized system of government.

Another book of the Bible set in this period is the book of Ruth—a love story that serves to prepare readers to receive the greatest of Israel's later kings, King David. The foreign-born widow Ruth leaves her native Moab to follow her widowed mother-in-law, Naomi, back to Naomi's home in Canaan. Naomi then proceeds to find a husband for Ruth from her own kin and Ruth and Boaz marry, becoming ancestors of King David and, further on in history, Jesus.

> **Read the book of Ruth.** It's only four chapters and a great story.

You may have heard a section of Ruth read at weddings. In Ruth 1:16–17 we hear,

> "Where you go, I will go; where you lodge, I will lodge; your people shall be my people, and your God my God. Where you die, I will die—there will I be buried. May the LORD do thus and so to me, and more as well, if even death parts me from you!"

The thing that generally isn't mentioned at the aforementioned weddings is that Ruth did not speak these words to Boaz but to her mother-in-law, when Naomi tried to convince Ruth to stay in her own homeland. Maybe if couples started reciting this to their new mothers-in-law, relationships would be easier down the road!

While placed after the book of Judges in the Old Testament, the Hebrew Bible places Ruth between the Song of Solomon and Lamentations as one of the five scrolls read at one of Israel's national feasts. The book of Ruth is traditionally read at the Jewish festival of Shavuot, perhaps because Shavuot celebrates the harvest, which is the setting for the story.

Didn't I Just Read That

One thing that confuses many Bible readers is the fact that entire books of the Bible cover the same basic material as other books. Of course the best known of these duplications are the four Gospels in the New Testament—each one telling about the life of Jesus with many similarities but also distinct differences. This repetition is found in the Old Testament as well.

In this chapter's material, the book of Deuteronomy retells the story of Exodus, and Numbers focuses in on the wilderness period, for a total of three portraits of those forty years in the desert. In later chapters we'll see that 1 and 2 Kings covers basically the same material as 1 and 2 Samuel, and 1 and 2 Chronicles covers the

Continued on next page

Didn't **I Just Read That** (Continued)

entire Old Testament period, although the period from Adam to Saul is covered only by genealogies (nine chapters of them!).

These duplicate accounts are similar, but they also have distinct differences. In some cases the same stories are told differently, and in other cases new stories and/or commentary are added. Why do we have them both—and why are they different?

Again, we have to toss out our modern, fact-based mindset. Those who wrote the books of the Bible (and, later, those who gathered the books together to form the official collection—or canon—of Scripture) weren't driven by the need to convey factual information. They certainly weren't averse to preserving facts, and I'm not saying the Bible is a work of pure fiction. I'm just saying that the transmission of a factual account wasn't the motivation of the people who wrote and compiled the books of the Bible. They wanted to preserve not **facts** so much as **meaning**. If the facts supported the meaning, they kept them. If they didn't, well, the meaning took precedence. This is especially true in the Old Testament.

We have the particular stories and books that we do, not because those were the only stories and books about ancient Israel that existed, but because those were the stories and books that explained **why** things were the way they were. In the Old Testament these re-tellings show us how the God of Israel is different from the gods of the surrounding cultures; they explain why certain people became great and why others floundered; and they search the history of a nation to try to discover why God allowed that nation to be enslaved, conquered, or marched into exile.

Continued on next page

Didn't **I Just Read That** (Continued)

So, first we get a book, like Exodus or 1 and 2 Samuel, that is primarily interested in telling the stories as they were first told—stories designed to highlight an aspect of the nature of Israel's God or the character of some of Israel's primary figures. But then we also get books that look back on those same stories from a later perspective—sometimes centuries later. In these later books, the details sometimes differ as the writers probe their history for meaning and relevance to their contemporary situation.

In the case of Deuteronomy, that look back is presented as a series of final speeches by Moses to the people before they enter the Promised Land, reminding them of the miracles and events that got them to this point. In the case of Kings and Chronicles, readers encounter a writer looking back at Israel's monarchy from the perspective of the Babylonian Exile many years later, as they search for clues to the divine displeasure that resulted in Jerusalem's destruction.

Extending the Covenant

When last we read about the covenant, God had established it with Abraham and continued it through Abraham's son Isaac (rather than Ishmael), through Isaac's son Jacob (rather than Esau), and then to all of Jacob's twelve sons. Lest it be forgotten that the purpose of a covenant was to extend the duties and privileges due to blood relations out to others, the sign of the covenant was carved into the flesh of the male reproductive organ. Blood was shed, and with the removal of the foreskin, the origins of family were very literally exposed to others.

Now it's been five hundred to eight hundred years since that covenant with Abraham. The book of Exodus opens with a new king in Egypt, a pharaoh who "did not know Joseph," the young Hebrew slave/government savior and the eleventh son of Jacob.

> ### Dating the **Exodus**
>
> As we saw in the first course of this series, there's considerable disagreement about the historical time period described in the Exodus narrative. Since the text doesn't name pharaoh (no, his name was not Yul Brynner), we're left to guess. The records of Egypt don't mention anything, but then again most nations conveniently omit records of being humiliated and trashed by enemies, unless they're able to come back and exact vengeance in the end.
>
> Ultimately the debate is interesting, but not critical either to an understanding of the text or to our ability to derive meaning and faith from the stories. Suffice it to say that one group of scholars insists that the events date to about 1400 B.C.E. under Amenhotep II (or even earlier) and another group is equally insistent that it all happened closer to 1250 B.C.E. under Ramses II. Cecil B. DeMille, director of the blockbuster film <u>The Ten Commandments</u>, opted for the latter interpretation, all of which ignores the fact that some scholars don't think the Exodus actually happened at all!

While we're not sure exactly how much time it's been since Joseph's whole family came to Egypt and took up residence in Goshen, it's been long enough that an extended family of about seventy (remembering that seven is another symbolic number) has turned into a multitude so numerous that they're making Pharaoh nervous. Pharaoh does a bit of fear mongering to convince people that these Semitic immigrants are a threat—and suddenly Jacob's descendants are slaves.

By the end of chapter two, the Hebrew slaves are crying out to God and in Exodus 2:24–25 we read,

> "God heard their groaning, and God remembered his covenant with Abraham, Isaac, and Jacob. God looked upon the Israelites, and God took notice of them."

While it's a bit disconcerting to think that the Israelites languished four hundred years in slavery because God just kind of forgot they were there, this point in Exodus marks a shift. From this point onward, God's covenant is not with an individual or even with a family. Exodus is the story of God's extension of the covenant from a family to a people—a nation—and the rest of the Old Testament chronicles both the successes and the failures of that extended covenant relationship. The full establishment of that covenant comes with the Ten Commandments and the giving of the Law on Mt. Sinai in Exodus 20 (and revisited in Deuteronomy 5).

> **Read the following chapters of Exodus: 19-20, 31-32.**
> Giving of the Law and the Golden Calf.

With the giving of the Law, we see the formation of Israel as a political entity. After Mt. Sinai they are a people, a nation, governed by a specific set of laws that are designed to set them apart from the other peoples of the region. That is, after all, what the Hebrew word "holy" (**qadosh**) means: to be set apart for a special purpose. While the covenant initially made with Abraham would continue to be literally carved into the flesh of all males, the outward sign of the new extended covenant would be evident in any person who was committed to following the precepts of the law.

Very specifically, the sign of the Mosaic covenant (as described in Exodus 31) would be the keeping of one particular law—the only one of the Ten Commandments that is not duplicated in the legal codes of any other nation:

The Adoration of the Golden Calf, Nicolas Poussin, 1633

"Remember the Sabbath day and keep it holy." This is the sign of the covenant precisely because it is unique. It sets both individuals and nations apart—makes them "holy." When other peoples came to the gates of an Israelite city to trade on the Sabbath and found all the shops closed, they noticed. Keeping the Sabbath was designed as a witness, a gift, and an invitation all at once.

As a gift, it represented rest—a day off. Israelite workers were not to be at the mercy of greedy bosses who wanted that extra day's profit. Everybody gets a day off every week. God says so. Every worker, every slave, every animal—even the land itself is to get a break from cultivation (spelled out in Leviticus 25). In the extension of the Sabbath to animals and land, we can hear the echoes of the universal covenant with Noah.

No other culture had such laws. Other gods either are harsh taskmasters themselves or tolerate others being so. Not the God of Israel. Not the God who put a rainbow in the sky for even the animals to see. As harsh as other laws of Israel might seem to our ears (Exodus 21:17 says you're supposed to stone children who curse their mother or father, for example), the sign of the covenant that other nations would notice is one of compassion, rest, equality, and freedom.

Sabbath Cartoon by Baloo

As we trace the history of the covenant, we can see that it has a mission, shown in the covenant with Noah in Genesis 9: God wants the kinship relation with all of creation—men, women, animals, birds, all of it. But you have to start somewhere, so God picks Abraham.

There was a covenant with particular individuals for only three generations: Abraham, Isaac, and Jacob. With Jacob the covenant got its first extension—God didn't pick just one of Jacob's sons, as was the case with Abraham and Isaac. The covenant was broadened to include all twelve of Jacob's sons.

With Moses at Sinai, we have the next major shift, as the covenant branches out again. Now the covenant is no longer limited to a person's ancestry. It is no longer about who you are but about what you do. Will you live the set-apart life, the "holy" life laid out in the law? Will you follow these instructions for living together? Will you remember the Sabbath and keep it holy? Will you recognize your God in these very public ways so that other nations can eventually be drawn in and the ultimate promise to Abraham be fulfilled?

The people answer in Exodus 24:3: "All the words that the LORD has spoken we will do."

Jews often look to the Sinai covenant as a marriage. The patriarchs presented their children at the altar. The vows were taken, the couple (God and Israel) were wed, and thus began a new covenant chapter. That image of God as the husband of Israel will surface again and again in the books that follow as Israel struggles to learn the meaning of faithfulness.

So We Promised To Do What, Exactly?

If you should be so bold as to read through the second half of Exodus and all of Leviticus, you will see that the law is both thorough and comprehensive. There's no aspect of life that isn't regulated in some way. The food you eat, the clothes you wear, your sexuality, your business practices, your treatment of others, what punishments are to be meted out for what crimes, what you can and can't plant in your fields, how much you can harvest and when, when you can do work and what constitutes "work"—the list goes on and on. After reading Leviticus you understand why a new group of scholars arose whose specialty was knowing and interpreting the Law—the lawyers or, as they were known in Jesus' day, the Pharisees.

Many people emerge from this section of the Bible overwhelmed, unable to imagine trying to keep up with

> **Read Leviticus 19:1-37.**
> A variety of laws.

it all or even why anyone would try. Those who decide to dive in and just read the Bible cover to cover usually lose their enthusiasm for the project at about Exodus 25. Others head directly to these sections, believing that if God laid down the law, it must be a law for all time, and attempts are made to re-create the early theocracy of Israel, at least on the level of a local faith community if not of a nation. The contemporary American movement of Christian Reconstructionism is precisely that kind of effort.

Mostly, however, what tends to happen with these laws is that people latch onto particular edicts that fit their own value system and either discard or ignore the rest. No matter how literally someone may read the Bible, a person who adheres to all these laws is a rarity.

> For a fun look at someone who decided to actually try following all the laws to the letter, check out The Year of Living Biblically[4] by A. J. Jacobs. As he sheepishly throws pebbles at people to try to live out the various commands to stone sinners, you get the picture.

The fact that people almost universally pick and choose which biblical laws to emphasize, however, does not mean that such selective implementation is a bad practice. Not all laws are created equal. There are many rabbinic discussions about which laws should be considered the most important. This is also reflected in the Gospels where Jesus (called a rabbi) is famously asked to name the greatest commandment. (Matthew 22:35–40, Mark 12:28–34, Luke 10:25–28) Jesus doesn't respond by saying that all the commandments are equal. He makes a selection—in fact he makes two selections:

> "'You shall love the Lord your God with all your heart, and with all your soul, and with all your mind.' This is the greatest and first commandment. [Deuteronomy 6:5] And a second is like it: 'You shall love your neighbor as yourself.' [Leviticus 19:18] On these two commandments hang all the law and the prophets." (Matthew 22:37-40)

---

[4] Simon & Schuster, 2007.

The chapter in Leviticus where we read the command to love your neighbor has sections that echo many of the Ten Commandments and many sections about being honest in business, impartial in judgment, and mindful of the needs of both the aged and the poor. Those passages ring out with contemporary relevance to all sides.

There are also passages that ring out in a more partisan fashion. In Leviticus 19, the left can shake their Bibles and recite, "The alien who resides with you shall be to you as the citizen among you; you shall love the alien as yourself, for you were aliens in the land of Egypt" (v. 34) to support amnesty for undocumented workers. The right can shake those same Bibles right back while quoting, "Do not turn to mediums or wizards; do not seek them out, to be defiled by them" (v. 31) and "You shall not practice augury or witchcraft" (v. 26) in support of banning books like Harry Potter and the Wizard of Oz. And yet neither side is particularly worried about our consistent violation of verse 19, which ends "nor shall you put on a garment made of two different materials" or the prohibition against a rare steak (v. 26) or tattoos (v. 28).

> **For Reflection**
>
> Do you agree that some laws are more important than others? Why or why not?
>
> Do you believe any of the biblical laws we've read about apply to us today?
>
> Do you think that Ten Commandments plaques and monuments should be on public display?

And that's just one chapter. Chapter 18 gets lifted up by those who oppose homosexuality (although the practice in v. 22 is about a very specific behavior), but the fervor doesn't seem to reach back three verses to go after those who have sexual relations with a woman during her menstrual period (v. 19), even though the text forbids both. Yet everybody is on board with the prohibitions against incestuous relationships (18:6–18), child sacrifice (18:21), and sex with animals (v. 23).

An Eye **For An Eye**

Leviticus 24:19–20 reads, *"Anyone who maims another shall suffer the same injury in return; fracture for fracture, eye for eye, tooth for tooth; the injury inflicted is the injury to be suffered."* The same thing is worded a bit differently in Exodus 21:23–25. While, in our heart of hearts, that kind of karmic retribution might be what we wish for when we or someone we love has been harmed, there aren't many today who would want such straightforward vengeance in our legal code. It sounds too barbaric. Rabbinic interpretation apparently thinks so, too, and considers the law to be about monetary compensation.

Because it sounds uncivilized to us, we often fail to realize that we are reading the first legal code of a new nation formed about 3,500 years ago. Even if we take it at face value, this law is actually a merciful improvement, considering the historical period in which it was written. Let's say a man attacks your sister and stabs out her eye. What is your response? Many if not most people want to kill the guy and, absent a law like this one, that's exactly what they did.

This law puts a lid on human vengeance, saying you may only take an eye for an eye. You can't take both his eyes, his tongue, and one leg. In other words, the punishment must match the crime. Jesus will famously take this law further in the Sermon on the Mount saying,

> *"You have heard that it was said, 'An eye for an eye and a tooth for a tooth.' But I say to you, do not resist an evildoer. But if anyone strikes you on the right cheek, turn the other also." (Matthew 5:38–39)*

For what it's worth, we don't much like Jesus' version either. "But, Jesus, can't I just poke him in the eye a few times—you know, not so it comes out or anything, just so it hurts…"

What often goes unnoticed in these laws is the reason given for establishing this set of laws and ritual practices.

> "Speak to the people of Israel and say to them: I am the LORD your God. You shall not do as they do in the land of Egypt, where you lived, and you shall not do as they do in the land of Canaan, to which I am bringing you. You shall not follow their statutes. My ordinances you shall observe and my statutes you shall keep, following them: I am the LORD your God." (Leviticus 18:2–4)

These are laws given to Israel to make them "holy"—that is, set apart from other nations. In reading what God forbids we are, by extension, reading what the gods of surrounding nations permit, or even command. These are not automatically eternal laws given in a vacuum for all time. They are the laws that will set Israel apart as a distinct nation with a distinct God. The word "holy" appears forty-six times in the book of Leviticus. Leviticus 20:26 says, "You shall be holy to me; for I the LORD am holy, and I have separated you from the other peoples to be mine."

Not only are the particular laws themselves set in contrast to the laws of surrounding nations, but there is an even deeper way that all this mind-numbing detail of ritual practices, tabernacle building, and law distinguishes both Israel and Israel's God.

Back in session one, we noted that in ancient cultures the overriding question was not, "Is there a God?" but rather, "What does God want?" The existence of a god or gods was a given, as was the underlying belief that everything that happened was a result of that god's pleasure or displeasure. Figuring out what your god(s) wanted was what stood between you and destruction, starvation, and all kinds of abject misery.

The kicker was that the gods of Egypt, Babylon, Canaan, and all the others were too busy competing with one another for control of the pantheon to bother to communicate with their worshippers about what they wanted. The surrounding cultures had a deep underlying angst because they had to guess and rely on trial and error to discover what on earth it was that their gods expected of them. They had laws, to be sure, but those laws were not considered to be god-given, as they were in Israel.

The wonder of these books of endless detail is that the God of Israel actually says, "I want you to do this and not that." This is a God who doesn't insist that you be a mind reader and, in fact, tells you to stay away from mind readers. The Law of Moses provided the comfort of knowing what would and would not be pleasing to God. And knowing what would please God would, they believed, ensure good crop yields, fertile wives, protection from enemies, and all the other blessings necessary for a culture to grow and thrive.

Consider detailed passages like this one:

> "Moreover you shall make the tabernacle with ten curtains of fine twisted linen, and blue, purple, and crimson yarns; you shall make them with cherubim skillfully worked into them. The length of each curtain shall be twenty-eight cubits, and the width of each curtain four cubits; all the curtains shall be of the same size. Five curtains shall be joined to one another; and the other five curtains shall be

LAYING DOWN THE LAW

joined to one another. You shall make loops of blue on the edge of the outermost curtain in the first set; and likewise you shall make loops on the edge of the outermost curtain in the second set. You shall make fifty loops on the one curtain, and you shall make fifty loops on the edge of the curtain that is in the second set; the loops shall be opposite one another. You shall make fifty clasps of gold, and join the curtains to one another with the clasps, so that the tabernacle may be one whole." (Exodus 26:1–6)

Diagram of the Tabernacle

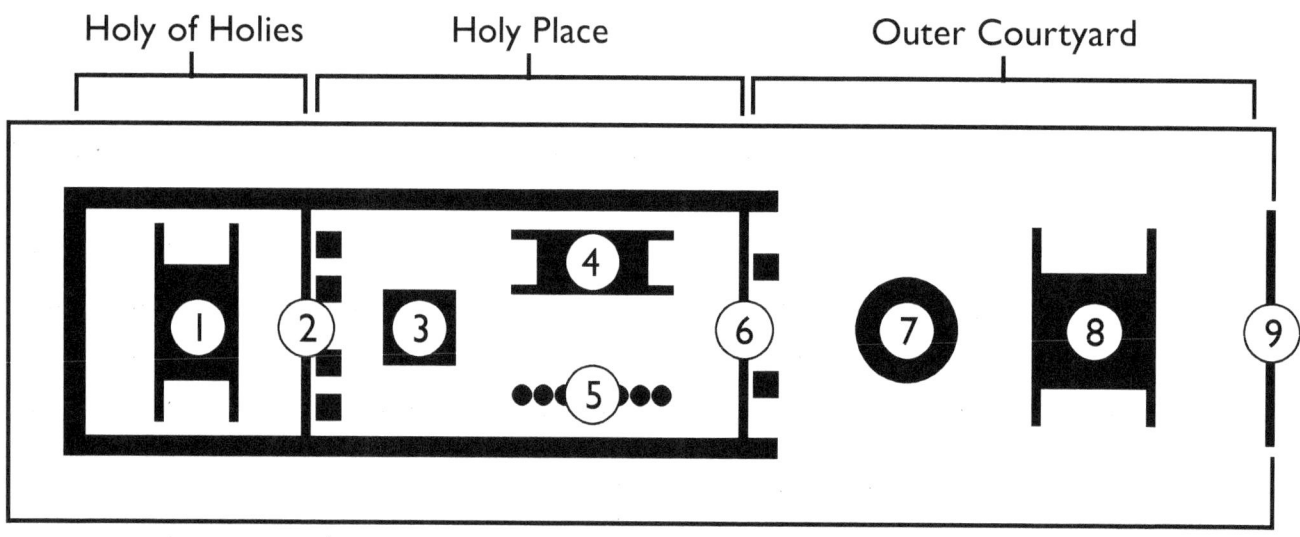

1 Ark of Covenant with "Szekhinah"
2 Veil
3 Altar of Incense
4 Table of Shewbread
5 Menorah
6 Door
7 Laver
8 Altar of Burnt Offerings
9 Entrance Gate

I don't know about you, but I read that passage and can only imagine what Monty Python would do with it: "Fifty loops shalt thou count, no more, no less. Fifty-one shalt thou not count, neither count thou forty-nine…" We look at it and think, "Come on, now. Is God going to open the trapdoor to hell if I put in fifty-one loops? Am I cast out of the covenant if I weave in some yellow or want pomegranates instead of cherubim? And linen…gosh…it wrinkles so easily!"

Of course, people who like to build things love it, and there's enough detail that full-scale replicas of the wilderness Tabernacle have actually been made. There are also people who get into the symbolism of the curtains and colors and cloth. But mainly the contemporary reader has to wonder…why is all that stuff in here? To what does it bear witness—not just this law, but all of it?

The answer is: It proclaims that Israel is in a relationship with a God who communicates. When someone asks, "What does God want?" in Israel, there is an answer that has come directly from God's lips—albeit mediated through the lips of Moses. And **that** makes Israel the envy of other nations and makes Israel's God appealing to those who encounter the Hebrew culture. After all, sticking to fifty curtain loops when HGTV advises fifty-five is a small price to pay for a bumper crop of grapes and six children who live into adulthood. And you get a day off every week to boot.

This theme that the God of Israel is knowable and desirous of intimate relationship with human beings cannot be overstated. It was there from the very beginning as God and Adam worked together to complete creation. It was there as Abraham bargained with God over how many righteous people it would take to save Sodom and Gomorrah. It was there when Jacob wrestled with an angel and got a new name as a blessing; and it was there as God and Moses worked miracles to thwart Pharaoh and free the

Hebrew slaves. Israel's God both wants relationship with human beings and is willing to seal and signify that relationship in covenant.

The proclamation of a relational God will continue to be a thread woven through all the stories that follow in both the Old and the New Testaments. St. Paul perhaps sums it up best when he visits Athens and is trying to figure out how to describe God to that polytheistic culture. Paul says to them,

> "For as I went through the city and looked carefully at the objects of your worship, I found among them an altar with the inscription, 'To an unknown god.' What therefore you worship as unknown, this I proclaim to you." (Acts 17:23)

The God of Israel can be known and wants to be known. The gods of other nations can't. That is the message.

Another **Great Book**

Although it is a work of historical fiction, <u>The Source</u>[5] by James Michener opens a detailed window into life in Canaan/Israel from its earliest times forward. This well-researched (and very long) novel follows an archaeological dig in Israel as the workers uncover the various layers of a tel.

Because water in the region has always been scarce, cities were built, conquered, and rebuilt on the same sites, wherever a reliable water source could be found. As a new city grew over the ruins of the old, the ground gradually rose underneath. The resulting mound is called a tel.

Archaeologists who dig at such a site uncover layer after layer and are able to learn much about the various cultures represented, the times that a city flourished, and often the means by which it was destroyed.

Michener's book was required reading for me in my biblical archaeology class, and I highly recommend it.

---

[5] Random House, New York, 1965.

The Story

Of course Cecil B. DeMille's epic film didn't send people dashing to the laws of Leviticus or even to the Ten Commandments themselves. That wasn't what made **The Ten Commandments** a hit movie. The jewel in the crown of this section of Scripture—arguably even of the entire Old Testament—is the **epic story** of an enslaved people escaping their captors, wandering in the wilderness, and finally entering the Promised Land.

There is really no way around the fact that you really need to just read the first half of Exodus. You should also watch the movie, although it does mix Hollywood license in with the biblical account. Truly, what part of the story are you going to skip? The decree of Pharaoh to kill any boy born to a Hebrew woman? The brave midwives who wouldn't do it? The Hebrew mother who hid the baby Moses in a basket and sent him floating down the Nile only to be found and adopted by Pharaoh's own daughter?

Will you skip the day that Moses realized his heritage, killed a cruel Egyptian, and had to flee Egypt for his life? Or how about when he saw the bush that was on fire but would not be consumed, went to investigate and ended up learning the name of God and learning that God wanted him to go back to Egypt and free his people? Even as you read you'll hear the echoes of the African American spiritual, "Go down, Moses, way down in Egypt's land. Tell ol' Pharaoh to let my people go."

You're certainly not going to skip the drama of Moses and his brother Aaron, time and time again paying a visit to Pharaoh and calling down plague after plague on Egypt, as the magicians of the Egyptian court tried to duplicate each plague to prove that the gods of Egypt were just as powerful as the God of Moses. Frogs, locusts, boils, gnats, darkness…

The Child Moses Trampling on the Pharaoh's Crown, ca. 1765.
Drawing by Francesco Bartolozzi after a painting by Nicolas Poussin

Moses and the Crown of Pharaoh

When God calls on Moses to free the Hebrew slaves, Moses presents almost an entire chapter of excuses about why he can't do it. The final excuse: He's not a good speaker: *"Oh my Lord, I have never been eloquent, neither in the past nor even now that you have spoken to your servant; but I am slow of speech and slow of tongue"* (Exodus 4:10). This really irritates God, who finally tells Moses to get his brother Aaron to do the speaking for him.

The passage, however, gave rise to the notion that Moses had a lisp, a stutter, or some other kind of speech impediment. The first-century historian Flavius Josephus explains this a bit further with a story that does not appear in the Bible. In it, three-year-old Moses is sitting with his adopted mother at Pharaoh's table. In fun, Pharaoh takes his crown and puts it on Moses' head. In a tantrum, Moses throws the crown down on the floor and steps on it.

This is problematic since doing such a thing is punishable by death, even if you're only three. But before such a sentence can be carried out, an angel intervenes, taking the shape of one of the wise men of the court. The angel then advises a test to see whether the child did the deed intentionally: Bring young Moses both hot coals and precious stones for him to choose between (apparently with the assumption that choosing the gems means malice of forethought). Moses (guided by the angel) picks up a coal and does what any three-year-old would do—tries to put it in his mouth. He burns his lips and voila! He now has a speech impediment.

the list of plagues goes on and on. It's almost comical at points, until it turns deadly and the firstborn of every household in Egypt—right up to the firstborn of Pharaoh himself—is struck down dead. I can still feel the dread that crept over me in the film when I saw the cloud that turns into the hand of the angel of death, crawling across the night sky. Things like that probably explain why the film won an Oscar for special effects.

You're not going to pass over Passover, the escape of the slaves into the night, the chase given by Pharaoh's army, or the parting of the Red Sea. Miracles and mayhem, manna (the word in Hebrew means "what is it?") falling from heaven, and poor Moses trying to run the show all by himself until his father-in-law orders him to delegate. And then the band of travelers arrives at the foot of a shaking, fiery mountain, enveloped in a cloud of smoke.

> **Read Exodus 1-18.** Just do it.

Just pour a glass of your favorite beverage, kick back, and read it. Rent the movie and see if you can spot the differences from the biblical account. But do look out for that cloud/hand of death thing. I wouldn't mess with it if I were you.

Of course there are great stories from this period in the other books as well. You'll look at the stories of Rahab, Deborah, and Jael in the class session, but there simply isn't time to get to them all. You should read Joshua 4–6, as the Israelites fully take control of the land, the new generation is initiated into the covenant, Joshua is formalized as the successor to Moses, and those ten-foot-thick, fourteen-foot-high walls of Jericho that had been standing for over **six thousand years** came tumbling down at a trumpet blast.

There's the story (and the movie—actually six movies—and the opera, and the song by the Grateful Dead) of Samson and Delilah, which you can always pull out when you don't like your son's girlfriend (Judges 13–16).

Shibboleth

Ever heard this term? It refers to a custom or belief (especially an outmoded one) that distinguishes one class or group of people from another. Its origin is in Judges 12, where Jephthah was taking revenge against the Ephraimites for not helping him in another battle. Since the Ephraimites were one of Israel's own tribes, it was difficult for Jephthah's men to tell who was friend and who was foe. They solved the problem by demanding that soldiers say the word "Shibboleth." The Ephraimites would invariably say "Sibboleth," and it would be the last thing they would say.

If you like mighty warrior stories there's Gideon in Judges 6–8, and if you need to remember to think twice before making a rash promise, read the tragic story of Jepthah and his daughter in Judges 11:29–40.

Personally I think you should also read Numbers 22, just because you should never pass up the opportunity to read about talking donkeys. Besides, if you skip it, you'll never understand all the Balaam's ass jokes.

That Other Ark

Apart from great stories, there's one more item to note before we move on. We need to stop and examine the furniture. We've seen God's concern with curtain loops and the very specific detail given for the creation of Israel's first national worship space: the Tabernacle. This set of instructions begins in Exodus 25, immediately after Israel has accepted the covenant relationship offered on Mt. Sinai. The Tabernacle was a moveable tent-shrine designed to be packed up and carried with the nomadic Israelites wherever they went.

At the heart of the Tabernacle was a large box—an ark, which you may recall means a place of safety. The details for this ark's construction begin in Exodus 25:10 and it is the single most important piece of furniture in the Bible.

Inside this ark are placed the stone tablets bearing the Ten Commandments, some manna from the wilderness sojourn, and a rod belonging to Moses's brother Aaron. (The story about that rod is found in Numbers 17.) With the law defining the covenant inside it, the ark became known as the Ark of the Covenant and, with the "mercy seat" on top of it, it becomes very literally the seat of law for Israel.

Balaam and the Angel, Gustav Jaeger, 1836

Over time, the ark takes on almost magical properties in the biblical accounts. It has poles so that it can be carried, and it is carried as a talisman into battle. Waters part before it. When it resides in a town, that town is blessed. If enemies capture it, the enemy town where it resides is cursed. One poor soul named Uzzah once reached out to steady the thing as the oxen carrying it stumbled and was struck dead for his efforts (2 Samuel 6:6–11).

A craftsman's artistic rendering of the Ark of the Covenant

Most contemporary Americans know the ark as the magical artifact that launched Indiana Jones to box-office gold, but the effort to find the Ark of the Covenant is a legitimate archaeological search. Once Israel switched from a moveable tabernacle to a fixed temple in Jerusalem, the Ark of the Covenant went inside the Temple and stayed there, and nobody knows what happened to it. If you took the first course in this series you did some research on the various theories of its whereabouts. Or maybe you've seen TV programming about it, since there's a tribe in Ethiopia that claims to have it.

We mention the ark here because it was created under Moses as the physical housing for the covenant symbols and because in the days of the kingdoms to come, it can almost be considered a biblical character in its own right. And, if you ever do stumble across it, for God's sake don't touch it!

The Story's Impact

The sweeping epic of the Exodus has resonated throughout the millennia, especially with peoples who have been oppressed or enslaved. The impact of the Exodus saga on the experience of African American slaves in the US was profound, with Harriet Tubman dubbed "Moses" for her work in helping slaves to escape.

Although white preachers were sent to the slaves to quote Bible passages about slaves obeying masters, that message was subtly undermined as slaves learned to read the only book they were allowed to have. They opened their Bibles to Exodus, and they heard the words of God saying to Moses,

> "I have observed the misery of my people who are in Egypt; I have heard their cry on account of their taskmasters. Indeed, I know their sufferings, and I have come down to deliver them from the Egyptians, and to bring them up out of that land to a good and broad land, a land flowing with milk and honey." (Exodus 3:7–8)

God, it seemed, was into freedom, and the message took hold. The Exodus story became their story, molded into both metaphor and spirituals that contained the code for escape opportunities.

Israel's wilderness wanderings also form the foundation for the Christian season of Lent and resonate with anyone going through a difficult stretch of life. The stories of the wilderness in Exodus, Numbers, and Deuteronomy have reassured millions that God cares for them even in the dry times and that enduring in such times will form them in new ways and prepare them for a land of promise.

Woodcut of Harriet Tubman, ca. 1869

Moses himself becomes enmeshed in Messianic prophecy when in Deuteronomy 18:15 he says to the people, "The LORD your God will raise up for you a prophet like me from among your own people; you shall heed such a prophet." Eyes would be on the lookout for the prophet like Moses from that time onward.

PREPARATION FOR CHECK-IN

(Prepare for the next group session by thinking about and writing a brief response to these two questions.)

What is one thing that was new to me in this material?

What is one question that this week's topic raises for me?

Homework (All students)

- ☐ Read the Student Text for Session 4 along with the associated Bible readings. **Plan ahead, as Session 4 has more reading than previous sessions.**
- ☐ Think about the reflection questions in the text.
- ☐ Review the assignment for the Extra Miles students. Find and listen to one musical setting of a psalm.

Extra Mile (CEU and Certificate Students)

Every single psalm has been put to music multiple times and some are quite famous. From classical works to rap, there are renditions of psalms in almost every musical genre.

- ☐ Find musical settings (in any style) for three different psalms to share with the class. Work with your group facilitator on how best to present what you find.
- ☐ Possible types of sharing could include:
  - Having the group sing the hymns/songs. Many are printed in denominational hymnals and songbooks.
  - Ask a musician in your group to play and/or sing them.
  - Play a music track.
  - Find a video performance of the music on YouTube and share that.
  - Invite a musician from your community to join you for this segment of the class and perform.

Note that if there are several Extra Mile students in your class, you may not have time to share all three, so you should pick a favorite song in case there is only time for one of the selections you have chosen.

UNITED WE STAND

Materials you will need for your fourth class session:

This student text

Your study Bible

Materials for taking notes

Your responses to the check-in questions on p. 145

A description of the Psalm setting you heard

Extra Mile Students: The music you will share with the group

Historical Era: 1030–922 B.C.E.

Parts of the Bible covered: 1 and 2 Samuel, 1 Kings 1–11, 1 Chronicles, 2 Chronicles 1–9, Psalms, Proverbs, Ecclesiastes, Song of Songs

Timeline for **Session Four**

☐ **World Events (Outside the Bible)**

1026 B.C.E.	Saul anointed as king by the prophet Samuel
1006 B.C.E.	David ascends the throne of Israel
1000 B.C.E.	**World population reaches 50 million** **Chinese develop counting boards (forerunner of the abacus)** **Wheeled battering rams first used by Assyrians** **Mounted cavalry first figure in combat** **Ancient Iranians enter Persia** **Latins come to Italy from the Danube region** **Beginnings of the Tamil language in India**
1000 B.C.E.	Portions of the Torah are first written down
970 B.C.E.	Solomon becomes king of Israel
957 B.C.E.	First Temple constructed in Jerusalem
931 B.C.E.	Death of Solomon
922 B.C.E.	Kingdom of Israel divides into the northern kingdom of Israel and the southern kingdom of Judah

The People's Choice

PEOPLE: "Give us a king!"
GOD: "What? You don't need a king. You have me."

PEOPLE: "Give us a king!"
GOD: "You'll be sorry. Kings are nasty."

PEOPLE: "Give us a king!"
GOD: "You don't love me anymore."

PEOPLE: "Give us a king!"
GOD: "Okay. You asked for it..."

Saul and David, William Reijers, Alkmaar, Netherlands

This chapter is about how it all went down. But first, let's catch up with the world, because it is precisely that early Iron Age world that makes Israel think kingship would be a good idea.

Boys in the Middle East have been able to attend school for about two thousand years now. For the first four hundred of those years there were just two of the three "Rs." Students could read and they could write. The Sumerians threw in the 'rithmatic about 2400 B.C.E., and for 1,600 years those poor early students were struggling without calculators. No longer. The Chinese gave the world counting boards (the forerunner to the abacus) around the year 1000 B.C.E. and India allowed traders to say that they didn't have any by inventing the number zero. The Chinese celebrated this milestone by inventing pasta, paving the way for the later arrival of SpaghettiOs.

In Israel, however, people are focused on their writing and it's during this period that the individual stories found in the first five books of the Old Testament are first written down. As we'll see in this chapter, this is also the period that saw some of Israel's greatest building projects, which only became possible when nomads decided to settle in one place, replacing the sporadic leadership of the judges with the more stable presence of a king.

As Israel came into contact with more and more of the outside world, it seemed good to them to settle down, build cities, and establish the worship of God in one place. Babylon, Ugarit, Egypt, Assyria—they all had kings and the kings were surrounded by their advisors and sages. What's wrong with that? Team up a prophet with a king and you've got a winning combination—or at least that was the theory. All of that happened during this period, with mixed results. It's a period marked by three kings and one prophet. We'll look at the prophet first.

Samuel

During the period of the judges, we didn't hear much about prophets. The word doesn't appear even once in the book of Joshua and it shows up only twice in the book of Judges. One of the latter references is to Deborah, one of the judges, and in the second reference, the prophet who is mentioned isn't even named. By contrast, in 1 and 2 Samuel, the word appears fourteen times and, of course, the prophet Samuel is a central character.

The story of Samuel begins with a now-familiar theme: a barren woman who is, nonetheless, a beloved wife. We saw it first with Abraham and Sarah, then with Isaac

> **Read 1 Samuel 1-3.**
> The birth and childhood of Samuel.

and Rebekah, Jacob and Rachel, and Manoah and his wife (the parents of Samson). Now this recurring motif appears again with Elkanah and his beloved Hannah.

The story of Samuel's origins are quite moving. Barren Hannah goes to pray for a child at the shrine in Shiloh and is so distraught that the priest, Eli, thinks she is drunk and reprimands her. Talk about adding insult to injury! When she explains her predicament, Eli softens and tells her that her prayer will be granted.

Hannah is thrilled, but the news must have come with an edge. A part of her prayer was that if God granted her a child, she would give him or her to God's service. That didn't mean he'd be a preacher one day when he grew up. It meant that as soon as Samuel was weaned, she'd have to give her only son over to a consecrated life and he would go to live with the priest Eli in Shiloh. After that, she'd see him just once a year.

It couldn't have been easy, yet the song of praise that Hannah sings as she gives away her toddler (1 Samuel 2:1–10) has been cited as a possible source for Mary's **Magnificat** in Luke 1:46–55. Remember that Mary was a young, Jewish woman. Why wouldn't the lovely song of Hannah inform her own song as Mary learned that she, too, was with child when no one thought it possible?

And so Samuel is born, weaned, and raised in the house of Eli. Once Samuel reaches adulthood, he naturally assumes that his sons will provide whatever leadership Israel needs, just as Samuel had. Samuel

Hannah Prays for a Son, from the Admont Giant Bible, located at Austrian National Library in Vienna, Austria

serves as both a prophet and a judge, much as Deborah had been. So as Samuel ages, he appoints his sons as judges.

Samuel's sons, however, are so bad at their jobs that the people decide they've had it with judges. Israel has had enough contact with other nations now to know there are other political games in town. The people bring a message to Samuel: *"You are old and your sons do not follow in your ways; appoint for us, then, a king to govern us, like other nations."* (1 Samuel 8:5)

Of course part of Samuel's job description is to bring this request of the people to God—and God is not pleased. If I were to guess, I'd say that it was the "like other nations" part of the request that stuck in God's craw. If you remember, we've had entire books devoted to laws and rituals whose purpose was to set the Israelites apart from other nations—to make and keep them "holy." Now the Israelites are petitioning God to be just a tad less holy and have something in common with other lands and peoples.

God doesn't like it, and Samuel's report back to the people says it all. Samuel describes all the nasty things that kings will require of them, finishing it off with this in verse 18: *"And in that day you will cry out because of your king, whom you have chosen for yourselves; but the* LORD *will not answer you in that day."* (1 Samuel 8:18)

> **The Role of the Prophet**
>
> While we tend to think of prophets as those who can foretell the future, that's not the primary role of the biblical prophet. In the Bible, a prophet is one who speaks messages from God to the people and who often intercedes with God on the people's behalf. Those messages from God sometimes involved warnings of what was to come, but "prophecy" in its biblical sense doesn't have to include that component.

The people, however, have had Samuel on mute and insist: *"No! but we are determined to have a king over us, so that we also may be like other nations, and that our king may govern us and go out before us and fight our battles."* You can almost hear Samuel's sigh as he takes the report back to God. God doesn't say much: *"Listen to their voice and set a king over them."* Not an auspicious beginning, but the deed is done and the search for an appropriate candidate begins.

The Holy City

Let's pause the story here for a moment to look further into why the idea of a settled city didn't sit well with either Samuel or God. Why was that aspect of the life of other nations so problematic? This comes up not only

Virupaksha Temple at Hampi, India

in settling down and having a king in a capital city. God has a similar reaction when building a permanent temple is proposed to replace the moveable tabernacle created in the wilderness. The two things are linked.

As we learned in Session 1, cities didn't originate as places of business or as secure housing for the population, even though they eventually provide both. The very first cities were built as dwellings for the gods. There was usually a central temple, and the entire city served as a temple complex.

Temple gardens symbolized the fertility given by the god, and their produce was used as an offering. Often water flowed out from the temple, signifying the waters of creation. In many places there was also something like the ziggurat, providing a means by which the god of the city could get down from the heavenly realms to receive the offerings of the people. These weren't stairways **to** heaven—people did not go up—but stairways **from** heaven. Because, you know, nobody had invented parachutes.

What's more, the design of ancient temples was meant to reflect the design of the cosmos. To take part of the Lord's Prayer completely out of context, "on earth as it is in heaven." While the primeval waters flowed around the temple gardens, the temple itself was the dry land that emerged and made human life possible.

There was some kind of representation of the deity inside each of these ancient temples, and the god it represented had to come down the stairs and give formal approval before the idol was thought to be effective. Once the god had flipped the on switch, it was believed that the god was present within the effigy. There was even a mouth-washing ritual to be sure the image could eat, drink, and smell the incense provided as offerings.

The temple wasn't where the people went to worship; the temple was where the god went to live. It was modeled after what people assumed the god's heavenly dwelling was like. Access to the god's house was strictly limited, especially when it came to the innermost chamber where the image of the god was located. People brought offerings to the priests, much as truckers deliver goods to the staff of a large estate. Lesser staff prepared the offerings and only the god's main man would actually set out the meal.

Once the god had shown up and was dwelling in the temple, well, a god's got needs. Other city structures and enterprises arose to meet those needs, including the housing for those who presented the offerings and maintained the sanctity of the temple and its environs.

With the god present in the image, the temple became the absolute center—not only of religious life, but of political and social life as well. Ancient temples were actually the first banks—all the wealth of the city or (if it was the capital city) of the nation was kept there, under the watchful eye of the god.

The City of the King

The temple in the capital city wasn't only the nation's bank, it was the home of whatever god headed that nation's pantheon. That was necessary because only the top god could properly evaluate and keep an eye on the king. If the king was not to the god's liking, then the god would abandon the temple, threatening  the nation with chaos—with "un-creation." A nation thrown back into the primordial waters would, according to the ancient criteria for existence, cease to be.

Moreover, the king needed access to the most important god, because the king was dealing with the most important matters of the state. If a leader in a village didn't properly honor the god of that village, the consequences were local. But if the king messed up and the god of the capital city was unhappy, then the entire nation was threatened with ruin.

That meant that if the nation enjoyed peace, or was at least winning its wars; if the crop yields were good throughout the land; if the people were not visited by plague or natural disaster, then the god of the nation (rather than the individual, household gods) must have been happy with what the king was doing, and they should keep him. If things went well in the land, then obviously the king had the god's approval. It's not a far step from this to believing that the king is a god.

It Was a Bad Idea

To contemporary ears, the longing for a king seems like a simple request for a different form of government when the system that had been in place seemed inadequate. And why not build a temple? We've had brick and mortar houses of worship for millennia, and it seems reasonable.

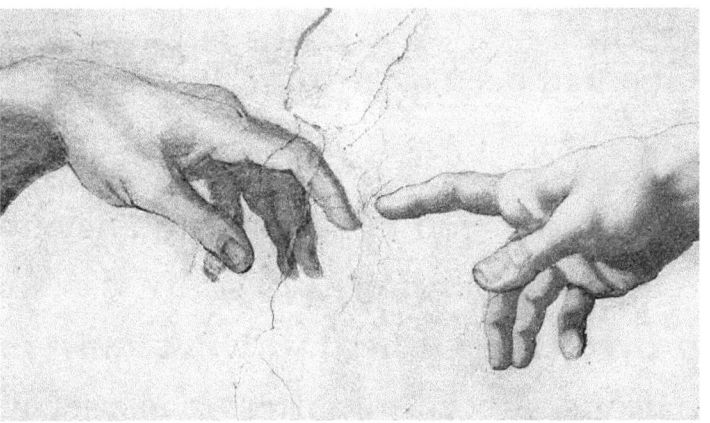

Detail from *The Creation of Adam*, Michelangelo

But for a people whose way of life was designed to model a view of God fundamentally different from the surrounding nations, the ancient understanding of both temples and kings was bound to undermine that witness.

The stories of the God of Israel to this point showed a God who was as likely to show up and wrestle a cheater as to fill the tabernacle with glory. The God of Abraham, Isaac, and Jacob never needed stairs to make an appearance and see what was happening, and it was Israel's God who even shared the process of creation with human beings by allowing Adam to name the animals. Israel bore witness to a God who communicated directly, who wanted to provide for the needs of people rather than the other way round, and who was willing to become family with anyone and everyone willing to accept the offer.

Most importantly, the witness of the Bible is that Israel's God is one—a point that often needed emphasis when some Israelites drifted into the worship of additional gods from the surrounding cultures. "No!" cry the stories of the Bible. The God of Israel didn't dwell here and not there—with the people of this city but not the people of that city. The one and only God was with the people, all the people, wherever they went—dwelling in the midst of those who were willing to enter covenant relationship. Moreover, God had been clear from the time that rainbow first appeared in the sky that the goal was to have the whole earth as part of that covenant family.

Every single thing about the ancient understanding of kingship and temples undermined that witness. And, as the next five hundred years proved, the witness was not only undermined in the eyes of other nations, it was forgotten by Israel itself. Ironically, even in this, the God of Israel is distinct. Israel is flying in the face of what God wants but, unlike other gods, Israel's God doesn't leave in a huff. God allows them to make their own mistakes and tries to work with them to make lemonade out of lemons.

With God's point made and the warning given, God is back with the program, telling Samuel about a young man who will come to Samuel looking for some lost donkeys. That young man's name is Saul, and he returns home both with his donkeys and with the promise that he will be the first king of Israel.

Annointing

The ritual that Israel used for the selection of a new king was anointing—that is, the pouring or smearing of oil (or other substance) in a ritual fashion. Other people and things were anointed as well, when they were set apart for sacred purpose.

Anointing Jar

The Hebrew word for "anointed one" is **mashiach**, translated in English as messiah. Christians often forget that the term messiah is used frequently in the Bible to refer to many people seen as serving a divine purpose. Even Cyrus the Great, the king of Persia, is called "God's anointed" in Isaiah 44:28. The Jewish expectation of a messiah was certainly for a very special "anointed one," but the expectation was for a great human being like Moses or Elijah or King David, not for a divine being come to earth.

There were definitely expectations of a "messiah" in the Hebrew Bible (although the word is not used in the Pentateuch); Christians should be very careful not to endow that word with our own interpretations. It meant and still means something very different to Jewish ears.

We Three Kings

Once God relented and allowed Israel to anoint a king, all the disparate tribes of Israel were united under one leader. First came Saul, then David, then Solomon, marking a period that became known as the United Monarchy. 1 and 2 Samuel (which are only one book in the Hebrew Bible) cover this period, as does the beginning of 1 Kings and 1 Chronicles 10 through 2 Chronicles 9. (See page 228 for more on the books of Chronicles.)

After Solomon's forty years on the throne, God pulls the plug on Solomon and the kingdom is divided into north and south. That "Divided Monarchy" will be the subject of the next chapter, but for now let's look at these three kings whose strengths first established (and whose flaws eventually unraveled) Israel as a united kingdom.

Saul

When last we saw Saul, he was out looking for his father's donkeys, deciding to visit the prophet Samuel to see if Samuel's powers of divination could succeed where plain old looking could not. This visit coincides with the back-and-forth between Samuel, the Israelites, and God over whether or not to have a king, and it seems that Saul is in the right place at the right time.

Why Saul? you might ask. The Bible doesn't give us any reason why God would select Saul above any other Israelite at the time. 1 Samuel 9:2 tells us only that Saul is the most handsome guy around and that "he stood head and shoulders above everyone else." There's no indication that he is a great warrior, has uncommon faith or wisdom, is well-connected, or

David Playing the Harp Before Saul, Lucas van Leyden, 1508

anything else that might make him a suitable candidate to be Israel's first king. In fact, when it comes time for Samuel to officially anoint him, Saul is hiding among the baggage and has to be dragged out. It doesn't really get better.

Given how unhappy both God and Samuel were about the request for a king, a cynical person might think that choosing Saul was a revenge pick, especially given the way things played out. Saul becomes king in 1 Samuel 10 and by chapter 13 he's blowing it. By the end of chapter 15, God and Samuel have both had enough of Saul, a sentiment echoed in the closing verse of that chapter: *"And the LORD was sorry that he had made Saul king over Israel."*

This is where things get tricky. God has dumped Saul from favor and in chapter 16 God has Samuel anoint a new king—David, son of Jesse the Bethlehemite. But the people as a whole aren't in on this arrangement. David may have been anointed by Samuel, but Saul is still the reigning monarch and will remain so until his death. That situation was awkward enough, but it got worse.

As it turns out, Saul wasn't just disobedient to God's commands. He was also mentally unstable:

> "Now the spirit of the LORD departed from Saul, and an evil spirit from the LORD tormented him. And Saul's servants said to him, 'See now, an evil spirit from God is tormenting you. Let our lord now command the servants who attend you to look for someone who is skillful in playing the lyre; and when the evil spirit from God is upon you, he will play it, and you will feel better.'" (1 Samuel 16:14–16)

God Did **What?**

In reading about the evil spirit tormenting Saul, some might be disturbed at the claim that the evil spirit was "from God." This is merely monotheism at work. While polytheistic cultures had good gods and evil (or at least mischievous) gods, statements like that one in 1 Samuel 16 reflect the claim that Israel has one God that has complete control over good and evil alike. To imply that an evil spirit of some other origin could take over God's anointed king would put that evil spirit at least on par with, if not greater than God. That would never do.

Well, guess who they found to play for King Saul? Yep—David. Thus began one of the most tormented love/hate relationships in the entire Bible.

Chapter 17 gives us the famous story of David and Goliath, establishing David's faithfulness over and against Saul's disobedience; David's military prowess above Saul's failures. (If you didn't read that story in the first course of this series, you should read it now.) By the time the armies are coming home from the battle, women are out dancing in the streets singing "Saul has killed his thousands, and David his ten thousands." It doesn't take a

Saul Attacking David, Guercino 1646

rocket scientist to imagine that this doesn't go over well with Saul. In fact, the very next day, as David is playing his lyre for King Saul, Saul hurls a spear at him.

The rest of 1 Samuel is basically the story of Saul trying to find a way to kill David, and David outwitting him, even as David consistently shows him mercy. They speak to each other like father and son—indeed, David is Saul's son-in-law, having won Saul's daughter Michal as a wife for killing Goliath. Saul's son Jonathan is also David's best friend. In fact, the language used for their relationship is so intense that some have suggested it was more than a friendship. Saul implies that himself in 1 Samuel 20:30.

With help from both Michal and Jonathan, David escapes from Saul's court and spends the rest of the book bolting from cave to cave with Saul in hot pursuit. Also out there are the Philistines, the Amalekites, and

> ***Read 1 Samuel 18-20, 24 and 28, 31, and 2 Samuel 1.***
> The relationship goes south.
> David spares Saul's life.
> Saul and the witch Endor.
> The death of Saul.

other enemies that both Saul and David have to contend with, and the text alternates between those battles and the various encounters between Saul and David.

Since the days when Goliath taunted the armies of Israel at Socoh, Saul had been afraid of the Philistines, and eventually they cornered Saul on Mt. Gilboa. Without the prowess of young David by his side, Saul, Jonathan, and two of Saul's other sons are killed. While Saul's death is merely described in 1 Samuel (albeit in gory detail), in 1 Chronicles it is retold with some commentary.

> "So Saul died for his unfaithfulness; he was unfaithful to the LORD in that he did not keep the command of the LORD; moreover, he had consulted a medium, seeking guidance, and did not seek guidance from the LORD. Therefore the LORD put him to death and turned the kingdom over to David son of Jesse." (1 Chronicles 10:13–14)

Samuel and Kings saw Saul largely as a military failure, Chronicles highlighted Saul's moral failings, but both finally agreed that it was time for a better king.

David

The story of David overshadowed the story of Saul in 1 Samuel, much as the young David overshadowed Saul's reign. As we move into 2 Samuel, however, it's David, front and center, for the entire book.

Before David ascended the throne, the primary stories about him focused on his faithfulness and his military prowess. Once the throne was securely in David's

> ***Read 2 Samuel 11-12, Psalm 51.***
> David and Bathsheba.

Death of King Saul, Elie Marcuse 1848

David, Michelangelo

hands, however, the primary narrative grew much darker. It begins in 2 Samuel 11 with the wife of one of David's elite soldiers taking a bath up where everyone took baths in those days—up where the water was warm—on the roof.

You can (and should) read the story for yourself, but the basics are that David sees Bathsheba, wants her, and takes her because he is king and he can. Her husband Uriah is out fighting in a battle with the Ammonites. Bathsheba becomes pregnant from the encounter, so David brings Uriah home in the hopes that he'll go relax with his wife and everyone will think the baby is his.

No such luck. Uriah is a faithful soldier—one of the reasons he is listed in the Bible as one of thirty soldiers on which David depended the most. Uriah refuses to even go home, let alone enjoy himself with his wife, while his men are in combat—in stark contrast to the warrior David who didn't even go into battle in the first place. David tries getting Uriah drunk. Still nothing.

Uriah goes back to battle and then David does the most despicable thing of all. He tells Joab, the commanding officer, to put Uriah into the thick of battle and then pull back support so that Uriah will have no hope of survival. The orders are carried out, Uriah dies, and David takes Bathsheba into the palace as his wife. Funny how all the famous artwork of this story seems to be limited to depictions of Bathsheba bathing.

Saul's missteps pale by comparison, and God is none too pleased with David, but he retains the throne and God's favor anyway. There is now a court prophet named Nathan, who uses a gut-wrenching story about a man and a lamb to call David to account. As the story brings David back to his own youth as a shepherd, the tactic works and David repents. The son born of the illicit union dies, but with Bathsheba, David has a second child—Solomon. Notes at the beginning of Psalm 51 indicate that the psalm was David's expression of remorse for the whole nasty business.

As you can tell from the Psalms (which we'll look at in a bit), David is a passionate guy, which becomes evident as his reign continues. He's also highly conflicted. Just as he was unwilling to kill Saul when he had the chance—even though Saul was trying to kill him—so David is unable to confront with his own sons who try to take his throne. David's son Absalom even goes so far as to sleep with David's concubines, yet David keeps directing his men to protect Absalom at all costs. Joab, David's commanding officer, finally has enough of all the drama and goes after David's son.

If you want your sons to keep their hair short, tell them about Absalom. As he flees from Joab, Absalom gallops quickly through the trees. But a low-hanging branch catches his long locks, leaving him hanging helplessly from the tree until Joab is upon him. Joab puts three spears through Absalom, and that is that.

Absalom Riding on a Mule, Chagall

At the end of David's life, it's another son, Adonijah, who pretty much announces that he's the new king, even holding a banquet to celebrate his ascension to the throne. Bathsheba, however, nips that plan in the bud by getting the bedridden David to name their son, Solomon, as David's successor. Solomon ruthlessly dispenses with Adonijah and all other threats. By the end of 1 Kings 2 we read, "So the kingdom was established in the hand of Solomon."

Solomon

King Solomon is known primarily for two things: his wisdom and his building projects. We'll look at the wisdom part when we discuss the book of Proverbs later in this chapter. Here we'll look at his greatest physical legacy—the Temple in Jerusalem.

It was actually David who wanted to build a temple. He brought up the matter to Nathan pretty early on (in 2 Samuel 7), apparently feeling guilty that he himself was living in a lovely palace while the Ark of God was stuck in a tent. Nathan tells him to go ahead and build a temple.

Nathan forgot the bit about checking with God first, however, and God interrupts Nathan with a dream that nixes the plan. "Did I ever ask you for a house?" God says, in essence. "Did I ever complain about being in a tent?" You can almost hear God sighing. Once again, though, God goes along with the plan and ends up promising untold blessings to David, saying that God will ensure that David's throne is established forever.

King Solomon With Plans for the Temple
Greek Catholic icon in Cathedral in Hajdúdorog, Hungary

It is David's son, God says, who will build God a house. The reason for the delay? David still wants a role in temple creation (or at least the author of Chronicles would like him to have one), so in 1 Chronicles 22, David starts collecting the building materials. He amasses a starter kit of 3,750 **tons** of gold, 37,500 **tons** of silver, and even more bronze, iron, and timber. (Just as a reference, there are currently about 4,600 tons of gold in Fort Knox.)

David also makes sure that Solomon knows he has a job ahead. It is in these instructions by David to Solomon that we hear a slightly different take on why David isn't the temple builder. He says to Solomon:

> "My son, I had planned to build a house to the name of the LORD my God. But the word of the LORD came to me, saying, 'You have shed much blood and have waged great wars; you shall not build a house to my name, because you have shed so much blood in my sight on the earth. See, a son shall be born to you; he shall be a man of peace. I will give him peace from all his enemies on every side; for his name shall be Solomon, and I will give peace and quiet to Israel in his days. He shall build a house for my name. He shall be a son to me, and I will be a father to him, and I will establish his royal throne in Israel forever.'" (1 Chronicles 22:7–10) (See page 228 for additional notes on the nature of the book of Chronicles.)

I'm not sure that the beginning of 1 Kings shows us a man of peace, but compared to the amount of blood that David shed across his career, Solomon probably looked like Gandhi.

In any case, Solomon did indeed build the Temple, which took seven years to complete. (Of course, since seven is the symbolic number of perfection, it is unclear whether it was actually seven years—could have been more or less.)

By contrast, the construction of Solomon's palace complex took thirteen years. In addition to those two grand projects, Solomon also built a citadel called the Millo, a palace for at least one of his wives (a daughter of Pharaoh), and entire cities devoted to storage, chariots, and horsemen. Imagine entire cities devoted to storage—makes me feel better about my stuffed closets.

King Solomon was reported to have 12,000 horses and 1,400 chariots, and archaeologists have confirmed that there were stalls for at least 450 horses in the city of Megiddo. Unfortunately, all that building was done with slave labor and funded through heavy taxation.

Artistic rendering of Solomon's Temple in Jerusalem

Solomon seems to have collapsed under the weight of his own success. With almost as many wives and concubines as he had chariots, he made strategic alliances. But those women came with the gods of their own nations and weren't about to give them up. Solomon not only tolerated their gods, he built shrines for them. Idolatry entered into the very house of the king of Israel, and God was not happy.

In 1 Kings 11, the seeds of rebellion are sown and God makes it clear that, while Solomon will remain king until his death to fulfill God's promise to David, after that all bets are off. An Ephraimite (one of those people who can't pronounce shibboleth correctly) named Jeroboam will take over the north and Solomon's son, Rehoboam, will rule just a small portion of the south. After just three generations, the united kingdom splits in two.

> **For Reflection**
>
> What are your thoughts about monarchy as a form of government?
>
> Are there advantages to centralized power? Disadvantages?
>
> Do you think Israel made the right move politically in moving to the kingship model?

Wine, Women, and Song

The stories of Saul, David, and Solomon are only part of the richness of this period. David and Solomon also left a legacy of music and literature that resulted in at least four additional books of the Bible: Psalms, Proverbs, Ecclesiastes, and Song of Songs (aka the Song of Solomon). While many consider either some or all of those books to be the work of others, their authors clearly wanted to link their work to the lives of these important biblical figures.

French writer and artist Jean Cocteau once said, "The poet is a liar who always speaks the truth." We've already considered the difference between truth and fact as we've tried to put ourselves into the minds of an ancient people whose main vehicle for transmitting truth to future generations was through myth, story, and song. These four works are entire books of the Bible that convey truth in just that way.

There have been a few scattered songs and poems in the books we've looked at so far. When the Israelites crossed the Red Sea in Exodus, Moses and his sister Miriam sang a song of victory. Most of Deuteronomy 32–33 is either song or poetry; Deborah sings in Judges 5; Hannah sings in 1 Samuel 2. But those are just the warm-ups.

> **Muslims and the Psalms**
>
> Muslim tradition also holds the Psalms in high regard, believing that God gave the Psalms to David in the same way that the Torah was given to Moses and the Qur'an was given to Mohammad.

Once a king has been established and the twelve tribes settle into the land as a united nation, music and poetry flourish, aided by the fact that King

David was himself a musician. The first seventy-two psalms (seventy-three in the Greek and Latin version of the Old Testament, which divides Psalm 9 of the Hebrew Bible into two) are traditionally linked to him.

Although many of the psalms come from a later period and the dating of some of the other poetic books is debated, the four books mentioned all have traditional connections to the people of this period, so we'll look at them here.

Not only are these books of a different genre than we've encountered so far, but they largely serve a different purpose. The stories, laws, and conquests that we've looked at until this point are presented over and against the faith and practice of the surrounding cultures. In short, they have told us about the nature of Israel's God by contrast.

In these books, however, the focus shifts a bit. While this type of "wisdom literature" can be found in nearby nations, they tell us less about God than they do about ourselves. In Israel's songs and poems we experience the wide range of human emotion. Joy, anger, grief, pride, depression, praise, lust, thanksgiving, fear, longing, malaise, judgment, love—it's all there. Each book holds up a mirror, allowing us to see yet another facet of the human psyche. It isn't always pretty, but there it sits in the middle of sacred Scripture, letting us know that whatever we see in that mirror, the God of Israel can handle it.

Psalms

First, the basics. The word "psalms" (don't pronounce the p) comes from the name of the book in Greek, **psalmoi**, which means music accompanied by a stringed instrument. The Psalms are not merely poems. They're lyrics to songs. This is the hymnal of ancient Israel and if you look closely, you'll see that many of the Psalms have introductions and/or instructions (set in italics in most translations) for the musicians. Did any of the actual music survive? Unfortunately, no—at least not that we've found.

There are 150 Psalms in Protestant, Catholic, and Hebrew Bibles. The Orthodox tradition has one more, and that tradition was validated when a Hebrew copy of that 151st Psalm turned up in the Dead Sea Scrolls. When included in a translation, it is labeled as Psalm 151 to avoid the confusion of re-numbering all the others. Sometimes you'll find it grouped with the books of the Apocrypha. It belongs with the first seventy-two (or seventy-three as explained above) Psalms of David as it recounts his battle with Goliath.

Lyres, British Museum

Psalm 151

My hands made a harp, my fingers fashioned a lyre.

And who will declare it to my Lord? The Lord himself; it is he who hears.

It was he who sent his messenger and took me from my father's sheep, and anointed me with his anointing oil.

My brothers were handsome and tall, but the Lord was not pleased with them.

I went out to meet the Philistine, and he cursed me by his idols.

But I drew his own sword; I beheaded him, and removed reproach from the people of Israel.

Dating any individual psalm is tricky, if not impossible. The consensus is that although they begin in King David's time (ca. 1000 B.C.E.), some were written centuries later, and there's even evidence that some psalms had sections that were added at various times in order to adapt the song for ritual use.

While we often think of the Psalms as songs of praise, they're filled with almost every human emotion you can think of. In addition to the praise psalms, there are laments as well as songs clearly meant to be used in a liturgical setting. Psalms 120–134, for example, are collectively known as the "Songs of Ascent" and scholars believe pilgrims used them as they approached the temple in Jerusalem. If you look at Psalm 136, you'll notice that the second half of every one of the psalm's twenty-six verses reads, "for his steadfast love endures forever." If that psalm is not a liturgical call and response, I'll eat my piano.

Some psalms even have an apparent educational goal in mind. The longest psalm is Psalm 119 (with 176 verses) and every set of eight verses begins with a successive letter of the Hebrew alphabet. Many Christians know only verse 105, which was popularized by Amy Grant's "Thy Word," which now appears in many hymnals. Just for the record, the shortest psalm is Psalm 117 with only two verses. Seven of the psalms are acrostics, with the first letter of each section spelling out a word or message—a characteristic not retained in English translations. There. Now you're ready for your **Jeopardy** appearance.

The poetic device generally retained in translation (in all Hebrew poetry, not just the Psalms) is the ancient Hebrew practice of parallelism. That refers to the appearance of two successive phrases where the second phrase provides a variation that expands or emphasizes the meaning of the first. Sometimes that goal is reached by saying something similar in the second phrase and sometimes by saying the antithesis. Here are examples of each:

Similar Emphasis

Psalm **27:1**

"The LORD is my light and my salvation; whom shall I fear?
The LORD is the stronghold of my life; of whom shall I be afraid?"

Proverbs **27:2**

"Let another praise you, and not your own mouth—a stranger, and not your own lips."

Song of Songs **1:7**

"Tell me, you whom my soul loves,
where you pasture your flock,
where you make it lie down at noon;"

Opposite Emphasis

Psalm **27:1**

"O let the evil of the wicked come to an end, but establish the righteous, you who test the minds and hearts, O righteous God."

Proverbs **27:2**

"The mind of one who has understanding seeks knowledge, but the mouths of fools feed on folly."

Proverbs **27:2**

"The heart of the wise is in the house of mourning; but the heart of fools is in the house of mirth."

You don't have to look very hard to find examples.

Clearly in the Psalms we're dealing with the truth of the poet and musician, not the truth of the historian or scientist. So what do we take from these ancient songs?

> Find examples of either kind of parallelism in ten different psalms.

To begin with, we take a boatload of our own music. From classical music to hymns to praise music, to chants, to musicals, reggae, and rock and roll, you can find the Psalms sung today all over the planet.

The Psalms still have a liturgical role in many church traditions and are central in most monastic communities. Even in the most non-liturgical traditions, you will hear at least Psalm 23 and perhaps others at a funeral.

What both the singing and the reciting of the Psalms in worship show us is that these poems have a greater power to move us when spoken or sung than when they are simply read silently to ourselves. While something similar could be said for narrative stories, the impact of speaking/singing/hearing poetry resonates in a unique way. If your only experience of the Psalms is reading them silently, try reading them aloud. It's an entirely different experience.

Church Music

The very first book printed in America was the Bay Psalm Book. For about the first hundred years of our history, the only singing that went on in churches was the chanting of the Psalms. It was a novel, and heavily resisted, idea to sing those new-fangled hymns from Britain (like "Amazing Grace," for example) that had churchgoers singing theology rather than Scripture. Eventually, of course, those hymns became the standard and people forgot that "Amazing Grace" was a new hymn once.

The Psalms, especially, are packages of condensed emotion. Their joy is infectious, their fear is palpable, their anger burns hot, and their questions are very frequently our own. The Psalms don't show us how God's people **should** pray; they show us how God's people **did** pray in the good, the bad, and the ugly of life. This, I think, is the kind of "truth" they offer us.

Take Psalm 137 as an example. The beginning of this psalm is a lament, reflecting the pain felt by those Israelites who were captured when Jerusalem was sacked in 587 B.C.E. and taken into captivity in Babylon. There are many beautiful musical works based on this psalm, from **Super Flumina** by Palestrina, to "Rivers of Babylon" by the Melodians, to my personal favorite, "On the Willows," from the musical **Godspell**.

While it's based on the experience of the calamitous siege of Jerusalem and subsequent exile (which we'll learn about in Session 6), there are so many people today who find that the cries of this psalm echo their own.

By the Rivers of Babylon in the Chludov Psalter, Mid 9th Century

> By the rivers of Babylon—
>> there we sat down and there we wept
>> when we remembered Zion.
> On the willows there
>> we hung up our harps.
> For there our captors
>> asked us for songs,
>> and our tormentors asked for mirth, saying,
>> "Sing us one of the songs of Zion!"
> How could we sing the LORD's song
>> in a foreign land?
> If I forget you, O Jerusalem,
>> let my right hand wither!
> Let my tongue cling to the roof of my mouth,
>> if I do not remember you,
>> if I do not set Jerusalem
>> above my highest joy. (v. 1–6)

For the refugee, for the immigrant, for anyone in a foreign land—or even just a situation that feels like a foreign land—and feeling the pangs of homesickness, this is a tearjerker of a psalm.

And then, as it so often does in real life, the psalm takes an abrupt turn as abject grief gives way to anger. The psalmist (who in this psalm is not identified) wishes for the wrath of God to avenge the wrongs they have suffered.

> O daughter Babylon, you
>   devastator!
> Happy shall they be who pay
>   you back
> what you have done to us!
> Happy shall they be who take
>   your little ones
>   and dash them against the rock! (v. 8–9)

Now there's a lovely thought. But, really, it isn't meant to be a lovely thought. This is not a religious teaching. This is an expression of pain and anger by someone who has experienced some of the worst that life can dish out. Descriptions of the siege that preceded the fall and destruction of Jerusalem include accounts of parents eating their dead children to stay alive. Then the city was burned, innocents were slaughtered, and anybody with a useful skill was marched off to Babylon. We're talking bad.

Psalm 137 is not a model prayer; it is an honest prayer, and I'm willing to bet that many similar cries to God were raised when the twin towers fell to the ground on September 11, 2001.

Of course most of the psalms do not contain that sort of violence and when we get to course number three of Exploring the Bible, I hope we can lay to rest the mistaken notion that the Old Testament is somehow more violent or vengeful than the New. It isn't. But I lift up this particular psalm because I have seen so many stumble on it.

If we look to the Psalms for the wrong kind of truth, we can be led astray. But if we hear in the Psalms the real cries of human hearts in all the joys and sorrows of life, we'll find these lyrics to be beloved, life-long companions.

Proverbs

The book of Proverbs is exactly as advertised. They are proverbial sayings and teachings about wisdom—some shorter, some longer—mostly in poetic form. The book attributes the wisdom in its pages to "Solomon son of David, king of Israel" (v. 1), and while the collection was probably not edited together until the time of the exile, there's no reason to question that at least a good portion of the material was preserved from King Solomon's court.

Remember the book of 1 Kings, chapter 3, when King David has died and the throne is given to David's son, the eighteen- or nineteen-year-old Solomon. God shows up and asks what gift Solomon would like to receive. Solomon requests wisdom, saying:

> And now, O LORD my God, you have made your servant king in place of my father David, although I am only a little child; I do not know how to go out or come in. And your servant is in the midst of the people whom you have chosen, a great people, so numerous they cannot be numbered or counted. Give your servant therefore an understanding mind to govern your people, able to discern between good and evil; for who can govern this your great people? (1 Kings 3:7–9)

God really likes this request and promises that Solomon will be the wisest person ever, and throws in riches and honor to boot. The stories of Solomon then focus on showing examples of that wisdom, like the famous case of the divided baby in 1 Kings 3:16–28. Word of Solomon's wisdom spread and the Queen of Sheba (modern Ethiopia and Yemen) came to Jerusalem to see for herself. We get descriptions of Solomon's vast wealth, both in treasure and in the coin of wives and concubines (of which Solomon reportedly had three hundred and seven hundred, respectively).

The point of putting all that in a sacred text is to show how God's promises to Solomon were kept. Many, if not most, of those wives were arranged marriages with kings and nobility of other nations, highlighting the high honor accorded Solomon across the known world. The treasure attests to his wealth, which came to him on account of his great wisdom. Given the role that wisdom played in Solomon's kingship, it would be no surprise if scribes were kept busy writing down his words for posterity.

The Judgment of Solomon, Gustave Doré, 19th century

Which is not to say that every proverb in the book—or even **any** proverb in the book—sprang from the lips of Solomon. Even in a strictly literal rendering, the book itself attributes some sayings to a person named Agur and another person named Lemuel. I also have to wonder whether the acrostic poem about the "good wife" that closes the book originated with Solomon. If that's what Solomon expected of his wives, I don't know how he ever got three hundred of them!

> **Read 1 Kings 3:16-28.**
> Solomon's Judgment.

The first nine chapters of Proverbs are a bit different from the rest of the book. This section is presented not as wise sayings but as poetic instruction about the nature of wisdom itself. Or—as wisdom is portrayed in the text—herself. Wisdom (**sophia** in the Greek) is personified in these first chapters as a woman who instructs the people:

Wisdom cries out in the street; in the squares she raises her voice. At the busiest corner she cries out; at the entrance of the city gates she speaks: "How long, O simple ones, will you love being simple? How long will scoffers delight in their scoffing and fools hate knowledge? Give heed to my reproof; I will pour out my thoughts to you; I will make my words known to you." (Proverbs 1:20–23)

I'm inclined to elect her to Congress.

A Word from the **Wise**

The following are some of the better-known sayings found in the book of Proverbs (KJV):

The fear of the LORD is the beginning of knowledge. (1:7)

Pride goeth before destruction, and a haughty spirit before a fall. (16:18)

As a dog returns to his vomit, so a fool returns to his folly. (26:11)

He that is slow to anger is better than the mighty; and he that ruleth his spirit than he that taketh a city. (16:32)

Even a fool, when he holds his peace, is counted wise. (17:28)

He that troubles his own house shall inherit the wind. (11:29)

Train up a child in the way he should go: and when he is old, he will not depart from it. (22:6)

A merry heart doeth good like a medicine: but a broken spirit drieth the bones. (17:22)

Trust in the LORD with all thine heart, and lean not unto thine own understanding. (3:5)

A soft answer turneth away wrath: but grievous words stir up anger. (15:1)

Reprove not a scorner, lest he hate thee: rebuke a wise man, and he will love thee. (9:8)

Pleasant words are as an honeycomb, sweet to the soul, and health to the bones. (16:24)

The teachings of Lady Wisdom go on until the end of chapter 9 at which point we get a shift from the longer poetic form to the more staccato proverbs of the rest of the book. Indeed, the text re-inserts the heading "The proverbs of Solomon" at the beginning of chapter 10.

Ecclesiastes

The Hebrew name for this book is **Qoheleth**, which means teacher or, perhaps, assembler. Rather than a teacher of a single pupil, the Hebrew word implies the teacher of some kind of assembly. Thus, when the text was translated into Greek, the word **ekklesia** (which means assembly) was used, giving us the English, Ecclesiastes.

Cemetery Gates, Chagall 1917

Who was this teacher? Well, the first verse says, "The words of the Teacher, the son of David, king in Jerusalem." This is repeated in verse 12, which reads, "I, the Teacher, when king over Israel in Jerusalem," and goes on to describe what is clearly meant to imply the life of King Solomon for the rest of chapter 1. As a result the work has been attributed to Solomon. Literary scholars, however, consider authorship by Solomon impossible due to the style of the writing, which matches the Hebrew of about 300 B.C.E.—some six hundred years after the time of Solomon.

Although the date of the book is uncertain, there is one thing we know for sure. This book was written before the development of Prozac. While Ecclesiastes 3:1–8 is the most famous section of the book (popularized by The Byrds in the 1965 hit "Turn! Turn! Turn!"), the next most familiar passages come from the first chapter, and are much more characteristic of the tone of the book: "Vanity of vanities, says the Teacher, vanity of vanities! All is vanity." (v. 2) and "What has been is what will be, and what has been done is what will be done; there is nothing new under the sun." (v. 9) It doesn't make you want to charge right out and change the world.

The Hebrew word for vanity here is **hebel** and means an emptiness—something that is transitory and/or unsatisfactory. The word is used thirty-four times in Ecclesiastes, which has only twelve chapters. Once the strains of "Turn! Turn! Turn!" fade away, we stop reading, but Qoheleth is still gearing up.

> I said in my heart with regard to human beings that God is testing them to show that they are but animals. For the fate of humans and the fate of animals is the same; as one dies, so dies the other. They all have the same breath, and humans have no advantage over the animals; for all is vanity. All go to one place; all are from the dust, and all turn to dust again. (Ecclesiastes 3:18–20)

That's pretty representative of the book. The person who penned the bumper sticker phrase, "Life's a b**** and then you die," was channeling his inner Qoheleth. Portions of the book are reminiscent of the book of Proverbs (one of the reasons I tend to think Solomon had something to do with it), but it really doesn't get much more encouraging. "If the snake bites before it is charmed, there is no advantage in a charmer." (10:11) Well, yes, there is that.

Some rabbis have pointed out that everything Qoheleth finds futile is to be found **under** the sun and it is therefore to the God who is **over** the sun that we should look for life's meaning and purpose. Perhaps.

I tend to think that Ecclesiastes is one of those books we just need to sit with for a while. It reminds us that life is not all sunshine and roses, that wickedness often wins the day, and that this earthly life has the same ending for all of us. Nobody gets out alive. That does not have to negate the promises and hope of other sections of the Bible, however. Ecclesiastes can helpfully serve as a counter-weight and foil to any attempt to see light without shadow.

SONG OF SONGS

> "Let him kiss me with the kisses of his mouth! For your love is better than wine, your anointing oils are fragrant, your name is perfume poured out; therefore the maidens love you. Draw me after you, let us make haste. The king has brought me into his chambers. We will exult and rejoice in you; we will extol your love more than wine; rightly do they love you." (Song of Songs 1:2–4)

And so begins "The Song of Songs, which is Solomon's." (Song of Songs 1:1)

Alternatively known as either the Song of Songs (sometimes the Canticle of Canticles) or the Song of Solomon, this book of the Bible is eight chapters of dripping sensuality. Shaped as a dialogue between a man (identified in the text as Solomon) and a woman (presumably one of Solomon's many wives or concubines), the book describes their love and longing for each other in unabashedly physical terms.

Book of Love, Jonathan Thorne

The date of the composition is unknown and authorship is ascribed to Solomon only from the first verse. Certainly it presents as being about Solomon and a ladylove, but the text (as well as scholarship) is vague about whether Solomon is actually considered the author.

There are really only two things you need to know about this charming ode to sexual love. The first is that both Jewish and Christian traditions view it as a metaphor for the love between God and God's people. Especially in the Old Testament, the image of God as the husband of Israel is writ large, something we'll examine more when we get to the prophet Hosea. Song of Songs is interpreted in light of that common metaphor.

The second thing to know is that such an interpretation is not even hinted at in this lusty text. I'm not saying it's wrong, I'm just pointing out that such a reading is 100 percent interpretation. "His Banner Over Me Is Love" is a praise song that I learned in church when I was a teenager. The song lyrics are taken from chapter 2:4, 16, and I sang them with gusto, hand motions and all, perfectly convinced that the banqueting table I was invited to was the Lord's. If my mother had known what was in the surrounding verses, however, she probably would have marched our whole family down the aisle and out the door. A preacher's son once confided in me how helpful this book was during his teen years as his hormones raged. "Just reading the Bible, Dad!"

One of the reasons I personally love the Old Testament is that it is inclusive of all aspects of life. To spiritualize everything the Bible has to say is to miss the key point that this is a book about faithful (and unfaithful) living in the real world. It is a world of wonder and mayhem, mercy and cruelty, war and forgiveness, betrayal and sacrifice, and—yes—the many faces of our sexual impulses. Part of the witness of the Bible is that God is the God of all of it and there is nothing common to human life that can be, or need be, hidden from that God. In our odd American culture that is at once highly sexualized and at the same time intensely puritanical, this little book reminds us that the God of the Bible doesn't hate sex or look askance at its pleasures within a loving relationship.

While you may not want to tell your own love that her teeth are "like a flock of shorn ewes" or that her nose is "like a tower of Lebanon," this celebration of body and heart is a welcome escape after all the "vanity" of Ecclesiastes. And it does remind us that Solomon was probably no more than twenty years old when he became king. Ah, youth.

Back at the Palace...

The years of Israel's united monarchy were mostly focused westward, trying to eradicate the Philistines who stood between Israel's new capital in Jerusalem and the sea. Preoccupied with Goliath and his minions, nobody noticed that to the east Assyrian soldiers were developing the boot, using the first battering rams, and taking mounted cavalry into combat. As the united kingdom splintered and became more vulnerable to outside powers, that inattention would cost them.

> ### For **Reflection**
>
> If you could add to the book of Proverbs more wise sayings that have been meaningful in your own life, what would you add?
>
> Saul, David, and Solomon all made major mistakes during their reigns, but God seemed more forgiving of David's mistakes than the others. Why do you think that was?

Preparation for Check-In

(Prepare for the next group session by thinking about and writing a brief response to these two questions.)

What is one thing that was new to me in this material?

| |
| |

What is one question that this week's topic raises for me?

| |
| |

Homework (All students)

☐ Read the Student Text for Session 5 along with the associated Bible readings.

☐ Think about the reflection questions in the text.

Extra Mile (CEU and Certificate Students)

☐ Choose one of the "Minor Prophets" from the period covered in Session 5:

Hosea	Obadiah	Habakkuk	Joel
Micah	Zephaniah	Amos	Nahum

☐ Research the prophet you have chosen—both the man and his writing—and prepare a report of about five hundred words on what you have found.

Be prepared to share the major points in the next class session.

DIVIDED WE FALL

Materials you will need for your fifth class session:

This student text

Your study Bible

Materials for taking notes

Your responses to the check-in questions on p. 192

Extra Mile Students: The information you will share about the prophet you have chosen

Historical Era: 931–586 B.C.E.

Parts of the Bible covered: 1 Kings 12–22, 2 Kings, 2 Chronicles 10–36, Isaiah, Jeremiah, Hosea, Joel, Amos, Obadiah, Jonah, Micah, Nahum, Habakkuk, Zephaniah

Timeline for **Session Five**

- Kings and Events in the North (Israel)
- Kings and Events in the South (Judah)
- World Events (Outside the Bible)
- Prophets in the North (Israel)
- Prophets in the South (Judah)
- *Important Event
- **Speculation on Date

931 B.C.E.	Jeroboam becomes king
931 B.C.E.	Rehoboam becomes king
913 B.C.E.	Abijah becomes king
911 B.C.E.	Asa becomes king
909 B.C.E.	Nadab becomes king / Baasah becomes king (after Nadab)
900 B.C.E.	Jerusalem builders create elaborate water supply system with reinforced subterranean tunnels
886 B.C.E.	Elah becomes king
885 B.C.E.	Zimri becomes king
*885 B.C.E.	Omri becomes king
*876 B.C.E.	Earliest known use of the symbol 0 (India)
*873 B.C.E.	Ahab becomes king (Jezebel is queen)
	Elijah 874 B.C.E.
871 B.C.E.	Jehoshaphat becomes king
853 B.C.E.	Ahaziah becomes king
	Elisha 853 B.C.E.
852 B.C.E.	Jehoram becomes king
848 B.C.E.	Jehoram becomes king

*842 B.C.E.	Jehu becomes king		
841 B.C.E.	Ahaziah becomes king		
840 B.C.E.	Athaliah becomes queen		
835 B.C.E.	Joash becomes king	Joel	**835 B.C.E.
*814 B.C.E.	**Carthage is founded**		
813 B.C.E.	Jehoahaz becomes king		
800 B.C.E.	**Homer writes Iliad and Odyssey** **Musical notation developed in Mesopotamia** **Chinese develop steam-propelled cart** **Egyptians develop sundials with six time divisions**		
797 B.C.E.	Jehoash becomes king		
796 B.C.E.	Amaziah becomes king		
*782 B.C.E.	Jeroboam II becomes king		
*776 B.C.E.	**First formal Olympiad**		
*767 B.C.E.	**First recorded world-wide plague**		
*767 B.C.E.	Uzziah (Azariah) becomes king	Amos	760 B.C.E.
*753 B.C.E.	**Rome is founded**		
753 B.C.E.	Zechariah becomes king		

			Hosea 750 B.C.E.
752 B.C.E.	Shallum becomes king Menahem becomes king		
742 B.C.E.	Pekahiah becomes king		Isaiah 742 B.C.E.
740 B.C.E.	Jotham becomes king		
			Micah 737 B.C.E.
732 B.C.E.	Hoshea becomes last king of Israel		
731 B.C.E.	Ahaz becomes king		
*723 B.C.E.	*Peking is founded*		
*722 B.C.E.	Assyria conquers Samaria ending northern kingdom		
*715 B.C.E.	Hezekiah becomes king		
*704 B.C.E.	*Capital of Assyria moved to Nineveh*		
701 B.C.E.	Hezekiah successfully revolts against Assyria		
700 B.C.E.	*Horseshoes invented in Europe*		
700 B.C.E.	Judah invents the first catapult		
687 B.C.E.	Manasseh becomes king		
*681 B.C.E.	*Assyria conquers Babylon*		
*668 B.C.E.	*Nineveh replaces Thebes as largest city in the world*		
*660 B.C.E.	*Founding of Japan*		
			Jeremiah 655 B.C.E.
650 B.C.E.	*Leprosy, tuberculosis, and gonorrhea first identified*		
642 B.C.E.	Amon becomes king		

*641 B.C.E.	Josiah becomes king	Zephaniah 640 B.C.E.
622 B.C.E.	Josiah finds missing book of the law in temple	Nahum 626 B.C.E.
*612 B.C.E.	**Babylon becomes the largest city in the world**	
609 B.C.E.	Jehoahaz becomes king	
608 B.C.E.	Jehoiakim becomes king	Habakkuk 608 B.C.E.
*605 B.C.E.	**Babylon conquers Nineveh, Assyria falls**	
600 B.C.E.	**Hanging Gardens of Babylon built** **Chinese invent printing** **First metal coins**	
598 B.C.E.	Jehoiachin becomes king	
597 B.C.E.	Zedekiah becomes king	
*590 B.C.E.	**Laws of Solon establish Athenian democracy**	
*587 B.C.E.	Babylon conquers Jerusalem	Obadiah 587 B.C.E.

Bas Relief of Phoenician Ship

It didn't last very long in the grand scheme of things. The Bible says Saul, David, and Solomon reigned for forty years apiece, although seeing that number forty might give us pause. It's generally a symbolic number (see p. 53), referring to a time of formative—and so ultimately positive—struggle. But that was then. This next historic period isn't positive at all; it will present Israel with the greatest test of its young national history.

Around the world things are moving quickly. The Phoenicians still dominate the seas (thanks to the addition of ramming capabilities to their galley ships) and are sailing around Africa and controlling the Straits of Gibraltar. They've also noticed that you can make some nifty purple dye from Mediterranean snails. God apparently foresaw this, since the divine decorating instructions for both the Tabernacle and the Temple called for purple yarn and cloth. While the Phoenicians rule the water, the Chinese are focusing on the land and develop the first steam-propelled cart. Yup, that's right: the Chinese have created a car in the year 800 B.C.E.

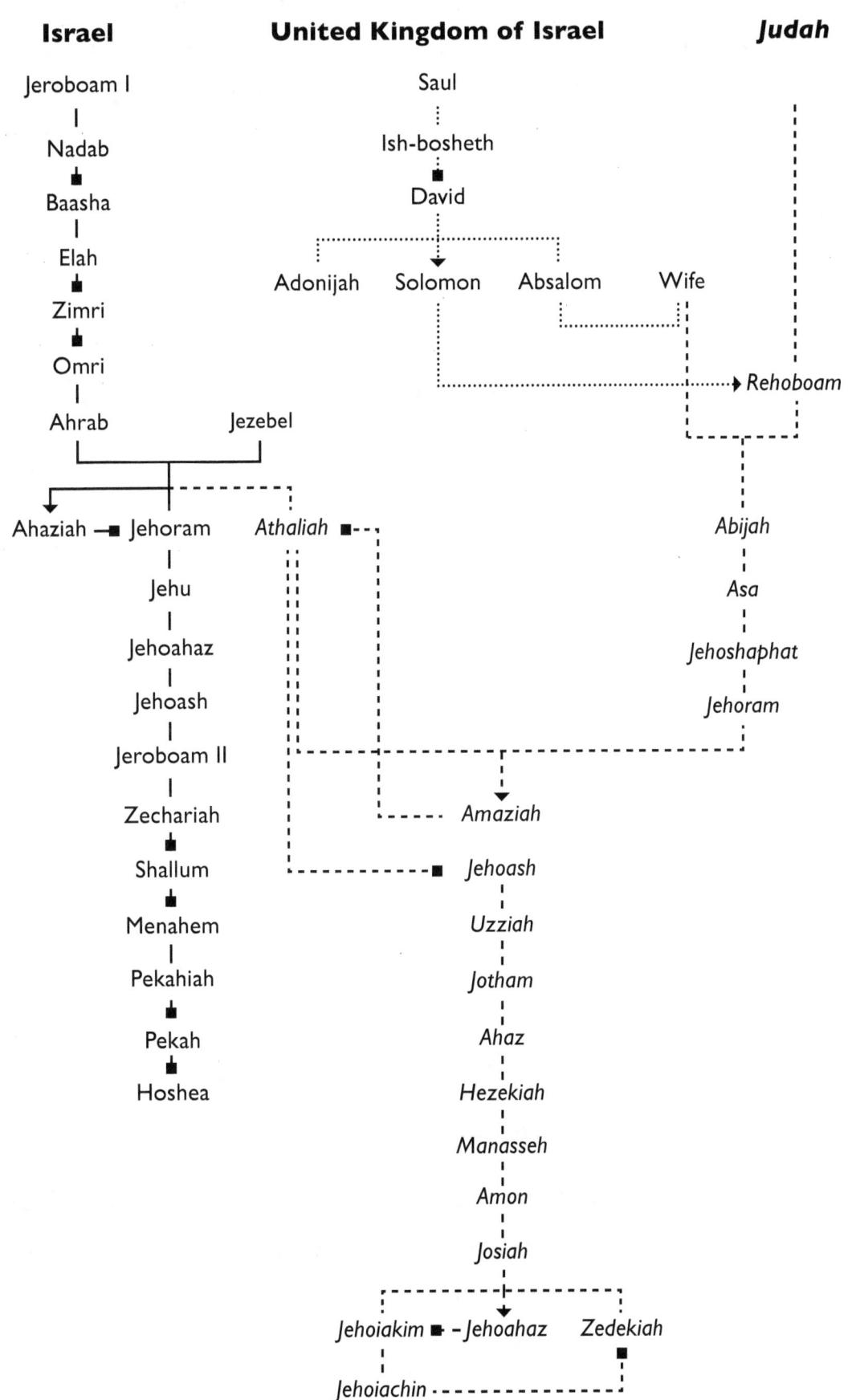

For their part, the Babylonians are looking up into the heavens and reporting a solar eclipse in 763 B.C.E., while the Egyptians have worked out sundials with six time divisions. But instead of gazing heavenward, perhaps the Babylonians and Egyptians should be looking at the Assyrians, who are busy putting metal wheels on their chariots. Further west a guy named Homer is writing his epic poems, The Iliad and The Odyssey, the first Olympiad is held, and the Europeans are inventing horseshoes. Oh yeah, and Rome is founded. Just founded, mind you. It wasn't built in a day...

Meanwhile, back in Israel, kings are multiplying—not doing arithmetic, but rather becoming numerous. The last 120 years have seen three kings: Saul, David, and Solomon. During the next 336 years there will be forty-one—well, forty kings and one queen regent—as what began as the single nation of Israel splits into two: Israel in the north and Judah in the south. Of all those many monarchs, just a few stand out. We'll look at them in this chapter, but the real stars of this period are not the kings but the prophets.

In the North

Cast your mind back to the time of Abraham, Isaac, and Jacob. Back then, God gave Jacob the new name of "Israel," and Jacob's twelve sons became the twelve tribes who comprised the eventual nation of Israel. (It's a little more complex than that, since the tribe of Jacob's son Joseph ended up becoming two half-tribes named for Joseph's sons, Ephraim and Manasseh, but you get the picture.)

When the united kingdom of Israel split in two after Solomon's death, ten of the twelve tribes became part of the northern kingdom of Israel, with Samaria as their capital, and two tribes (Judah and Benjamin) comprised the southern kingdom of Judah, with Jerusalem as their capital. After the death of Solomon, the rest of the books of Kings and Chronicles tell the stories of these two kingdoms—and of the kings and prophets who served them. We'll turn our attention first to the north.

It's notable that though there were twenty kings of the northern kingdom, the biblical writers didn't give them much respect, labeling all of them as "bad" kings. But let's take a look at what they meant by "bad." First, the label was religious, not political. To read the Bible, you'd think that Judah was a mighty kingdom and that Israel in the north was just an idolatrous afterthought. If you ask an archaeologist or historian, however, you'll discover that two of the most biblically derided kings of Israel, Omri and Ahab, actually formed a dynasty so well known that the Assyrians called the Kingdom of Israel the Kingdom of Omri, even well after his rule was over.

Politically, the northern kingdom was the powerhouse and the southern kingdom almost a vassal of the north—which is what you might expect when you divide a kingdom up ten tribes to two. Looking through the lens of the Bible, however—especially through the lens of those writers who were looking back at this period years later, from the perspective of their Babylonian Exile—the sins of the north are exactly what led to its destruction. To these writers, leading the people into the worship of other gods and establishing worship centers outside Jerusalem angered God enough to use the Assyrians to wipe the northern kingdom off the map forever. The northern rulers had abandoned "true" worship; that's what made them "bad."

How It Got This Way

Let's go back for a minute and look at the splitting of the kingdom, because it didn't really need to happen. While King Solomon was praised for his great wisdom, the Bible tells us that by the end of his life he was having an idolatry problem himself. Attempting to establish political connections with other nations and tribes, he married bucket-loads of wives, who came with their own gods, for whom Solomon, the solicitous husband, built shrines. But when your job is to witness to the world about monotheism, encouraging the worship of other gods isn't such a good idea.

In the last session, we learned that God disapproved, allowing Solomon to live out his reign in peace because of the promise to David, but keeping Solomon's son from inheriting the throne—or at least not much of one. Because of all the promises God had made to David about establishing his throne forever, God had to leave a bit of the family line in charge somewhere—but it wasn't much.

> ### Counting the **Years**
>
> Since the Bible tells us the number of years of a king's reign, it can seem like an easy task to simply tally it all up to determine how much time has passed. It is simple to add up, but your total will be wrong. There are two things to consider.
>
> The first thing is a topic we've already talked about—the ancient Israelite inclination to convey some of their truth through numerology. This extends both to genealogies (with the number of generations from one important person to another sometimes adjusted to support a symbolic reading) and to the length of a king's reign. When you see seven or twelve or forty or their multiples, your radar should always go up.
>
> The second thing to consider is the way that the number of years of a monarch's reign was counted. Let's say a king ruled for only three months. If those three months all fell within the same calendar year, his reign would be recorded as three months. However, if the three months happened to fall on both sides of a new year, the reign would be recorded as two years. A "year" didn't necessarily mean twelve months. It meant that the ruler reigned for at least a portion of the number of calendar years listed.
>
> Continued on next page

Counting the **Years** (Continued)

Complicating matters further, years were often identified in pretty confusing ways—for example, "the second year of King Joash son of Joahaz of Israel." Sometimes, though, as one king died and another took his place, you'd end up with two kings in one year, so rules were developed to determine which king the year would be named for: The outgoing king took precedence. Add to that practice the complexity of a divided kingdom. Once that happens, every year has not one but two labels—year x of King y of Israel and year b of King c of Judah. Add in co-regencies and different reign numbers in the Hebrew Bible and the Septuagint and you have a royal mess. I think math word problems probably can be traced to this period.

It's still the prophet's job to anoint kings and this time it's the prophet Ahijah who has the task of anointing Solomon's replacement. At the end of 1 Kings 11 we get a scene much like we had back when Samuel anointed David as king while Saul still ruled. This time, with Solomon still on the throne, Ahijah finds the able and industrious Jeroboam, one of Solomon's trusted leaders, and proclaims that God has given the vast majority of the kingdom to him.

Prophets were rarely content in those days to merely say something. They tended to illustrate their message with some kind of action or object lesson. In this case, Ahijah takes off his garment and tears it into twelve pieces, giving ten of them to Jeroboam to indicate the number of tribes that would be in his part of the kingdom. Probably Ahijah held the remaining two pieces over strategic parts of his anatomy as he walked home without a garment.

DIVIDED WE FALL

Of course Solomon doesn't take to this news any better than Saul had, and he responds in much the same way: He tries to kill Jeroboam. Jeroboam flees to Egypt, where we find him when Solomon dies and Solomon's son, Rehoboam, ascends to his father's throne. When Jeroboam hears the news, he returns to Israel, presumably with his ten garment pieces in hand. At that moment there is still one kingdom and everybody has shown up in Shechem to crown Rehoboam. And here is the turning point.

> **Read 1 Kings 12.**
> The Kingdom is divided.

What happened next should be required reading in any class on leadership. Even though the prophet told Jeroboam that God had chosen him as king, Jeroboam appears willing to give up his throne if it will keep the kingdom united—a very kingly move. Jeroboam speaks to Rehoboam on behalf of the people saying,

> "Your father [Solomon] made our yoke heavy. Now therefore lighten the hard service of your father and his heavy yoke that he placed on us, and we will serve you." (1 Kings 12:4)

The "yoke" they're talking about was the burden of forced labor and heavy taxation that had been imposed for all of Solomon's building projects. So everybody, even Jeroboam, is willing to get behind Rehoboam and keep the kingdom intact if Rehoboam will simply recognize and fix the oppressive burdens on the people. Rehoboam tells everybody to go away for three days while he thinks about it.

During those three days, Rehoboam consults two groups of advisors—the older advisors of his father and a group of his own peers. The older group says,

"If you will be a servant to this people today and serve them, and speak good words to them when you answer them, then they will be your servants forever." (v. 7)

Rehoboam's buddies, on the other hand, have different advice. This is what they tell him to say:

"My little finger is thicker than my father's loins. Now, whereas my father laid on you a heavy yoke, I will add to your yoke. My father disciplined you with whips, but I will discipline you with scorpions." (v. 10–11)

Rehoboam takes the advice of his peers, and the results are totally predictable. The vast majority of people say, "Ummm…no thanks," foreswear the House of David, and look to Jeroboam to lead them. The rest—there aren't many—follow Rehoboam back to Jerusalem.

So you'd think that Jeroboam and the new northern kingdom would be the favorites. After all, the prophet picked him, the people picked him, and an idiot with a tyrant complex is reigning in Jerusalem. But no. As Jeroboam surveys the new political reality, he decides that if his people still have to go to Jerusalem to worship, he won't ever be able to establish anything permanent in the north. So he builds two new shrines, one at Dan and one at Bethel. In each he puts a golden calf and tells the people, "Here are your gods, O Israel, who brought you up out of the land of Egypt."

Jeroboam should have known that things that begin with golden calves don't end well, and it didn't. Eventually even Ahijah, the prophet who had anointed Jeroboam in the first place, condemned him for idolatry. When all was said and done, although Jeroboam successfully consolidated the northern kingdom and ruled for twenty-two years (give or take), he was labeled a "bad" king of a divided kingdom.

On Golden **Calves**

The Golden Calf, Bernd Lauer

Whether it's Aaron or Jeroboam, when we hear that somebody sets up a golden calf as a god, we're puzzled. What were they thinking? These men weren't dime store leaders—they were pretty astute folks who should have known better.

The first we encounter, of course, is Moses's brother Aaron, who sets up a golden calf in the wilderness when the people decide that Moses has been so long up on the fiery, shaking Mt. Sinai that he's probably not coming back. (Exodus 32) And now we have Jeroboam, who has just proved himself to be a pretty savvy leader, doing something similar. Why didn't they see this coming?

One suggestion is that the calf wasn't meant to be a god, but rather a steed for Israel's God to ride. Since the making of images of God was forbidden, the suggestion is that the invisible God is riding the very visible steed. Well and good, but why would they think God needed a ride? Easy: because Baal had one.

Wait—who?

Continued on next page

On Golden **Calves** (Continued)

The stories of this period are rife with concerns about the surrounding Canaanite culture—especially Canaanite religion—seeping into Israel. The word **Baal** means "lord" or "master," and it was often affixed as a title before the name of a god in the polytheistic religions of the area. Thus the Bible often speaks of "the Baals" in the plural. In the Canaanite pantheon, the chief god in this period is Baal Hadad—that's the Baal meant when you see the word in the singular. And it just so happens that Baal Hadad rode a bull.

Consider the problems Aaron and Jeroboam faced. Aaron, left in charge of thousands of ex-slaves in a desert wilderness, wasn't sure if Moses was ever going to return. And Jeroboam had just taken the majority of people in a kingdom and seceded from the union, and he needed to start from scratch with religious practice. Both Aaron and Jeroboam would have been familiar with Canaanite culture and religion, and so would the people they were trying to lead.

So…if **their** god rode a bull, you could possibly make a statement about Israel's God (who couldn't be portrayed by any image) and give people a symbol they would understand (the steed of the top god) by making a calf with no rider. I can see how both men might have reached that conclusion.

On the flip side, Baal Hadad didn't always ride a bull. Sometimes he **was** a bull. So the golden calves may have been true idols after all. In any case, all of this was the kind of bull God doesn't put up with.

As Israel's history progresses, we'll see that some wounds don't heal—they just grow and fester. One of those festering wounds is the relationship between Judea and Samaria, the new capital of the northern kingdom. Remembering that the Bible has nothing good to say about any king who ruled from Samaria, we have the first rumblings of the split between Jews and Samaritans that will become deep enmity by the time of Jesus.

When it comes to the kings of the new northern kingdom, the only ones beside Jeroboam who warrant a mention here are Ahab, son of Omri (whose reign is dated somewhere around 869–850 B.C.E.), and Jehu, who brought the Omride dynasty to a screeching and bloody halt.

Ahab, Jezebel, and Elijah

You can always tell the truly colorful stories and characters of the Bible because Hollywood and/or Broadway make shows out of them. Ahab might be king, but it's his queen, Jezebel, who gets the movie (and a 1951 hit song by Frankie Laine). As a result, the name Jezebel has become synonymous with a scheming, idolatrous, seductive woman.

Bette Davis as Jezebel in the 1938 film by that name

That portrayal of Jezebel isn't just Hollywood fiction. The Bible paints her as the shrewd and corrupting voice behind a weak and easily compromised king. Her character is perfectly illustrated in the story of Naboth's Vineyard, which describes an event that will partly inspire Jehu's vengeance later on.

At the end of the Naboth story, the chief enemy of Ahab and Jezebel is the prophet Elijah, a towering figure in the Old Testament and the second prophet (after Moses) to become associated with Messianic prophecy (see the section on Malachi beginning on page 226). To this day families celebrating Passover pour a cup of wine for Elijah and open the door to

Read 1 Kings 21. Naboth's Vineyard.

welcome him to the Seder in the hope of his return.

Most of 1 Kings revolves around either Elijah's attempts to rid the northern kingdom of idols—or around Ahab and Jezebel's attempts to kill Elijah for doing so. Beneath that main narrative the text records a number of Elijah's miracles, which serve as signs to the people that this prophet has been sent by God.

Statue of Elijah on Mt. Carmel

The most notable of these miracles is the spectacular contest on top of Mt. Carmel between Israel's God and the prophets of Baal. If you're looking for a my-God-can-beat-the-pants-off-of-your-God story, it doesn't come any better than this.

Each side has erected an altar and prepared identical sacrifices. The challenge is to see which god will show up and accept the sacrifice by engulfing the altar in flames.

As the prophets of Baal pierce themselves and dance around their altar to the point of exhaustion, Elijah is over at his altar, whistling to himself and upping the ante. He douses the whole thing with water three separate times, making fire more unlikely, and taunts the prophets of Baal, asking

> **Read 1 Kings 18:17–1 Kings 19.** Contest on Mt. Carmel and its aftermath.

The choice of words for the English translation of Elijah's taunt is the work of translators who know the prudishness of English-speaking congregations. The words in Hebrew have Elijah asking whether Baal has wandered off to attend to certain bodily functions, perhaps with a good stack of reading material.

whether their god is perhaps away on vacation, sleeping, or has wandered off to meditate.

Of course it's Israel's God who wins the Mt. Carmel contest and Elijah decides the best way to end the day is to slaughter all the prophets of Baal. But those were Jezebel's folks, and she's none too pleased about the execution of her prophets. She vows to kill Elijah and the chase is on.

At the end of 1 Kings, Ahab goes into battle against the Arameans (a loose group of peoples in what is modern-day Syria) and tries to save his skin by having someone else dress up as king in the battle. While the ruse works for a little while, Ahab gets killed anyway by a stray arrow. As he is brought back to Samaria for burial, the blood on his chariot is washed off and the dogs lick it up, fulfilling the prophecy of Elijah about the death of Ahab. (1 Kings 21:19) The more dramatic ending of Jezebel comes later.

Elijah is a deeply passionate character, and the stories in 1 Kings allow us to see both his fire and his ice. We also get to see him pretty depressed, sitting under a broom tree and complaining to God that he's the only one on the planet trying to do anything about the idolatry in the land. God sends Elijah out to find both some help and an eventual successor in the prophet Elisha. Yes, you will confuse those two names and their stories early and often.

Elisha, Jehu, and the End of the House of Ahab

The transfer of prophetic power is made at the beginning of 2 Kings in an exit as dramatic as Elijah's life had been. He's taken up to heaven in a chariot of fire (minus the music) as Elisha looks on and cries, "Father, father! The chariots of Israel and its horsemen!" (2 Kings 2:12). The lack of an actual "death" for Elijah contributes to the belief that he will one day return.

From Elijah's dramatic departure through chapter 8, we're treated to a series of Elisha's miracles, again designed to prove to the people that the favor of God that was with Elijah had been duly transferred to Elisha. This notion of miracles as "signs" will surface again in the New Testament, especially in the Gospel of John.

By chapter 9 it's time for a new rendition of a now-familiar story—anoint a new king while the previous king is still ruling and watch the mayhem ensue. Elisha is still chief prophet, but he sends one of his underlings on a mission: Find a military commander named Jehu and anoint him king of Israel. The prophet underling is also given a message for Jehu: Wipe out the house of Ahab. Jehu does this without hesitation for several bloody chapters until there isn't a relative remaining. Jezebel finally meets her end.

> *Read 2 Kings 9:30-37.*
> The death of Jezebel.

Prophetic Books of the North

While Elijah and Elisha rule the narratives from this period, there were other prophets at work in the northern kingdom. Most go unnamed, but three of them have had their writing preserved, becoming part of the canon of Hebrew scripture. We'll take a quick look at each in turn. The dates beside each prophet's name represent the general period of the prophet's activity, not the time that the prophet's words were fixed in their biblical forms.

Amos (ca. 760–750 B.C.E.)

From Moses on down, many of the prophets report coming into their role with at least a bit of hesitation—if not kicking and screaming. After all, they rarely had good news to report. The phrase "Don't shoot the messenger" comes out of the historical reality that bearers of ill tidings often had a hostile if not deadly reception.

The Prophet Amos, James Tissot, ca. 1888

The prophet Amos had to deliver messages of God's dissatisfaction with Jeroboam II (not the Jeroboam who first split the kingdom), messages that Jeroboam found treasonous. The priest at Bethel advised Amos to get out of Dodge and go prophesy in the south somewhere (where Amos was originally from). Amos responds: *"I am no prophet, nor a prophet's son; but I am a herdsman, and a dresser of sycamore trees, and the LORD took me from following the flock, and the LORD said to me, 'Go, prophesy to my people Israel.'"* (Amos 7:14-15)

Apparently nobody told Amos that tending sheep was the preferred training program for God's leaders. Amos, however, doubled down on his condemnations.

The book of Amos is nine chapters long, almost all of it poetry. The most famous passage is best known to Americans from the "I've Been to the Mountaintop" speech by the Rev. Dr. Martin Luther King, Jr.: "Let justice roll down like waters, and righteousness like a mighty stream." (Amos 5:24)

Hosea (ca. 750–735 B.C.E.)

Following closely behind Amos in the north is the prophet Hosea, again in a book whose twelve chapters are almost entirely poetic. The most notable thing about the book of Hosea is not a particular famous passage, but rather the type of object lesson that God asks Hosea to use.

Prophet Hosea, Ducciodi Buoninsegna, ca. 1311

While Amos just compares Israel to a basket of fruit, Hosea starts out with this command from God:

> When the LORD first spoke through Hosea, the LORD said to Hosea, "Go, take for yourself a wife of whoredom and have children of whoredom, for the land commits great whoredom by forsaking the Lord." (Hosea 1:2)

This from the author of "Thou shalt not commit adultery."

The entire book revolves around this connection between adultery and idolatry. One of the strongest metaphors for the relationship between God and the people of Israel in the Old Testament is that of husband and wife. Hosea's words show a God who is a cuckolded lover, angry and ready to punish Israel for infidelity, but also longing for a day when the relationship can be restored.

> **Read Hosea 1-3.**
> Israel's infidelity and God's faithfulness.

In light of what we've learned about covenants, pay special attention to chapter 2:18, which hearkens back to that very first inclusive covenant with Noah:

"I will make for you a covenant on that day with the wild animals, the birds of the air, and the creeping things of the ground; and I will abolish the bow, the sword, and war from the land; and I will make you lie down in safety."

Jonah

If you took the first course in Exploring the Bible, you have already read the four chapters that comprise the book of Jonah. While one of those four chapters is poetry, the rest is a prose narrative familiar to anyone who has come through the ranks in Sunday School. If you didn't read it before, read it now. You're not allowed to say you're literate in the Bible without knowing the story of Jonah.

Jonah himself seems to have been an obscure prophet during the time of Jeroboam II (2 Kings 14:25)—roughly the same time as Amos. The story about him, however, was probably penned a good bit later, perhaps combining an older legend with a current message. Instead of stern oracles about **Israel's** shortcomings, like we have in the other prophets, in Jonah we have a story of the **prophet's** shortcomings.

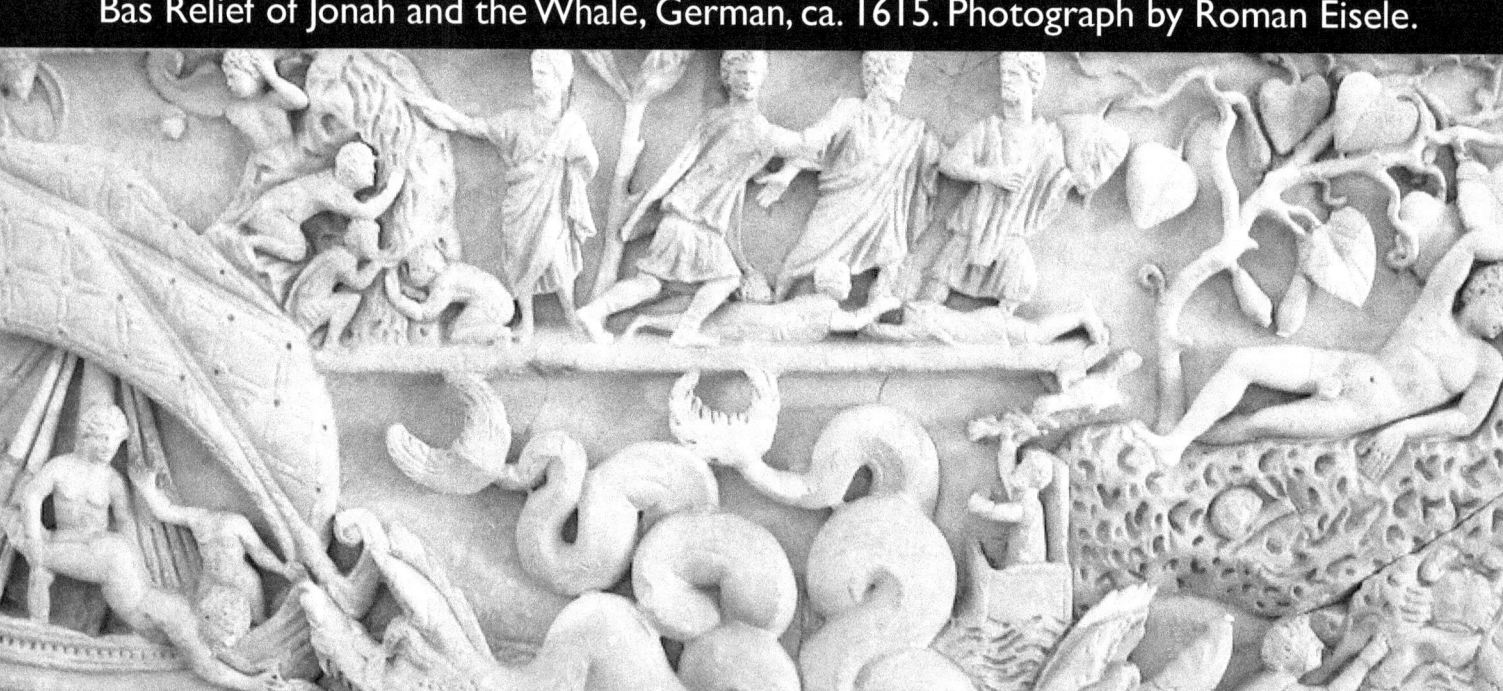

Bas Relief of Jonah and the Whale, German, ca. 1615. Photograph by Roman Eisele.

Like the other prophets, however, the book of Jonah shows us the grace of God in the face of disobedience. Yes, getting swallowed by a big fish and vomited up three days later isn't a picnic (Jonah might well have wanted to swap jobs with Hosea), but all the prophets show us that sin has consequences. Most of the prophets also show us something else, however: God's steadfast love. Even the dire words of Amos end in a paean of hope and restoration. And so it is with the redemptive story of Jonah.

And Then There Were None

We've seen that for centuries the activity in Assyria was defined by inventions and refinements in warfare. During the period of the divided kingdom in Israel the Assyrians put that superior war machine to work in expanding their empire. Under Ashurnasirpal II, the Assyrian Empire's borders are pushed to the Mediterranean. Tiglath-pileser III (I know, I know…I didn't name them) conquers Syria and gains control of Babylon. And in bits and pieces the next two kings, Shalmaneser V and Sargon II, take Samaria and complete the conquest of the northern kingdom of Israel.

The Israelites in the north are carried off to various parts of the Assyrian Empire, and the Assyrians take up residence. 2 Kings 17 provides a long justification for Israel's punishment. Notice as you read that the cities of the northern kingdom are called the "cities of Samaria." We are told that the new people who move in are also idolaters and that "to this day they continue to practice their former customs." This section of the Bible shows us not only why Israel believed God punished the northern kingdom, but also why they (those who are writing about the past from a future date) are justified in opposing the new residents of Samaria—the Samaritans.

In the biblical report, the ten tribes of the north no longer exist—even in exile—and they become known as the "Ten Lost Tribes." The account written by later Samaritans would, of course, tell the story differently.

For now, however, let's go back and see what's been happening south of the border in the smaller kingdom of Judah.

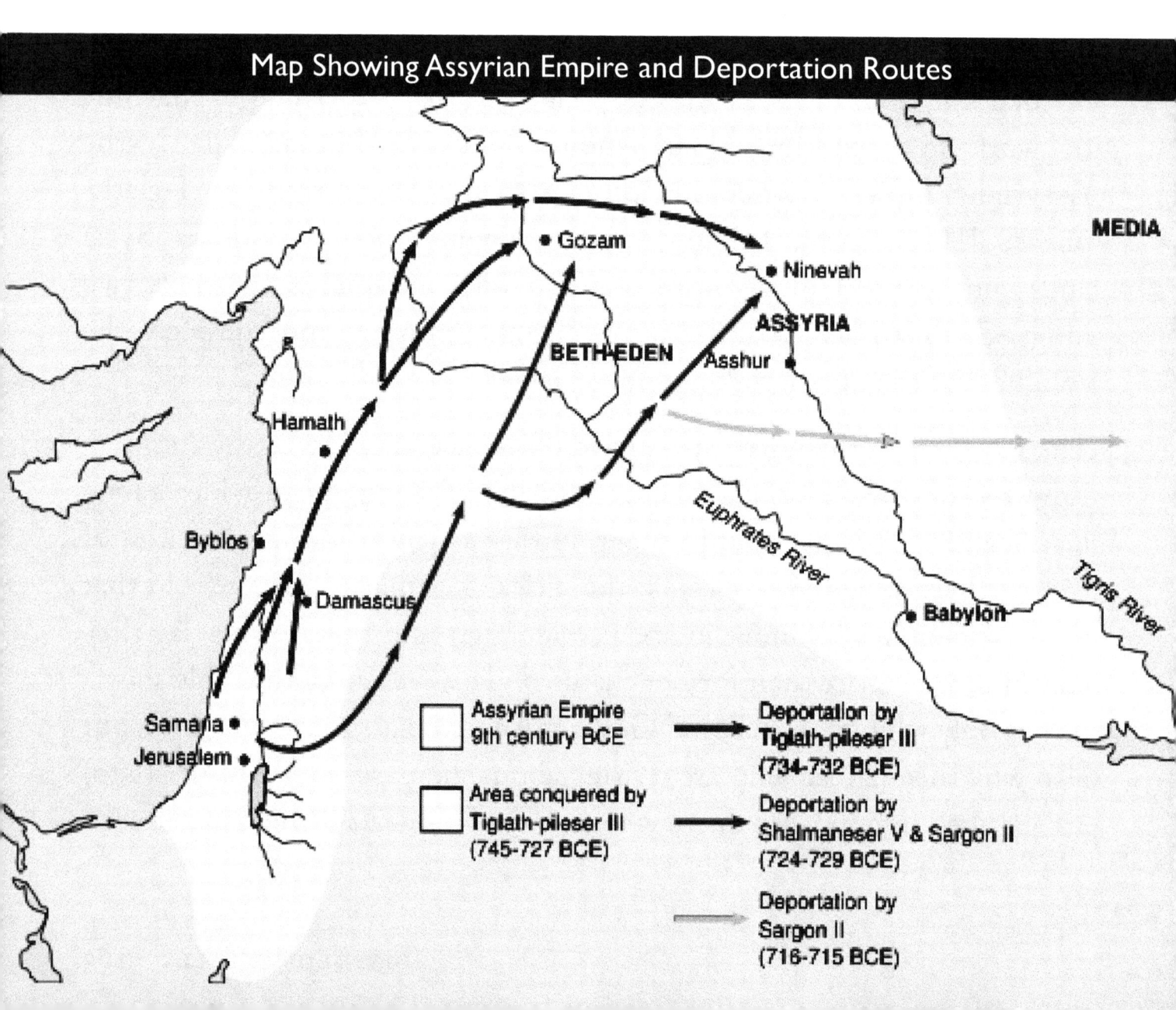

In the South

The history of the southern kingdom of Judah is similar to that of the north in that there were a similar number of kings and only a couple of standouts. As in the north, it's the prophets who take center stage, and, once again, the tale doesn't end well. The southern channel in our Bible show is kind of like the Weather Channel—there's usually a storm brewing somewhere. Let's start with the kings.

Hezekiah

Soon after the fall of the northern kingdom, Assyria sets its empire-minded sights on Judah. Our southern-kingdom story opens in the fourteenth year of good king Hezekiah of Judah, as King Sennacherib of Assyria harries the towns in the southern kingdom, where Isaiah is the chief prophet.

Portrait of Hezekiah, 17th century

Fearful for Judah, Hezekiah sends for a word from Isaiah, who tells Hezekiah to hang tight, for God has it in for Assyria in general and Sennacherib in particular. That night 185,000 soldiers in the Assyrian camp are mysteriously struck dead and King Sennacherib hobbles home to Nineveh.

Problem solved. Hezekiah and Judah are spared for the moment, but Isaiah later warns Hezekiah:

> Days are coming when all that is in your house, and that which your ancestors have stored up until this day, shall be carried to Babylon; nothing shall be left, says the LORD. Some of your own sons who are

born to you shall be taken away; they shall be eunuchs in the palace of the king of Babylon. (2 Kings 20:17–18)

How does Hezekiah respond to this dire prediction about his heirs? He says, in essence, "Meh…better them than me," and goes about his business. Although Hezekiah's words seem callous, historical evidence implies that he did seem to take the warning seriously. Hezekiah is best known to archaeologists for major improvements to the water supply in Jerusalem, including a conduit running from the Gihon Spring outside the city wall to the Pool of Siloam inside—well before the invention of dynamite and PVC pipe. Hezekiah's Tunnel, as it would be later known, ran 1,700 feet through solid rock, a significant engineering feat for its time.

> **Read 2 Kings 20.**
> Time goes backward for Hezekiah.

While 2 Kings pays little attention to the beginning of Hezekiah's reign, the writer of Chronicles has a different agenda. The writer spends much more time with all the kings of Judah, focusing on whether a Judean king was able to avoid the snares of idolatry. Hezekiah was a "good king" because he was a great reformer, and Chronicles spends much more time on this than the book of Kings.

In 2 Chronicles 29, Hezekiah begins his reign and immediately sets about cleansing the temple from the idolatrous practices of his father and predecessor, King Ahaz. Everything and everyone is re-consecrated, culminating in a great Passover celebration that lasted an extra seven days, much to the dismay of the two thousand bulls and seventeen thousand sheep who ended up on the wrong side of the celebration.

Nehushtan

Back when the Israelites were wandering in the desert with Moses, the people whined about their condition one time too many and God got mad. To shut them up, God sent them poisonous snakes. Moses pleaded with God, who told Moses to create a bronze snake and put it up on a pole. Anyone who looked at the bronze serpent was healed. The story is in Numbers 21 and is referred to by Jesus.

Brazen Serpent, Giovanni Fantoni

In 2 Kings 18:4, we learn that the Israelites didn't leave that bronze snake out in the wilderness. It came along with them into the Promised Land and long ago had stopped becoming a solution and had become part of the problem. By the time of Hezekiah, the Israelites were worshipping the thing and giving it offerings. It even had a name—Nehushtan—and Hezekiah had to destroy it.

Josiah

Hezekiah's son, Manasseh, apparently took after his grandfather, earning him the "bad king" label, and Manasseh's son Amon was no better. Amon was so rotten that his own servants killed him at home, leaving his eight-year-old son, Josiah, in charge of the kingdom.

King Josiah, Julius Schnorr von Carolsfeld

Like his great-grandfather, Josiah becomes known for his reforms, getting rid of idols and

DIVIDED WE FALL 173

Canaanite shrines throughout the land. He also orders the high priest to count the money in the temple, then spend it on repairs. While doing this, the high priest finds an old copy of the book of the Law of Moses, which most believe was some form of the book of Deuteronomy. The book is brought to Josiah and his secretary reads it to him.

High Places

Kings in Israel and Judah were always either building or tearing down "high places" and "Asherah poles." High places were Canaanite open-air worship spaces, usually on top of a hill of some kind. These were generally places where fertility rites were practiced. Usually there was also a stone altar for other sacrifices as well as a pole signifying the fertility goddess, Asherah, the consort of Baal. Note the bulls surrounding her in this image.

Asherah and Bulls

Listening to Deuteronomy, Josiah flies into a panic, realizing that his kingdom has been disregarding many—if not most—of the laws of God. This can't be good. Josiah sends servants to find a prophet and see how things stand with God. They find one of the few female prophets mentioned in the Bible, Huldah.

Huldah has a mixed message for Josiah. Much as it did with Hezekiah, the word of the Lord for Josiah indicated that because Josiah was penitent about not having followed the Law, he would have a peaceful reign. But after that, Huldah warns, Judah would be toast.

The warning notwithstanding, Josiah does all he can to change God's mind about Judah's fate. He reads the newly discovered book to all the people of Judah and sets about trying to follow it to the letter.

> Before him there was no king like him, who turned to the LORD with all his heart, with all his soul, and with all his might, according to all the law of Moses; nor did any like him arise after him. (2 Kings 23:25)

The die is cast, however, and once the Babylonians have freed themselves from the clutches of Assyria, capturing Nineveh and wiping Assyria off the map, they set the dial for Judah.

There were other kings, of course, but in the eyes of the writer(s) of Kings and Chronicles, the bad ones outweighed the good ones. Why else would Judah have fallen?

And it isn't like they weren't warned. The south had more than their fair share of prophets.

Isaiah (ca. 742–687 B.C.E.)

We've already met Isaiah, which isn't surprising, since his work spanned about sixty years and covered the reign of four kings: Uzziah, Jotham, Ahaz, and Hezekiah. We learn of some of Isaiah's actions in reading the accounts of the kings under whom he served. But it's in the book that bears his name that we get a glimpse into Isaiah's inner life. There he remembers his vision of God calling him to be a prophet, despite

The Prophet Isaiah, Michelangelo, 1509

Isaiah's own reluctance and fear that he wasn't good enough. This passage is a favorite of the coal industry.

Isaiah as a book is incredibly complex. It is mostly poetic and has almost as much famous music attached to it as the book of Psalms. Ink makers have been kept in business by those debating whether the prophet who served Hezekiah and his forebears wrote all the sixty-six chapters that bear his name. Those who lean toward a more literal interpretation of the Bible insist that the prophet is responsible for all of it.

> **Read Isaiah 6:1-8.**
> The call of Isaiah.

Those who favor literary and historical criticism find that suggestion impossible and believe there were at least two and possibly three "Isaiahs." Their reasoning is complex, but you should be able to find an overview of the arguments in the introduction to the book in your study Bible or in the Wikipedia article on the prophet Isaiah.

Innumerable books and countless multi-volume works have been written about the book of Isaiah—the work is that complex. We surely can't wrap our brains around it in a few paragraphs, but here are two things we should note.

How Many **Isaiahs?**

Everybody is pretty comfortable putting chapters 1–39 into the period when the prophet Isaiah lived. Those who think there were two primary writers label chapters 40–66 as "Second Isaiah," and those who go still further cut off Second Isaiah at chapter 55, giving the final ten chapters to "Third Isaiah."

When dealing with the debate over how many fingers were in the Isaiah pie, it's helpful to remember the concept of "schools of thought." You have one influential person and a band of people who follow the teachings of that person, adding their own thoughts and insights in new work.

Continued on next page

How Many **Isaiahs?** (Continued)

For example, today in the field of psychology you have Jungians and Freudians just to name two of many. They bear the label of the psychologist who has most influenced their thinking, and that original person's influence informs all their work, even as the new person expands, adjusts, and applies the thought in new situations.

This was even truer in the ancient world and especially in the ancient near east, where the relationship between master and disciple was especially close. We've seen already that prophets in this period came in groups. Although there tended to be one main court prophet, there were bands of prophets serving the king as well as others roaming about the countryside.

I don't see that the book of Isaiah is compromised in any way by the suggestion that other prophets associated with Isaiah, either by proximity or by deep appreciation for his work, produced prophetic works in his name. Though today our legal sensibilities impel us to define authorship and footnote sources, Jews in Palestine in 740 B.C.E. didn't feel that same compunction. In fact, if your chief inspiration and material came from your interaction with Isaiah (either personally or through study), then putting Isaiah's name on it was your means of source citation.

Ultimately, it wasn't intellectual property rights that mattered. The focus belonged on the message—the prophecy—the word of the Lord.

> *"The grass withers, the flower fades; but the word of our God will stand forever." (Isaiah 40:8)*

First notice the presence of a character suggested in the second half of the book. Portrayed as a servant, he's first introduced in chapter 42. There are four "servant songs" in the second half of Isaiah, and debate swirls around the servant's identity. A common Christian interpretation has been that the servant songs are talking about Jesus. But the Jews (as well as a number of Christians) don't see it that way, instead viewing the servant as a depiction of the nation of Israel.

> **Read Isaiah 52:13–53:12.**
> The suffering servant.

Which is it? You'll have to decide for yourself. The four servant songs can be found in: Isaiah 42:1–4, 49:1–6, 50:4–9, and 52:13–53:12.

Interestingly enough, when Jesus is teaching in his hometown synagogue (Luke 4:16–21), he reads from Isaiah and to identifies himself with the passage he selects. He does not, however, choose one of the servant songs. He reads from Isaiah 61:1–2a and then tells the congregation that the words he has just read have been fulfilled in their hearing:

> "The spirit of the Lord GOD is upon me, because the LORD has anointed me; he has sent me to bring good news to the oppressed, to bind up the brokenhearted, to proclaim liberty to the captives, and release to the prisoners; to proclaim the year of the LORD's favor."

Second, note that Isaiah introduces a new type of writing: apocalyptic literature. We looked at this genre briefly in the first course of Exploring the Bible when we learned about the book of Revelation. Apocalyptic literature is a highly symbolic form of writing that generally portends an impending disaster, usually the end of the world as we know it. This literary genre is much more common in the period of the exile and beyond.

Jesus Unrolls the Book In the Synagogue, James Tissot, 1894

While most of Isaiah isn't written in this style, chapters 24–27 have several of the characteristics of apocalyptic writing, although this section doesn't really use the heightened symbolism common in later examples. These chapters paint a bleak picture, but there are no multi-headed beasts, goat horns that grow tall enough to knock down stars, mysterious kings, and other decidedly odd symbols more common to the genre.

Some scholars spend a lifetime in the book of Isaiah, and there's beauty, comfort, reproach, and much that puzzles in its pages. Plus, Isaiah walks around naked for several years (Isaiah 20:1–6). But he's just one of the "Major Prophets" speaking for God in this period. Let's look at some of the others.

Jeremiah (ca. 655–586 B.C.E.)

The longest prophetic book in the Bible is Jeremiah, clocking in at over forty-two thousand words. Just for reference, a literary work must have at least forty thousand words to be considered a novel. Because the majority of this long book is prose narrative rather than poetic oracle, we have a much clearer picture of the man behind the book than we do with Isaiah and most of the other prophets.

Jeremiah Lamenting the Destruction of Jerusalem, Rembrandt, 1630

Jeremiah himself came from a priestly family, and he began his prophetic work under Josiah, continuing through the fall of Jerusalem. Its history as a book of the Bible is complex, with the ordering of the chapters different in the Hebrew Bible. The ordering in the Old Testament comes from the Greek Septuagint (edited in Egypt), which also leaves out some passages included in the Hebrew Bible (edited in

Babylon). If you like investigating such matters, you'll have your work cut out for you. Both versions can be found among the Dead Sea Scrolls. But for most of us, the discrepancies don't have any great impact on our understanding of the book.

What is clear is that Jeremiah is both a reluctant and, as time goes on, very unhappy prophet. Isaiah's call from God doesn't come until the sixth chapter of that book, but Jeremiah's call comes right away. God claims to have appointed Jeremiah from the womb, Jeremiah complains that he's too young to have the requisite speaking skills, and God touches his lips (without coal this time) to fix it.

As you might expect from a prophet immediately before an unprecedented national disaster, Jeremiah seldom has anything positive to report from the Lord—even though he begins his work under the reforms of Josiah, which God really should have been happier about. Remember how hard young Josiah worked to follow the Law? Remember how he tore his clothes and wept when the book of the Law was found and he heard what he and his people should have been doing? What does God have Jeremiah say to all that? First he recalls the faithlessness of the northern kingdom of Israel (using the whore/adultery metaphors we saw in Hosea) and how God punished Israel. Then he says,

Read Jeremiah 1:4-10.
The call of Jeremiah.

> Yet for all this her false sister Judah did not return to me with her whole heart, but only in pretense, says the LORD. Then the LORD said to me: Faithless Israel has shown herself less guilty than false Judah. (Jeremiah 3:10–11)

Ouch! You can just see Josiah passing out on his throne.

This is what life is like for Jeremiah—always the bearer of bad news, even to the good kings. Now and then he complains to God that other prophets get to say wonderful things and give hopeful messages. God just tells him that those are false prophets—then gives him some other dire message to relay.

In these last years, Jeremiah isn't going out for a few beers with the other prophets after work. Instead, he's getting beaten, put in the stocks, starved, and thrown into cisterns. And yet he must go on. If you've ever heard someone speak of a fire in their bones, here it is from Jeremiah's own lips.

> For **Reflection**
>
> Have you ever had to deliver and/or receive bad news? What was that experience like?
>
> Can you think of any modern-day prophets who deliver necessary messages that are unpopular and difficult to hear?

> "O Lord, you have enticed me, and I was enticed; you have overpowered me, and you have prevailed. I have become a laughingstock all day long; everyone mocks me. For whenever I speak, I must cry out, I must shout, 'Violence and destruction!' For the word of the LORD has become for me a reproach and derision all day long. If I say, 'I will not mention him, or speak any more in his name,' then within me there is something like a burning fire shut up in my bones; I am weary with holding it in, and I cannot." (Jeremiah 20:7–9)

Jeremiah continues the gut-wrenching cry for the rest of that chapter, ending with cursing the day he was born. The last verse of the chapter asks, "Why did I come forth from the womb to see toil and sorrow, and spend my days in shame?" I mean, really. You have to feel for the guy—and he still has thirty-two chapters to go!

There are a couple of moments of respite, and readers are drawn to these passages as much as the initial hearers must have been. Chapters 30–31 are sometimes called the book of Consolation as Jeremiah reports that God will restore the fortunes of Israel and make a new covenant. This is followed by the one hopeful symbolic action that Jeremiah gets to make. Just as the nation is about to fall to Babylon, God tells Jeremiah to go out and buy a plot of land. Why? "For thus says the LORD of hosts, the God of Israel: Houses and fields and vineyards shall again be bought in this land." But this light of consolation is much briefer than is typical of the other prophets.

Jeremiah Thrown in the Cistern by the Princes of King Zedekiah, Marc Chagall, 1956

Soon Jeremiah is right back at the doom and gloom. With Babylon knocking, Jeremiah is saddled with the unenviable job of trying to convince King Zedekiah to surrender to the enemy rather than put the city through a disastrous siege. You don't need a degree in political science to know that suggesting surrender to a king won't earn you brownie points. Jeremiah is imprisoned for his efforts.

> **Read Jeremiah 31:31-34, 32:6-15.** The promise of a new covenant.

It's actually the conquering king of Babylon who frees him and orders him to be treated well. Jeremiah isn't deported to Babylon but is allowed to live wherever he wants. Hmmm…maybe Jeremiah **did** have a degree in political science. He ends his days in Egypt.

Joel (date uncertain)

Putting the prophet Joel in this period is a complete crap shoot. We know nothing at all about him, other than his own note in the first verse that he was the son of Pethuel—but nobody's ever heard of Pethuel either. Joel was a common name (the name means "YHWH is God") and this prophet isn't to be equated with any other Joel mentioned in the Bible apart from Acts 2:16, where this book is quoted.

The Prophet Joel, Michelangelo, 1512

Because the book of Joel doesn't mention anything about the destruction of either Samaria or Jerusalem, it's generally assumed that Joel wrote either well before or well after those events. He seems to be more concerned for the area around Jerusalem, and most scholars assume he lived there. Linguistic scholars see similarities between Joel and Amos, Micah, and several others who wrote before the fall of Jerusalem, so this is as good a place for him as any.

The book of Joel can be summed up in one word: locusts. Lots and lots of locusts. The three chapters of this book describe a plague of locusts and use that plague as a metaphor for God's terrible day of judgment. Even here, though, there's a promise of restoration after the destruction.

When people turn to the book of Joel, it is usually to this passage:

> Then afterward, I will pour out my spirit on all flesh; your sons and your daughters shall prophesy, your old men shall dream dreams and your young men shall see visions. Even on the male and female slaves in those days I will pour out my spirit. (Joel 2:28–29; in NAB it is Joel 3:1)

It's also worth noting that although both Isaiah 2:4 and Micah 4:3 talk about turning swords into plowshares and spears into pruning hooks, Joel 3:10 takes the opposite position and recommends, "Beat your plowshares into swords and your pruning hooks into spears." I guess to everything there is a season.

Obadiah (date uncertain)

The book of Obadiah is only one chapter long, so we don't have a lot to go on to help us identify this prophet. Like Joel, Obadiah was a common name and the book itself doesn't even give us his father's name. Dating the book is solely reliant on interpreting what events are being referred to in verses 11–14. Jerusalem is being attacked, so it would either be the Philistine attacks when Jehoram ruled (making Obadiah a contemporary of Elisha) or the Babylonian destruction (teaming him up with Jeremiah).

What is certain is that this is a message to the people of Edom (the descendants of Jacob's brother Esau). Obadiah condemns them for gloating over Israel's destruction, deserved though it might have been. He also scolds Edom for withholding aid in Israel's hour of need, since the people of Edom are kin to Israel.

The Prophet Obadiah, James Tissot, ca. 1888

Remember that the people of Edom are descended from Jacob's twin brother, Esau. Those original expectations of kinship that governed the ancient world are still in force. If your kin are in need, you help. Period. Obadiah warns that Edom's own day of reckoning is at hand.

Micah (ca. 750–686 B.C.E.)

Micah is a little more forthcoming in identifying both himself and the time during which he served. From the first verse of the book, we know that he was a slightly younger contemporary of Isaiah, serving under the rule of Jotham, Ahaz, and Hezekiah. He says he is from Moresheth, a small village in southern Judah.

Micah, the Prophet, James Tissot

Like most other prophets, Micah brings messages of both doom and hope with a heavy emphasis on the futility of idolatry and the call for social justice. Unlike the highborn Zephaniah, Micah comes from humble stock and his concern for those who struggle to receive justice comes from one who clearly knows the plight of the poor.

If you hear people quoting the book of Micah, they are likely referencing one of two places. If you hear it in church near Christmas time, you'll most likely hear Micah 5:2,

> But you, O Bethlehem of Ephrathah, who are one of the little clans of Judah, from you shall come forth for me one who is to rule in Israel, whose origin is from of old, from ancient days.

Since Jesus was born in Bethlehem, Christians usually see this as a prophecy about him.

Prophetic **Plagiarisms?**

If you're reading carefully you might notice that Micah 4:1–3 is identical to Isaiah 2:1–4. Why? Well, we don't exactly know. It could be that one is quoting the other, and cries of plagiarism arise because neither references the other. It could also be that they are both

Continued on next page

> **Prophetic Plagiarisms?** (Continued)
>
> quoting something from a third source that we don't know about—maybe another prophet or maybe something from a temple liturgy or something in the public sphere. Of course it could just be that God thought it was a nice turn of phrase and gave it verbatim to multiple prophets. Students of literary and historical criticism delve into these things and use them to help date biblical texts and generally find out what's going on. For the rest of us, however, it doesn't really impact the meaning, beauty, or faith represented by the words.

The other passage that many people highlight is Micah 6:6–8:

> "With what shall I come before the LORD, and bow myself before God on high? Shall I come before him with burnt-offerings, with calves a year old? Will the LORD be pleased with thousands of rams, with ten thousands of rivers of oil? Shall I give my firstborn for my transgression, the fruit of my body for the sin of my soul? He has told you, O mortal, what is good; and what does the LORD require of you but to do justice, and to love kindness, and to walk humbly with your God?"

Especially the last verse can be found in a number of songs and is as eloquent a summary of true worship as any in the Bible.

Nahum (ca. 626–612 B.C.E.)

While the book of Jonah tells us of a prophet who successfully convinced the people of Nineveh (the capital of Assyria) to repent, the book of Nahum shows us that the repentance was short lived. The harsh words of Nahum have nothing to do with Israel or Judah. They represent God's condemnation of Nineveh and, by extension, the Assyrian empire for its cruelty.

Russian Orthodox icon of the prophet Nahum, 18th century

Again we have little information about the prophet himself, other than that he was from Elkosh—and nobody's sure where Elkosh is. What we do know is that, like Jonah, there was no love lost between Nahum and the Ninevites. This is no solemn warning to a people, no lament for their loss and destruction. This is Nahum dancing on the grave of Assyria. There is not a shred of hope or encouragement offered, and the book's three chapters can perhaps be best summarized by the book's final verse:

> There is no assuaging your hurt, your wound is mortal. All who hear the news about you clap their hands over you. For who has ever escaped your endless cruelty? (Nahum 3:19)

Habakkuk (ca. 608–598 B.C.E.)

Habakkuk is also only three chapters and, like so many others, we know basically nothing about the prophet apart from placing him as a contemporary of Jeremiah.

There is a lot going on in this little book, so much so that some scholars think it's a composite of several genres and was never initially a unit. Others believe it fits together just fine, so you'll have to judge for yourself.

Prophet Habakkuk, Donatello

The beginning has Habakkuk offering a complaint to God about how the wrong guy always wins and how justice is perverted. Next comes a series of five woes—a classic form of judgment that we see in both the Old and New Testaments. "Woe to you, who…"

Then, lastly, there is a lovely hymn. We know it's a hymn because chapter 3:1 says, "A prayer of the prophet Habakkuk according to Shigionoth." That last word is the plural of Shiggaion, a technical term used to instruct musicians, and the last verse of the book ends with "To the leader: with stringed instruments." Whether it is actually a hymn he wrote or just one that seemed a fitting close to this little book is hard to say, but perhaps the most quoted verse from Habakkuk comes from this faith-filled concluding hymn:

> Though the fig tree does not blossom, and no fruit is on the vines; though the produce of the olive fails and the fields yield no food; though the flock is cut off from the fold and there is no herd in the stalls, yet I will rejoice in the LORD; I will exult in the God of my salvation. GOD, the Lord, is my strength; he makes my feet like the feet of a deer, and makes me tread upon the heights. (Habakkuk 3:17–19)

Zephaniah (ca. 640–609 B.C.E.)

Apparently several of these prophets got together and decided that they would compose works of identical lengths. Again we have a book of three chapters. Maybe it was a contest.

Zephaniah is good enough to let us know that he is actually the great-great-grandson of Hezekiah and that he was working as a prophet during the reign of Josiah. Probably this particular work reflects the earlier part of Josiah's rule, since it's

Russian Orthodox icon of the prophet Zephaniah, 18th century

hot on the trail of idolatry and doesn't seem to be aware of any attempt at reform. Zephaniah's themes should be familiar by now: It's going to get really, really bad. And then it will be much, much better. He also takes a swipe at Nineveh.

I'm not forgetting to mention the well-known verses. I'm just not finding any.

The End

As the Babylonians recovered from their Assyrian thrashing and built an empire of their own, it was only a matter of time before they, too, came calling at the gates of Jerusalem. As we mentioned long ago, Israel occupied strategic land with access to the trading routes of the Mediterranean. Any empire worth its salt wanted to control it.

While the Assyrians were well known for the cruelty, the Babylonians didn't seem to have the same need to completely flatten their enemies. If they could just annex the territory and get tribute from the resident kings, all would be well and good. If Zedekiah had been willing to accept his place as a tribute king to King Nebuchadnezzar of Babylon (as Jeremiah told him to), life would have been easier.

But that's a hard pill for any king to swallow, and when Zedekiah tried to forge an alliance with Egypt against Babylon, Nebuchadnezzar showed Zedekiah that he meant business. The siege of the city lasted a full thirty months, and even with the sophisticated water systems built by Hezekiah and others, the city simply couldn't bear up.

By all accounts it was horrific, with reports of cannibalism of the dead as food supplies ran out. When Jerusalem finally fell in 587–586 B.C.E., it fell

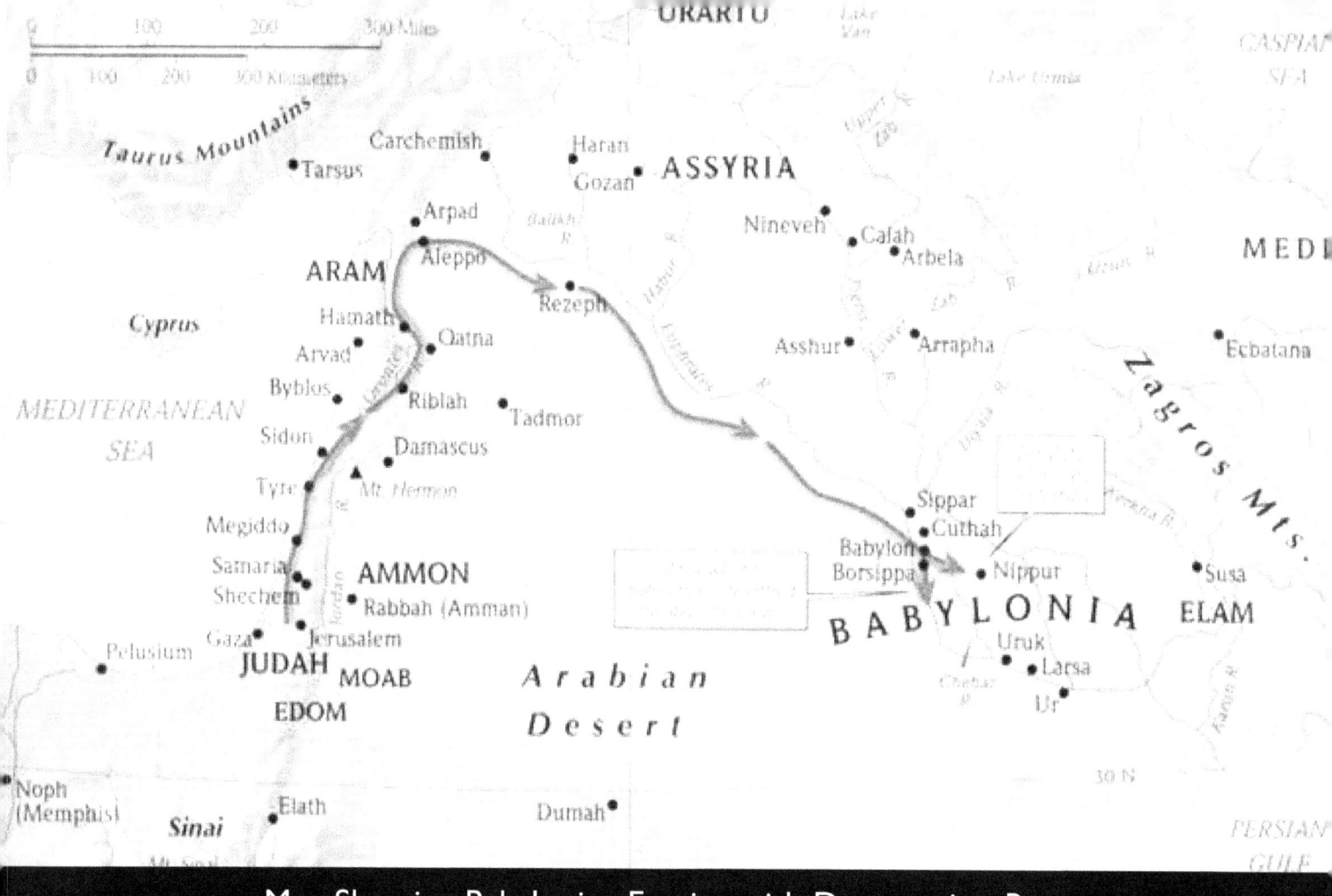

Map Showing Babylonian Empire with Deportation Route

hard. Those who hadn't already been carted off as exiles to Babylon were taken, leaving only a few of the poorest people to till the land. Solomon's grand temple? Burned to the ground. The king's house? Burned along with every great house in the city. The walls were broken down. And King Zedekiah himself?

> Then they captured the king and brought him up to the king of Babylon at Riblah, who passed sentence on him. They slaughtered the sons of Zedekiah before his eyes, then put out the eyes of Zedekiah; they bound him in fetters and took him to Babylon. (2 Kings 25:6–7)

Jerusalem. The city where God had promised to dwell forever. The Temple. The only place where sins could be forgiven; the only place for right worship; the place of which God said to Solomon,

> "I have heard your prayer and your plea, which you made before me; I have consecrated this house that you have built, and put my name there forever; my eyes and my heart will be there for all time." (1 Kings 9:3)

Gone.

Bleak, Mark Goldstein

For **Reflection**

Have you ever had to leave a place you considered home for any reason?

Has there been anything in your life that helps you connect with the feeling of exile?

Preparation for Check-In

(Prepare for the next group session by thinking about and writing a brief response to these two questions.)

What is one thing that was new to me in this material?

What is one question that this week's topic raises for me?

Homework (All students)

- ☐ Read the student text for Session 6, including all Bible reading.
- ☐ Think about the reflection questions.
- ☐ You've read a lot of stories throughout the Old Testament. You've also seen some major thematic arcs: covenant, exile and return, captivity and freedom, sin and repentance. Select either a particular story or a broad theme that stood out for you and plan to share your selection with the group at the final class session. You will be asked to share in the following ways:

  - Identify the story or theme, including (for particular stories) the chapter and verses in the Bible where it can be found.
  - Was this a story/theme that was familiar to you before the course or was it new to you?
  - Why did this particular story/theme stand out for you? Was it just a good story? Did it either connect with or challenge something you had believed or experienced in your own life? Did it generate new understanding in some way?
  - Is it a story you would tell your children or grandchildren or do you think it is best kept for adult discussion?

Extra Mile (CEU and Certificate Students)

- ☐ In five hundred to seven hundred words, write out your response to the last set of questions.

AGE OF EMPIRES

Materials you will need for your last class session:

This student text

Your study Bible

Materials for taking notes

Your responses to the check-in questions on p. 238

The story or theme from the Old Testament you wish to share with the group

Historical Era: 606–4 B.C.E.

Parts of the Bible covered: Ezra, Nehemiah, Esther, Job, Lamentations, Ezekiel, Daniel, Haggai, Zechariah, Malachi, Apocrypha

Timeline for **Session Six**

☐ **World Events (Outside the Bible)**

606 B.C.E.	Daniel is taken captive to Babylon along with others of the Jewish intelligentsia prior to siege of Jerusalem. Works in Babylonian court.
605 B.C.E.	Nebudchadnezzar II becomes king of Babylon. King at the time of the destruction of Jerusalem.
593 B.C.E.	Ezekiel begins prophetic ministry
582 B.C.E.	Baruch works independently from Jeremiah
563 B.C.E.	**Siddhartha Gautama (the Buddha) is born**
559 B.C.E.	Cyrus II (the Great) becomes king of Persia
556 B.C.E.	Nabonidus becomes last king of Babylon. Often left rule to his son, Prince Belshazzar, mentioned in the book of Daniel.
551 B.C.E.	**Confucius is born**
538 B.C.E.	Persians conquer Babylon Decree of Cyrus, freeing Jewish captives in Babylon and allowing the return to Jerusalem Ministry of Ezra begins
521 B.C.E.	Darius I (the Great) becomes king of Persia
520 B.C.E.	Foundations of second temple in Jerusalem begun Haggai begins prophetic ministry
519 B.C.E.	Zechariah begins prophetic ministry

500 B.C.E.	**Chinese invent the crossbow**
485 B.C.E.	Xerxes I becomes king of Persia. Likely setting for the biblical book of Esther.
484 B.C.E.	**Herodotus, the "Father of History" is born in Greece**
465 B.C.E.	Artaxerxes I becomes king of Persia
450 B.C.E.	Malachi begins prophetic ministry
447 B.C.E.	**Building of the Parthenon is begun in Greece**
445 B.C.E.	Nehemiah oversees construction of new walls in Jerusalem
424 B.C.E.	Xerxes II becomes king of Persia
423 B.C.E.	Darius II becomes king of Persia
400 B.C.E.	**Zodiac circle and practice of astrology is begun in Babylon** **Festival of Samhain first celebrated in Ireland. Later becomes Halloween.**
399 B.C.E.	**Socrates poisons himself by drinking hemlock**
390 B.C.E.	**Gauls sack Rome**
387 B.C.E.	**Plato founds his academy in Athens**
332 B.C.E.	**Alexander the Great conquers Jerusalem** **City of Alexandria founded in Egypt**
330 B.C.E.	**Alexander conquers Babylon**

325 B.C.E.	**Art of War written by Sun-tzu in China**
312 B.C.E.	**First stone aqueduct begun in Rome**
305 B.C.E.	**Library at Alexandria founded**
300 B.C.E.	**Cast iron invented in China**
264 B.C.E.	**Beginning of First Punic War between Rome and Carthage**
214 B.C.E.	**Great Wall of China begun**
200 B.C.E.	**Romans develop concrete**
167 B.C.E.	Antiochus orders a statue to Zeus to be placed in Temple in Jerusalem sparking revolt. This revolt and its aftermath are the primary subject of the books of the Maccabees.
165 B.C.E.	Jerusalem is freed from foreign rule by Judas Maccabeus First celebration of Hanukkah
150 B.C.E.	**Chinese invent paper**
146 B.C.E.	**Carthage is destroyed by Rome in the Third Punic War**
63 B.C.E.	Rome conquers Palestine and destroys the temple
51 B.C.E.	**Rome conquers Gaul**
47 B.C.E.	**Library at Alexandria burns**

46 B.C.E.	**Julian calendar is introduced**
44 B.C.E.	**Julius Caesar is assassinated**
30 B.C.E.	**Library at Alexa Antony and Cleopatra commit suicide in Alexandria ndria founded**
6-4 B.C.E.	Likely time frame for the birth of Jesus of Nazareth
4 B.C.E.	Herod the Great dies

Your Move

If you've ever played the board game Risk, then you understand what this biblical age was about: empire. There were many players on the board, and most of them had more armies than Israel. First the Assyrians moved their pieces onto Israel's part of the map, taking the northern kingdom of Israel as we saw in Session 5. All of the Jewish pieces were moved to the southern kingdom of Judah.

Risk board game

While the Assyrians stretched their armies thin, leaving only one or two armies on most places on the board, the Babylonians built up their forces. Soon it was the armies of Babylon that dominated the territories, and although it took a thirty-month siege, Jerusalem finally lost all their pieces and the Babylonians took over.

But the world was growing and now other nations are afoot. While the Assyrians and Babylonians were battling it out in the Fertile Crescent, the power of Greece on the other side of the Mediterranean was growing and the new kid on the block, Rome, was making its mark on the world. But Babylon wasn't looking over there much. They were focused closer to home as the Persians began to put more and more armies on the map.

Everybody in this ancient game knew that, to win at the game of empire, you needed Jerusalem and environs so you could have unfettered access to trade routes. And so empire after empire stomped across their territory, ruling the land of Abraham, Isaac, and Jacob from a foreign capital.

There was an exception. For one brief and shining moment the revolt of Judas Maccabeus freed the Israelites from Greek rule and ushered in a century of self-rule under the Hasmonean dynasty. The festival of Hanukkah celebrates this victory, and it's arguably the memory that fueled many of the expectations of what Jesus would be and do. Rome, however, was unimpressed and stamped it out almost as quickly as it had begun.

As empires came and went, Israel struggled to maintain its identity as a nation and as a people. Perhaps their biggest struggle, however, was to re-establish their covenant relationship with the God of their ancestors—the God who had brought them into the Promised Land and then, as with Adam and Eve in the Garden, had apparently seen their sin and cast them out.

It was in this tumultuous and unsettled time that the remainder of the Old Testament came into being and that most of what had come before began to be collected, refined, and given authoritative status. We'll look at that process as we look at the influence and events of each empire in turn.

Babylon (586–538 B.C.E.)

In China, Confucius was alive and teaching. In India, the Buddha lived. Babylon built the second of the seven wonders of the ancient world, the Hanging Gardens of Babylon. To Israel, however, this period of seventy years was simply known as the Babylonian Captivity.

When last we saw Israel, Jerusalem had been burned to the ground and all but the poorest agricultural workers had been marched off to Babylon as captives.

Flight of the Prisoners, James Tissot, ca. 1896

This is trauma of the first magnitude for a number of reasons. The Jews who went to Babylon were physically and emotionally traumatized by the war and especially the siege. They had physical wounds and diseases. Many if not most were malnourished. They had lost loved ones, and some of them had even eaten their own dead children to stay alive. Their homes were gone and they were taken from the only land they knew. It's not like you get over that stuff.

In addition to the physical and mental trauma, the Babylonian Captivity presented an enormous spiritual crisis. Most of us have no frame of reference for the notion of one particular place being not just nice, but necessary for worship. Remember all those sacrificial laws back in Leviticus? The command of God was that for the sins of anyone to be forgiven, certain sacrifices had to be made. They had to be made in just

Diaspora

Remember that some Jews didn't go to Babylon. Nebuchadnezzar wanted to benefit from the land in any way he could so some of Judah's poor were left behind to till the fields. A few others, like Jeremiah, had earned favor with the Babylonians and were allowed to stay if they wished.

Nebuchadnezzar also appointed a governor over the area—a native of Judah named Gedaliah. Gedaliah encouraged any Jews who had fled to surrounding areas before the siege to return, and a number did just that. But it didn't last long. After five years or so Gedaliah was assassinated and, fearing the wrath of Babylon, many of those who had repopulated the area, including Jeremiah, fled to Egypt. Thus a significant Jewish presence developed in Egypt, and a number of biblical texts that were compiled and/or edited in one way by the Jews in Babylon were compiled and/or edited differently by the Jews in Egypt. Examples of this dual editing can be seen in the texts found among the Dead Sea Scrolls in Qumran.

But not everybody went to Egypt, either. Some stayed in Judah even after Gedaliah's assassination, and still others had remained with the descendants of the Assyrians in the areas around Samaria. Conflicts about the nature of Jewish identity were bound to surface sooner or later. And sure enough, they did.

the right way at just the right time by an approved priest at an approved location. The only approved location, however, was the Temple in Jerusalem—and that had been burned to the ground.

According to 1 Kings, God promised to dwell in that temple forever and see that David's line would continue on the throne. But the last king had been blinded and taken to Babylon where he died in captivity, his last moments of vision filled with watching the execution of his sons and heirs. With king and Temple gone, Israel had some serious soul-searching to do. Had God invalidated the covenant? Was the promise null and void?

Surely God had done this because of the sin and idolatry of the people, they thought, but how could they atone for those sins without bringing sacrifices to the Temple? A people who were given very specific instructions about how to please their God were suddenly without any of the means to do so at the very moment they most needed to make amends.

The only light in this dark period was the fact that, although they were forcibly held captive in Babylon, the Israelites were not otherwise mistreated. They were not slaves nor kept in prisons, but allowed to congregate and to dwell together in communities along the Chebar River, where they could farm and otherwise earn an income. The biblical accounts tell us that some became important figures in the palace. Others made a good enough life for themselves that they declined to return to Jerusalem when they were finally free to do so. It's not freedom when you aren't allowed to go home, but certainly the conditions of their captivity could have been worse.

This relative autonomy allowed for reflection and for the development of new forms of faith that would carry them forward. Since Nebuchadnezzar made it a point to bring the best, brightest, and most skilled of Judah into captivity, the Jews in Babylon had the human resources to buckle down and face the task of reinvention that lay before them.

Imaginative reconstruction of the Hanging Gardens of Babylon, one of the Seven Wonders of the Ancient World

Some exiles used the time to record their stories and their history in a way that would be beneficial to future generations. New books were written, old stories were recorded, and books from previous generations were combined, compiled, sorted, and edited. Even a new Hebrew script was developed, resulting in the Hebrew alphabet we know today.

Without the Temple, the role of the priest became less important than the roles of the scholar and sage, and instead of gathering at the Temple to make sacrifices, Jews began to gather at the synagogue to learn. The people of the Temple became the people of the Book. The organizing principle was no longer sacrifice, but law. If it was failure to follow God's commands that got them into this mess, then obedience would get them out. Never again must the book of the Law be lost and forgotten in a dusty trunk in the Temple treasury. Judaism was fundamentally changing.

Ezekiel

The prophet Ezekiel was also a priest and the book that bears his name speaks of events both before and after the fall of Jerusalem. Ezekiel was taken with the others into exile in Babylon in 597, which is where he received his call to prophesy.

Ezekiel's Wheel in St. John the Baptist Church in Kratovo, Macedonia

The book opens with Ezekiel describing himself as being among the exiles by the River Chebar, the irrigation channel where the Israelites deported to Babylon developed a community. We know from the text that, although forbidden to leave Babylon, he had his own home, a wife, and could go about his business with relative ease. So, although the first twenty-four chapters describe events that occurred before the siege, all of it is being recorded after the fact, from the perspective of the exile. Don't let the fact that Ezekiel had a wife and a house lure you into thinking that Ezekiel was just your normal prophet in exile.

As you read Ezekiel, remember that LSD is as yet unknown. This is not Woodstock in 1969—Ezekiel is simply…different. We visited a section of the pre-fall Ezekiel during the last group session. What was he doing? He was building a model of the city of Jerusalem on a brick, laying siege to the brick, and lying on the ground next to it for more than a year. Where are Legos when you need them?

To be sure, other prophets also got instructions to use this sort of object lesson to communicate God's message to the people. But Ezekiel definitely gets the stranger batch of these instructions. He also gets visions—and who wouldn't after lying next to a brick for 430 days? Ezekiel's visions are also very odd, and yet so vivid that they captured the imagination of musicians and UFO enthusiasts alike.

Look at the first chapter of Ezekiel. That's where he records his vision of the cryptic wheel in the air, immortalized in the spiritual, "Ezekiel Saw de Wheel." He describes four living creatures in the middle of the wheel. These creatures each have four faces: one human, one like a lion, one like an ox, and one like an eagle. About six hundred years later, these four living creatures make another appearance in the vision that became the New Testament book of Revelation (Revelation 4:7). In that version, instead of each creature having the same four faces, each creature has a single, different face, but they are identical to these four: the human, the lion, the ox, and the eagle. These four faces became associated with the four writers of the Gospels in the New Testament: Matthew the human, Mark the lion, Luke the ox, and John the eagle.

> ***Read Ezekiel 1:1-28.***
> Ezekiel's Wheel.

As alluded to above, those seeking evidence for the existence of UFOs also picked up on this vision. There's even a 1974 book by Josef F. Blumrich titled <u>The Spaceships of Ezekiel</u>.

So some people are really into the wheel, but my favorite vision comes later, in chapter 37. This vision also became an African American Spiritual, and some people think it's a song to teach anatomy (it isn't). I'm referring to the greatest Halloween story in the Bible, the Valley of Dry Bones.

Although it's fun to play with both the wheel and the Valley of Dry Bones visions, I prefer the dry bones because it's comprehensible as a potent, vivid, and moving message of hope. When Ezekiel calls, "Come from the four winds, O Breath, and breathe upon these slain that they may live!" something deep within me stirs. It's an amazing text to use on both Pentecost and Easter in the Christian tradition.

> **Read Ezekiel 37:1-14.**
> The Valley of Dry Bones.

But it's even more powerful in its original context. Remember that those dwelling with Ezekiel along the Chebar knew the identities of those skeletal remains—they had been the mothers and fathers, friends and lovers, sons and daughters of the surviving exiles, slaughtered or starved by the horrors of war. Moreover, many who survived probably felt like dry bones themselves, with no more tears to cry and nothing but a shell of a life remaining to them.

When God carries Ezekiel to that Valley of Dry Bones, Ezekiel witnesses the resurrection of Israel, bringing to the exiles a vision of new life, hope, and a return home. It's the promise not only that things will get better, but also that God hasn't given up on them, as the Spirit of God animates the dry bones and God promises, "I'll be back."

There are many other visions within the forty-eight chapters of this book, and some of them definitely fall within the genre of apocalyptic literature that we began to see in Isaiah and that will reach full bloom in the New Testament book of Revelation. But there are also more accessible oracles, promises, and indictments that are more in keeping with what we've seen in other prophetic books.

Remembering that the image of the shepherd was a common Near Eastern metaphor for kings, the indictment of the shepherds in Ezekiel 34 is as stinging—and as timeless—as it is clear. The "shepherds" were the nation's political leaders. Does this sound familiar?

> "Ah, you shepherds of Israel who have been feeding yourselves! Should not shepherds feed the sheep? You eat the fat, you clothe yourselves with the wool, you slaughter the fatlings; but you do not feed the sheep. You have not strengthened the weak, you have not healed the sick, you have not bound up the injured, you have not brought back the strayed, you have not sought the lost, but with force and harshness you have ruled them. So they were scattered, because there was no shepherd; and scattered, they became food for all the wild animals. My sheep were scattered, they wandered over all the mountains and on every high hill; my sheep were scattered over all the face of the earth, with no one to search or seek for them." (Ezekiel 34:2–6)

I remain baffled by those who want nothing to do with the Old Testament. How do you not love this stuff?

Daniel

While Christian Bibles place Daniel with the prophets, in the Hebrew Bible the book is considered part of the section called "the Writings" and is placed between Esther and Ezra/Nehemiah (which are one book in the Hebrew Bible). As you read this book, you can see why it might be placed in either location. The name Daniel means "God is judge" in Hebrew.

As Ezekiel spanned the time just before and just after the fall of Jerusalem, the stories in the book of Daniel overlap the empires of Babylon and Persia and give us both narrative stories (chapters 1–6, 13–14) and apocalyptic visions (chapters 7–12). Since the book describes Daniel as achieving great prominence in the court at Babylon, you might expect that he'd be mentioned elsewhere—and sure enough, he is. In the Bible he's twice mentioned by Ezekiel (14:14 and 28:3) and in other sources, his name is found in the clay tablets discovered at Ras Shamra, a city on the Syrian coast and the site of the ancient Canaanite city of Ugarit.

> *Read Daniel 3, 5-6.*
> The Fiery Furnace, The Writing on the Wall, Daniel in the Lion's Den.

If languages interest you, it's notable that almost half of the book of Daniel is written in Aramaic (Daniel 2:4b–7:28) and the other half in Hebrew. The two languages are quite similar, but Aramaic accounts for only about 250 of the over 23,000 verses of the Bible. Most of those Aramaic verses are found in either Daniel or Ezra, and their main function seems to be making scholars argue over when this particular form of Aramaic was spoken and, by extension, when those sections of the Bible were written.

If you ever went to Sunday School, you know most of the stories of Daniel: Daniel in the lion's den, the men in the fiery furnace, the writing on the wall. If you aren't familiar with them, you need to fill in the gaps and read them now. If you were learning about Daniel as a Protestant, however, you missed another great Daniel story. While we're throwing around important-sounding Bible words like apocalyptic, let's see if we can confuse the matter by recalling the word "apocrypha."

We looked at both apocryphal literature in general and the Apocrypha in particular in the first course of Exploring the Bible, <u>What Is the Bible?</u> But in the Apocrypha (those books

Daniel in the Lion's Den, Abbaye de la Sauve Majeure

recognized as authoritative in the Orthodox and Roman Catholic traditions but not in Protestant traditions) Daniel has fourteen chapters as opposed to the Protestant versions, which have twelve.

In the first course you were asked to read the engaging story of Susanna in Daniel 13. Daniel 14 contains the very fun story of Bel and the Dragon. If you don't have Daniel 13 and 14 in your Bible (some Protestant Bibles now put the Apocrypha in a separate section in the middle rather than in place in the text), just do an Internet search on "Susanna Daniel 13" or "Bel and the Dragon" and you'll find links to the texts.

> **Read the story of Bel and the Dragon.** It is found in Daniel 14 (part of the Apocrypha) and can be found online if you don't have that chapter in your Bible.

They're short and worth the read. The Apocrypha also has sixty-eight additional verses to Daniel 3, recording a prayer spoken by Azariah in the midst of the fiery furnace.

210 **INTRODUCING THE OLD TESTAMENT**

Job

The first thing you need to know about the book of Job is how to pronounce it. It isn't job, like employment—it has a long o sound. That will save you the kind of embarrassment suffered by one of my fellow seminarians who announced that he was preaching from the book of Collisions (instead of Colossians).

Unlike the prophets, Job the man isn't the author of the book bearing his name. Nobody has a clue who wrote this book, and it could have been penned anytime from the reign of Solomon through the exile. The setting for the story is much earlier, probably sometime during the second millennium B.C.E.

Job and His Wife,
Oil on panel in Frankfurt,
Germany, ca. 1504

Structurally, Job is a long poem framed by a narrative folktale. It's not history and isn't categorized that way in either the Hebrew or Christian Bible. It begins with the Hebrew language equivalent of "once upon a time." The language gives translators fits with its mix of styles and many unusual words. Translations of this book can vary widely. The Septuagint (the early Greek version of the Old Testament) is about four hundred lines shorter than the Hebrew version, and some see that as the Greek translators just throwing up their hands and admitting defeat on those lines.

For a long time my favorite verse in the book of Job was 13:15, which reads, in the King James Version, "Though he slay me, yet will I trust him." Imagine my dismay when I turned to that verse in the New Revised Standard Version and read, "See, he will kill me; I have no hope." A bit of a difference!

In the story itself, Job is a righteous man whose faith is tested by an unprecedented string of disasters. The tale is set up as a challenge. God is at a heavenly staff meeting bragging on the goodness of Job. Satan[6], more cynical, claims that Job is only good because God keeps blessing him with health, wealth, and happiness. Satan insists that Job is only into God as a way to get good stuff—and if that good stuff is taken away, God will see that Job isn't really good, just selfish. Satan's challenge to Job's motives is stated clearly in Job 1:9–11:

> "Does Job fear God for nothing? Have you not put a fence around him and his house and all that he has, on every side? You have blessed the work of his hands, and his possessions have increased in the land. But stretch out your hand now, and touch all that he has, and he will curse you to your face."

Many people think that the book of Job is trying to answer the question of why good people suffer and then get all bent out of shape because the book doesn't answer the question. But the setup in chapter one makes it clear that the central question is not "Why do bad things happen to good people?" but rather, "Why are good people good?" The first question is certainly important—and it's one that Job keeps asking throughout the book. I just don't think it's the right question for the story.

When you hear someone talk about "the patience of Job," they're referring to this poor man who, despite living a blameless life, gets hammered with every disaster imaginable and yet still bears up.

---

[6] The character of Satan (in Hebrew *ha satan* means "the adversary") evolves over time. At the time Job was written, "the satan" was not yet equated with the pitchfork-wielding devil of the Christian era. Here he simply has a role to play—to roam the earth like God's personal justice department and test the faithfulness of those he finds.

A second reference that occasionally pops up in Western culture is a reference to Job's friends. When Job is at his most miserable, having lost not only his wealth and his children but his health as well, several of his friends show up. Many of the forty-two chapters of this book are the speeches of these friends, who seem determined to get Job to admit to some unacknowledged sin.

Job Suffering, Syracuse University

In the theology of the friends, bad things happen as a result of God's displeasure with your sin, so if life isn't going well, you're somehow to blame. This, of course, was the theology of the Israelites during the exile. They looked back to the "bad" kings and the idolatry of the people as the reason that God allowed first Assyria and then Babylon to almost stomp them out of existence. It's also a very common theology today. Every time you hear a religious leader announcing that a natural disaster has befallen a certain area because of some sin, you're hearing this theology. It also works in the reverse. If you've ever had a great day and said, "I must be living right," you're expressing the theology of Job's friends.

> **For Reflection**
>
> Have you ever had so many things go wrong at once that you felt like Job? Why do you think bad things happen to good people?

It isn't surprising, however, that Job finds this annoying. He knows he hasn't done anything wrong, and the setup in chapter one as well as the resolution at the end of the book affirms that. God actually speaks to one of the friends, Eliphaz, saying:

> "My wrath is kindled against you and against your two friends; for you have not spoken of me what is right, as my servant Job has. Now therefore take seven bulls and seven rams, and go to my servant Job, and offer up for yourselves a burnt offering; and my servant Job shall pray for you, for I will accept his prayer not to deal with you according to your folly; for you have not spoken of me what is right, as my servant Job has done." (Job 42:7–8)

I can think of at least a couple of people today who need to be offering up quite a few bulls and rams.

The other main speech in the book comes from God. Job has been complaining loudly about his condition and demanding that God explain how all this has anything to do with justice, mercy, and all the other great qualities for which God is renowned. God's response begins in chapter 38 and continues all the way through chapter 41. It's beautiful, majestic poetry, and the main message seems to be that Job really has no business questioning God because his puny brain couldn't understand the answer even if he got one.

The book closes with God giving back all Job has lost—and more. Perhaps not surprisingly, Satan is nowhere to be seen. He's lost the challenge. Job proved to be good for goodness' sake.

Lamentations

Traditionally attributed to the prophet Jeremiah (and thus its placement in the Bible right after Jeremiah), the book of Lamentations is just that. It is five chapters of poetic lament for Jerusalem and the agonies endured in its fall. These verses were most probably used in public rituals on days of fasting and mourning and would have been composed sometime between the fall of Jerusalem in 586 B.C.E. and the return and reconstruction of the Temple in 516 B.C.E. The language is raw and graphic, causing many to argue for a date much closer to the fall than to the restoration.

> One aspect of the book of Lamentations lost in translation is the fact that the first four chapters are an acrostic poem, with a stanza for each of the twenty-two letters of the Hebrew alphabet.

And of course there are those who think it is a combination of materials from several periods.

The tone of the book is one of extreme emotional pain, coming to an end with a fear-tinged plea:

> "But you, O LORD, reign forever; your throne endures to all generations. Why have you forgotten us completely? Why have you forsaken us these many days? Restore us to yourself, O LORD, that we may be restored; renew our days as of old—unless you have utterly rejected us, and are angry with us beyond measure." (Lamentations 5:19–22)

Lamentations goes from misery to misery, but smack dab in the middle is an amazing little passage of hope, which serves as the foundational text for the 1923 hymn "Great Is Thy Faithfulness":

> The thought of my affliction and my homelessness is wormwood and gall! My soul continually thinks of it and is bowed down within me. But this I call to mind, and therefore I have hope: The steadfast love of the LORD never ceases, his mercies never come to an end; they are new every morning; great is your faithfulness. (Lamentations 3:19–23)

As we saw in the book of Job, the faith reflected in these verses isn't fire-insurance faith. It doesn't represent a self-serving belief in a God who exchanges a set of protections and benefits in return for worship and obedience. The author of Lamentations is very clear that God is the one who has blasted Israel to kingdom come and who has inflicted their current misery. But the writer doesn't turn away from God mad, as Satan would have predicted in the Job challenge. No. Instead the writer turns **to** God, voicing confidence in God's mercy even in the midst of describing God's wrath.

Other Segments of the Apocrypha

In addition to the additional portions of the book of Daniel, there are three other books from the Apocrypha[7] that represent this period in either their composition or in the events described.

Baruch/Letter of Jeremiah

The first is the book of Baruch, named for Jeremiah's secretary; it often (but not always) includes the Letter of Jeremiah as a final chapter. Baruch is set during the period of the Babylonian Captivity, although it was probably written several centuries later. Just the presence of Baruch in Babylon gives us a window into conflicting traditions, since other traditions have Baruch accompanying Jeremiah to Egypt.

Most of the book of Baruch echoes or paraphrases sections of Daniel, Job, and Isaiah, and its five chapters are about half prose and half poetry. The Letter of Jeremiah is either considered chapter 6 of Baruch or, in some manuscripts, stands on its own as a letter composed by the prophet

---

[7] For an explanation of this term, see the section from the first course in Appendix 1 on page 256.

for those about to be taken into captivity in Babylon. The letter is a long prose warning to the exiles not to be seduced by the idols they will find in Babylon.

Prayer of Manasseh

In the succession of the Kings of Judah that we examined in Session 5, right before good King Josiah there was the very, very bad king—Manasseh. As a punishment for his sins, the Assyrians put him in shackles and carted him off and the experience brought about a change of heart. We are told in 2 Chronicles 33:13 that Manasseh prayed, but the prayer is not recorded—at least not in the book of Chronicles.

But there were other books from the period that have never been recovered. Two of them are described in 2 Chronicles 33:18–19:

> Now the rest of the acts of Manasseh, his prayer to his God, and the words of the seers who spoke to him in the name of the LORD God of Israel, these are in the Annals of the Kings of Israel. His prayer, and how God received his entreaty, all his sin and his faithlessness, the sites on which he built high places and set up the sacred poles and the images, before he humbled himself, these are written in the records of the seers.

This indicates that Manasseh's prayer was recorded in at least two other sources: the Annals of the Kings of Israel and the records of the seers. While we don't have those other sources, we do have a document, fifteen verses long, that purports to be the prayer.

The Prayer of Manasseh is an example of a work that is accepted as part of the canon by the Eastern Orthodox traditions, but not by the Roman Catholics or Protestants.

End of an Empire

The Babylonians controlled Jerusalem (and, by extension, the Jews) for a scant seventy years. We've seen that the kings of Babylon weren't particularly cruel, but as the stories from the Babylonian court in the book of Daniel show, neither were they particularly wise. Sources outside the Bible also attest that the kings of the Babylonian Empire were caught up in themselves, had stretches of severe mental illness, and didn't seem to govern well.

Belshazzar's Feast, Rembrandt

In fact, the last king of the Babylonian Empire, Nabonidus, didn't even bother to show up in his own capital for ten years, instead taking a long vacation in a southern oasis. Remember that the king of Babylon had a key religious role, and keeping the gods happy was believed to be the key to a nation's security and prosperity. When Nabonidus failed to show for even the most important religious festivals, the city grew both nervous and impatient.

Taking care of matters in the king's absence was his son, Belshazzar, who hosted the feast recorded in Daniel 5, when the finger of God wrote a message on the wall. Tellingly, that feast began with Belshazzar getting the bright idea to bring out all the sacred vessels taken from the Temple in Jerusalem and use them in the revelry of the feast. The words written on the wall were **"Mene, mene, tekel, and parsin."** Those words didn't form a sentence—they were simply a listing of weights and measures.

Belshazzar called for Daniel to interpret the message and the interpretation he gave Belshazzar is not surprising:

"God has numbered the days of your kingdom and brought it to an end. You have been weighed on the scales and found wanting. Your kingdom is divided and given to the Medes and Persians." (Daniel 5:26–28)

The people of Babylon knew that the Persians to their north had a much better king, Cyrus, who had recently taken over the nearby Median Empire and seemed to have his act together. While the Babylonian army fought and lost to Cyrus outside the walls of Babylon, Belshazzar feasted inside. The Persian forces waltzed right in, wading into the city through an irrigation channel. The Bible records that Belshazzar was killed that night. The rest of the city, however, danced. Babylon was taken peacefully.

Persia (539–333 B.C.E.)

Detail of Cyrus the Great Monument in Olympic Park, Sydney, Australia, 1994

Daniel tells us it was Darius I, the third king of the Persian Empire, who conquered Babylon. But a quick fact-check shows that it was actually Cyrus who took the city, and thereby the empire, much to the delight of the Babylonian people. Even more delighted were the Jews. Cyrus was not only a brilliant tactician, he was an honest and generous king, respecting the customs, religions, and human rights of the peoples he conquered. Perhaps he got word of what Confucius was teaching right about this time in China: "What you do not want done to yourself, do not do to others." It was Cyrus who issued the edict (related in Ezra 1:2–4) to free the Jews and allow them to return home.

Cyrus would become known as Cyrus the Great and in the Bible he has the rare distinction of being called "God's anointed," even though he was a Gentile. Remember that word in Hebrew is **meshiach**—messiah in English. Cyrus had many grand titles, including "King of the Four Corners of the World." The empire that he built eventually encompassed 44 percent of the world's population, making it the largest empire ever seen, and the political system he put in place allowed for just the right balance between autonomy and centralized power. Cyrus ruled the Persian Empire for about thirty years. A Greek teenager named Alexander was one his biggest fans and studied him closely.

Unlike the unstable Babylonians, the Persian Empire lasted for centuries, but only one thing mattered to the Judean exiles along the Chebar River—they were going home. Two entire books of the Bible tell us how it all went down: Ezra and Nehemiah.

Ezra and Nehemiah

We're looking at these two books together because most scholars believe they were originally one book. Together they give us two views of the same period of reconstruction.

Ezra Reads the Law to the People, Gustave Doré

The book of 1 Esdras, found in the Apocrypha, also describes this time period, with some sections reaching all the way back to the reforms of Josiah. This work describes the details differently, with Nehemiah getting the boot and all the work attributed to him in the books of Ezra and Nehemiah given over instead to Ezra.

The book of Ezra tells us about the restoration of worship, laying the foundation for the new Temple in Jerusalem, and protecting the faith from the corrupting outside influences that had made them exiles in the first place. Nehemiah tells us about the political reconstruction, especially the rebuilding of the fortification walls of Jerusalem. But those are generalities. Ancient Israel knew no boundary between religion and politics and both overlap in these two books.

What we see in these accounts are the strict protections put in place to keep the past from repeating itself. As the Jews turned to the Law during the exile, they became more and more convinced that it was a failure of obedience to the law of God that led to the horrible destruction and exile of the prior generation. They looked back and saw that even the great reforms and repentance of Josiah couldn't avert the wrath of God incurred by the evil kings who had come before. Such sin could, therefore, not be tolerated even in the slightest, and to be sure that no one fell into sin, every temptation needed to be removed from their midst. It wasn't just the physical walls that needed to be rebuilt; spiritual walls needed to be put up as well, and these books chronicle the construction of both.

> ### Ezra
>
> Christians generally don't pay much attention to Ezra—neither the book nor the man. For the Jews, however, Ezra is a major figure, believed to be the founder of the Great Assembly, a group of scholars and prophets that would eventually become the Sanhedrin (the supreme court of ancient Israel). It was the Great Assembly that instituted many features of traditional Judaism known today, including the feast of Purim, Torah reading, and the Amidah, the central prayer of Jewish liturgy.
>
> Tradition attributes the writing of the book of Chronicles to Ezra.

It was an understandably emotional time for the returning exiles. We read this mixed reaction to the laying of the Temple foundation:

> "And all the people responded with a great shout when they praised the LORD, because the foundation of the house of the LORD was laid. But many of the priests and Levites and heads of families, old people who had seen the first house on its foundations, wept with a loud voice when they saw this house, though many shouted aloud for joy, so that the people could not distinguish the sound of the joyful shout from the sound of the people's weeping, for the people shouted so loudly that the sound was heard far away." (Ezra 3:11–13)

There's much debate about whether Ezra and Nehemiah were contemporaries or whether one came before the other (different scholars put different people first), but the results were the same. The Temple foundations were laid, the walls were rebuilt, and the process of purging Israel of all foreign influence and restoring the Law of God was begun.

But Which Was It?

Many events in the Bible are lumped together, transposed, or otherwise mixed up because the writers weren't primarily interested in establishing firm dates and chronologies. They were writing history in these books, but it was religious history. What was accomplished to allow the people of God to re-establish the covenant was far more important than detailing exactly how that came about. When we bring our need for historical accuracy to these ancient texts, we're asking them to give us something they never meant for us to have. We're demanding that the texts reflect *our* literary values rather than the values of the authors.

The Bible tells us that Ezra was a scribe, descended from Moses's brother Aaron, and that Nehemiah, a cupbearer for King Artaxerxes, asked for permission to return to his homeland and rebuild the walls. Permission was granted and Nehemiah became the governor of the region, eliminating political corruption even as Ezra sought to purge religious corruption.

For a small example of what that purging looked like, let's look at this account at the end of Nehemiah:

> "In those days also I saw Jews who had married women of Ashdod, Ammon, and Moab; and half of their children spoke the language of Ashdod, and they could not speak the language of Judah, but spoke the language of various peoples. And I contended with them and cursed them and beat some of them and pulled out their hair; and I made them take an oath in the name of God, saying, 'You shall not give your daughters to their sons, or take their daughters for your sons or for yourselves. Did not King Solomon of Israel sin on account of such women? Among the many nations there was no king like him and he was beloved by his God, and God made him king over all Israel; nevertheless, foreign women made even him to sin. Shall we then listen to you and do all this great evil and act treacherously against our God by marrying foreign women?'" (Nehemiah 13:23–27)

In Ezra 10 we read that all foreign wives and children were actually cast out, and there's a whole list of all the men who had sinned in marrying foreign wives. But I always end up wondering why the fall to idolatry was the fault of the women. How come the men didn't convince their wives to worship the God of Israel? Why were they so spiritually powerless? I wouldn't be surprised if they blamed their weakness on the women's too-revealing robes. You have to wonder.

We'll Do It Ourselves

The only other noteworthy event occurs at the beginning of Ezra 4. The rebuilding of the Temple has begun and since they're gathering materials from all over, everybody in the surrounding regions knows about it. Remember that throughout those surrounding regions are Jews who were either left behind by the Assyrians or who fled during the onslaught of Babylon on Jerusalem or after the assassination of Gedaliah.

These folks weren't necessarily physically exiled, especially if their original home was in the north country. But they had experienced a kind of spiritual exile, dating all the way back to the dividing of the kingdom under Jeroboam. If everybody was starting over and even the Temple had to be rebuilt from scratch, maybe this could herald the return of a single, united kingdom as the prophets before the exile had foretold.

It was also true that when the Assyrians sent some of their own folks to occupy Samaria, they began to worship the God of Israel (must have been those foreign Jewish women!). While they also kept the Assyrian gods, Israel's God was a significant addition to the mix, and when the Jews from Babylon returned, even those with roots in other nations felt a common bond because they shared a god.

So the leaders from the surrounding areas came to Jerusalem and said, *"Let us build with you, for we worship your God as you do, and we have been sacrificing to him ever since the days of King Esarhaddon of Assyria who brought us here." (Ezra 4:2)*

Their offer is rebuffed, however. *"You shall have no part with us in building a house to our God; but we alone will build to the* LORD, *the God of Israel, as King Cyrus of Persia has commanded us." (Ezra 4:3)*

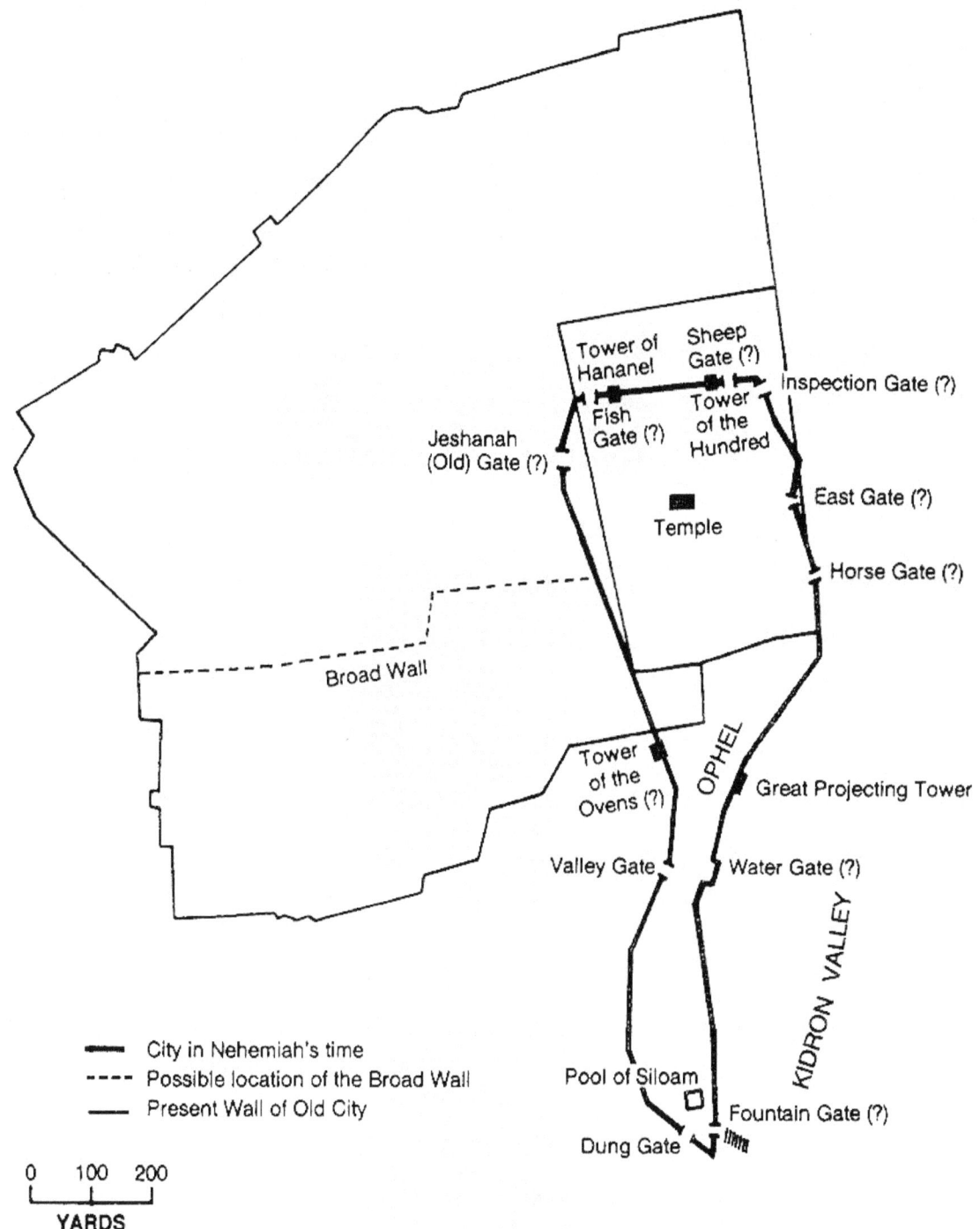

JERUSALEM IN THE TIME OF NEHEMIAH

Not surprisingly, those who have been rebuffed try to make the rebuilding of both the Temple and the wall difficult and tensions between Israel and her neighbors grow. This continues the development of the conflict between Jews and Samaritans that began with the establishment of separate temples in the divided kingdom and reaches a fever pitch by the time of Jesus.

AGE OF EMPIRES

Esther

Set during Persian rule, the book of Esther is a great read. The wonderful storytelling, however, hasn't protected the book from criticism—mostly because the book doesn't contain a single mention of God. The Persian king gets 190 shout-outs, but God gets nary a one in the Hebrew. This led to some later additions to the book to give it a more religious tone. These additions are considered to be part of the Apocrypha.

> **Read the book of Esther.** You won't be sorry.

Written several centuries after its Persian setting, the book of Esther as we have it represents the joining of three independent stories: a harem tale about Vashti, a palace intrigue story revolving around Haman and Mordecai, and the deliverance story starring Esther/Hadassah.

Queen Esther and Her Maids, Edwin Long, 1878

The book also has earned detractors who claim that its moral tone is lacking, and both Jews and Christians were fairly late in giving it full acceptance into the canon. Though the hatreds, vengeance, and bloodletting found in Esther are hardly foreign to the Old Testament, I suspect they're problematic only because there's no religious voice in the book to point out their inconsistency with Jewish values.

Despite all that, the book of Esther provides the origins of the Jewish festival of Purim, although the festival isn't commanded or even predicted in the book itself. In 2007 I was in Jerusalem during the festival of Purim.

It is a time of major gift giving, especially to the poor. And, of course, no festival is complete without a special meal.

Purim is also a time when people dress up. The custom began with people dressing up as the characters in the book of Esther—the book is read in its entirety during the festival—and that was still evident in the celebrations that I witnessed. But over time the holiday has branched out to include other costumes as well, and I probably saw as much Disney as I did Esther. (I'm still trying to process the fact that I saw a grown man dressed as a giant chicken going through the metal detectors to get to the Wailing Wall.)

Like the book from which it springs, Purim is more of a national holiday than a religious one, but it's been incorporated into Jewish religious life, just as the book of Esther finally made it into the canon of Jewish and Christian Scripture.

Haggai and Zechariah

As a teenager I was very involved in church and that included helping the congregation with a project to paint the church walls. As it happened, my family had also decided to do some painting at home during the same period. While my parents labored to turn our living room from Seaside Blue to Taco Tan, I was AWOL from the family project, working instead at the church to get their walls painted. My father complained about this and I responded with a quote from Haggai 1:4, *"Is it a time for you yourselves to live in your paneled houses, while this house lies in ruins?"*

Prophet Haggai, Russian icon from the 18th century

Prophets are never popular.

The two chapters that comprise the book of Haggai represent that prophet's efforts to spur the returned exiles—and especially their leadership—to get the new temple completed, including all the attendant purification rituals. Haggai insisted that this was necessary for a new messianic age to come.

The message was actually proclaimed in stereo, as the prophet Zechariah was delivering basically the same message to the same people at the same time—in about 520 B.C.E. The book of Zechariah is both longer and more complex than Haggai. Haggai simply addressed the leaders in Jerusalem and told them to get a move on it. Zechariah was more like Ezekiel, conveying his message in visions and metaphors.

Zechariah saw four horns, a mysterious man with a measuring line, Satan standing next to the high priest Joshua, golden lampstands, and flying scrolls. To the core message of "Get it done" is added the reminder that the work is accomplished *"not by might, nor by power, but by my spirit, says the LORD of hosts." (Zechariah 4:6)*

The elements of apocalyptic literature appear in Zechariah, and chapters 9–14 probably come from the Greek rather than the Persian period and were likely the work of Zechariah's disciples rather than the prophet himself.

Malachi

The final book of the Old Testament (Chronicles closes it out in the Hebrew Bible) is Malachi, who was probably a contemporary of Nehemiah. The name Malachi means "my messenger," and some question whether it was the actual name of a prophet or whether it is a title, as we saw in Qoheleth (the Hebrew name of Ecclesiastes that was simply a title meaning "teacher"). As with most such questions, however, it doesn't change the message of the book one bit.

In Malachi, covenant language returns to the fore, and the author writes in a question-and-answer style, rather than in the visions and images of some of the other prophets.

Malachi the Prophet, James Tissot, 1896

Evoking the covenant, Malachi tries to lay to rest the question that had haunted Israel since the people watched Jerusalem burn: Does God still love us? Is the covenant so badly broken that God has abandoned us? Is there any possible way to restore the relationship? Malachi answers,

> "See, I am sending my messenger to prepare the way before me, and the Lord whom you seek will suddenly come to his temple. The messenger of the covenant, in whom you delight—indeed, he is coming, says the LORD of hosts. But who can endure the day of his coming, and who can stand when he appears?
>
> "For he is like a refiner's fire and like fullers' soap; he will sit as a refiner and purifier of silver, and he will purify the descendants of Levi and refine them like gold and silver, until they present offerings to the LORD in righteousness. Then the offering of Judah and Jerusalem will be pleasing to the LORD as in the days of old and as in former years." (Malachi 3:1–4)

Like most of the prophets throughout Israel's history, Malachi presents the "if—then" oracles of God. The covenant will stand, but only if Israel renews her vows and keeps up her part of the bargain. Sin must be acknowledged; there must be honest repentance that leads the people to turn in a new, God-ward direction.

There's the promise of blessing for the righteous: *"But for you who revere my name the sun of righteousness shall rise, with healing in its wings. You shall go out leaping like calves from the stall." (Malachi 4:2; 3:20 in the New American Bible)*

And destruction for the wicked: *"And you shall tread down the wicked, for they will be ashes under the soles of your feet, on the day when I act, says the* LORD *of hosts." (Malachi 4:3; 3:21 in NAB)*

There's a reminder: *"Remember the teaching of my servant Moses, the statues and ordinances that I commanded him at Horeb for all Israel." (Malachi 4:4; 3:22 in NAB)*

And a prediction whose fulfillment is awaited until this day: *"Lo, I will send you the prophet Elijah before the great and terrible day of the* LORD *comes. He will turn the hearts of parents to their children and the hearts of children to their parents, so that I will not come and strike the land with a curse." (Malachi 4:5; 3:23 in NAB)*

And those are the final words of the Old Testament.

Chronicles

In the Hebrew Bible, the book of Chronicles (which, like Samuel and Kings, is only one book in Hebrew) was the original conclusion. It was moved to its present location after Samuel and Kings (and was divided in two) by the Greek translation known as the Septuagint. The Greek title of the Chronicles means "the things omitted," which explains the thinking behind its placement at the end of the Bible. Jewish tradition holds that Ezra wrote Chronicles, but that has never been independently established and the book itself claims no particular author.

Continued on next page

Chronicles (Continued)

It's easy to see that Chronicles is intended as a summary of the entire history of Israel, right from its very first word, which is "Adam." It doesn't retell all those early stories, but it fast-forwards through Israel's history by means of genealogies. There are nine full chapters of genealogies before the actual stories, which pick up with the death of Saul and Jonathan on Mt. Gilboa and end when the exiles in Babylon are given permission to return home. Some scholars believe that the books of Ezra and Nehemiah were originally part of the book of Chronicles, but that's disputed.

What anyone who reads Chronicles can see, however, is that material from Israel's history is edited, quoted, and rewritten here, often with significant differences from the sections of the Torah, Samuel, Kings, and other biblical books that it duplicates. Chronicles also includes material from books outside the Bible that are now lost to us.

If we remember the place of Chronicles at the end of the Hebrew Scriptures, it's easy to see it as we might see an elder remembering how things were "back in the day." Despite the well-documented moral failures of King David, Chronicles lifts up those times as the golden years, remembering the characters with longing and looking forward to their return.

Meanwhile, Across the Mediterranean...

As the Buddha was achieving enlightenment in India, Confucius in China was teaching, "If a man takes no thought about what is distant, he will find sorrow near at hand." Persia should have heeded the words of Confucius, for there was much happening in the distant lands to the west, especially in Greece.

During the Persian period the Athenians established their democracy. Plato founded his famous academy at Athens, the Parthenon was built, Pindar began writing poetry, Herodotus began writing history, Hippocrates developed the Hippocratic oath, Socrates poisoned himself, and Pythagoras came to the striking conclusion that the earth is a sphere.

Things seemed pretty comfortable in Greece, and mostly they were. The Gauls took care of Greece's western border by sacking Rome and the Celts further north were just enjoying the first observance of Samhain—the festival that we know today as Halloween. The Persians seemed content to remain on their side of the Mediterranean, leaving lots of time for a philosopher named Aristotle to tutor a promising young man named Alexander, who had been studying Cyrus the Great very closely.

Greece (Seleucids) (332–166 B.C.E.)

Born in 356 B.C.E. in Pella, Greece, Alexander was one of the greatest military commanders of all time, ascending to the throne in Macedon after the assassination of his father in 336 B.C.E. Probably you learned about him in your high school history classes. Undefeated in battle, Alexander was a boy wonder, creating one of the largest empires in the ancient world by age thirty, founding twenty cities that bore his name and another city named after his horse. The most notable of these is the Egyptian city of Alexandria.

We could fill pages with his exploits, but here we'll note that he took Jerusalem from the Persians in 332 B.C.E., the same year Alexandria in Egypt was founded, and took the Persian capital of Babylon two years

Ruins of the Parthenon in Athens, Greece

later. Alexander didn't even have to "conquer" Jerusalem. They saw him coming and, perhaps with a nod to the grave of Jeremiah, opened their gates to him in surrender. When Alexander entered the city, they showed him part of the book of Daniel that predicted a mighty Greek king who would overthrow the Persians. Alexander just checked Jerusalem off his list and moved on to the south.

Samaria, too, accepted Alexander's conquest, but only briefly. In 331, the nobles of Samaria revolted, expressing their displeasure by burning Alexander's appointed prefect alive—definitely a bad idea. Alexander marched some troops back north, massacred the population of Samaria, and established a firmer Greek colony there.

A sudden illness took Alexander's life (some suggest he was poisoned) at the tender age of thirty-two, before he could really establish a coherent system of government for the new empire as a whole. Had he lived, the Greek Empire might have lasted centuries longer. As it was, the empire held together, albeit tenuously, for more than twice the duration of the Babylonians.

Bust of Alexander the Great, ca. 335 B.C.E.

The part of Alexander's legacy that most affects the world of the Bible is the way that he spread not just Greek power, but Greek culture. Alexander had studied Cyrus well, and saw that you didn't have to be a tyrant to be successful. Like Cyrus, Alexander wanted to rule the territories he conquered as the absolute monarch, but he had no desire to squash or alienate the population along the way. Because Greek culture was not imposed, it could be observed without defensiveness in the various parts of the empire. People generally liked what they saw, and willingly adopted the Greek language and way of life.

Even as other empires came and went, Greek language and culture flourished in the areas touched by Alexander, not just for centuries but for more than a millennium. Alexander is the reason the Hebrew Scriptures were first translated into Greek, even though the translation (the Septuagint, or LXX) was sponsored by the Egyptian court. It was the Jews of Alexandria who did the translation that, even more than the Hebrew version, became the basis for the format of the Christian Old Testament.

Even though during the life of Jesus it was the Roman Empire that controlled Palestine, it was still Greek—or Hellenistic—rather than Roman culture and language that was preferred. Throughout the New Testament we'll see conflicts between Jews who were Hellenistic and those who saw Hellenism as a corrupting foreign influence.

During this period, a number of the works from the Persian era were collected, edited, and redacted, and works **about** the Persian era, like the book of Esther, were likely recorded. The Septuagint was begun in Alexandria and three other books that are now part of the Apocrypha were created: Tobit, the Wisdom of Solomon, and Sirach. Tobit is yet another great story, and the latter two books fit into the category of wisdom literature.

Hasmonean (165–64 B.C.E.)

While we closed out the Old Testament two empires ago, Christians are at a disadvantage if they don't know something about what went on between the time Malachi finished his message and the time Matthew opens his Gospel.

Today not many people name their sons Judas, but in Jesus' day that was a name of renown. It was Judas Maccabeus, the son of a Jewish priest, who led a revolt against the Greeks in 165 B.C.E. and secured a hundred years of self-rule for the Jews. It's this successful revolt and the consequent reconsecration of the Temple in Jerusalem that's celebrated in the feast of

Hanukkah. Handel composed an oratorio that bears his name, and Judas Maccabeus went down in Jewish history as a warrior on par with Joshua, Gideon, and David.

Menorah from Peter Fjellstedts Bibel, 1890

The dynasty of rulers from the family of Judas Maccabeus became known as the Hasmonean dynasty, and you can get a wonderful (if gory) picture of this period by reading the four books of Maccabees that are part of the Apocrypha. The book of Judith in the Apocrypha also dates to this time. If you're not yet convinced that Judaism has one of the best storytelling traditions around, maybe the book of Judith will convince you.

As we begin to round the corner toward the time of Jesus and the New Testament, this period becomes most important for two things that we'll encounter there. First is the intense and relatively recent memory of a revolutionary who overthrew foreign occupation. As the ministry of Jesus cranks up, there's no doubt that at least some of the population—if not a significant portion—wanted Jesus to be another Judas Maccabeus.

The second impact of this period is the final nail in the coffin of Samaritan-Jewish relations. The nephew of Judas Maccabeus was John Hyrcanus, who became the high priest and military leader in Jerusalem during a period when there was no king. As in the period of Ezra and Nehemiah, John Hyrcanus was eager to wipe out all vestiges of idolatry and deviance from the Law of Moses. He was willing to use force if necessary, and he raided the treasures of King David's tomb to finance his efforts. Yes, he violated Jewish law to get the funds to enforce it. Gotta love it.

Meanwhile, during the era of Greek rule, a temple had been erected in

Samaria on Mt. Gerizim; there's some evidence that Alexander himself ordered the construction. The Jewish historian Josephus reports that there was a statue of Zeus in that temple, which supports the theory of Alexander's involvement. After all, according to the cultural dictates of antiquity, the main god goes in the main temple. The head of the Greek pantheon was Zeus, so if Alexander established Samaria's main temple, he would naturally put Zeus in it. But you also don't have to call in Sherlock Holmes to figure out why the Jews would have a problem with that.

It was already bad enough that Samaria had its own shrines, but a major temple with Greek's top god sharing space with the God of Israel was too much for the Jews in Jerusalem. John Hyrcanus lost no sleep in deciding to destroy it (along with most of Samaria), going so far as trying to forcibly impose the Judean form of Judaism on all Samaritans. Still weakened from their opposition to Alexander, the Samaritans easily but unhappily came under the rule of Jerusalem. Once the invasion of the Romans released them from the grip of the high priests in Jerusalem, the antipathy between Jews and Samaritans was fully formed.

Rome (63 B.C.E.–390 C.E.)

The Hasmoneans were a family dynasty, not an empire. John Hyrcanus certainly tried to get an empire going, attempting to conquer (and convert) any weakened remnants of the Seleucid Empire that he could find. He was, however, an anomaly in that regard. Israel definitely wanted and fought for all of the area they believed God had promised to Abraham and later to Moses, but seeking to conquer areas outside of that territory was an aberration.

Back in the West, the Romans had recovered from their sacking by Gaul, had dealt with the Carthaginian Empire in Tunis, and had began to look eastward. Pompey marched east and took Jerusalem in 63 B.C.E. Samaria, released from the grip of Judean priest kings, greeted Pompey as a liberator. Jerusalem, however, was another story.

The residents of Jerusalem didn't welcome Pompey as they'd welcomed Alexander, and an ugly siege ensued. Twelve thousand Jews were slaughtered and Pompey himself entered the Holy of Holies in the Temple, desecrating it, although he didn't destroy it or steal the contents. The Romans left a Hasmonean puppet king on his throne, and that petty dynasty continued. Just thirty years later, Herod the Great (himself a Jewish convert), with the aid of Mark Antony, laid siege to the city yet again, ending all vestiges of Hasmonean rule. Just to be sure, Herod hunted down and killed all remaining descendants of the Hasmonean line.

Desecration of the Temple of Jerusalem by Pompey and His Soldiers,
Jean Fouquet, ca. 1470

As Herod surveyed his new territory, he seemed to agree with the elderly Jewish exiles who wept when the new temple was constructed under Ezra. It was not, he decided, quite grand enough, so in 20–19 B.C.E., he greatly expanded it. The temple itself was finished in a year and a half, but it took a full 80 years for his massive plans for the entire temple complex to be completed.

Herod was known for his building projects, and for executing people, including members of his own family. Perhaps he's best remembered, however, for the New Testament account of Herod executing all children in Bethlehem under two years of age when some Babylonian astrologers followed a star to his doorstep, seeking the newly born "king of the Jews." (Matthew 2:13–23)

Preparation for Check-In

(Prepare for the next group session by thinking about and writing a brief response to these two questions.)

What is one thing that was new to me in this material?

What is one question that this week's topic raises for me?

Extra Mile Wrap-Up

☐ In a concluding essay of five hundred to seven hundred words, describe your experience with the Old Testament in this course. How familiar were you with it when you started? What was the most important thing you learned during the course? Which chapters did you find the most challenging and why? If you could take just one book of the Old Testament with you to a desert island, which one would it be? Why?

Appendix 1

What is the Bible?
Session 3: Overview of the Old Testament

This is the chapter introducing the Old Testament in the first course of Exploring the Bible, <u>What Is the Bible?</u> If you have not taken that course, you should read this chapter before beginning this course.

The Organization of The Bible

The Bible begins with the creation of the universe and ends with the destruction of that universe and the establishment of a new heaven and new earth. That has led many people to believe that the Bible is organized chronologically. It isn't.

Testaments

The major divisions within the Bible are the Old and New Testaments. The word "testament" comes from the Latin **testamentum**, which means to bear witness to a formal, written agreement. Another English word that comes from the Latin **testamentum** is "testimony." Outside of religious circles, the only place you regularly hear the word "testament" today is in relation to someone's "last will and testament"—the witnessed document showing how a person would like his or her assets distributed after death. The testaments in the Bible are documents that were recorded to bear witness to the way God's people have lived out their relationships with God, with one another, and with the world in which they lived.

When looking at the Old and New Testaments in the Bible, you can say that **those** are arranged chronologically. "Old" in this case doesn't mean outdated; it simply means that it came first. All the material in the Old Testament (OT) was written and describes events that are earlier than any of the material in the New Testament (NT). The words **old** and **new** should not lead us to believe that the new replaces the old, but simply that the old came first and the new came later.

> **Supersessionism**
>
> The view in some Christian traditions that the New Testament has greater authority and therefore "supersedes" the writing and teaching in the Old Testament. The supersessionist believes that the covenant with Israel described in the Old Testament was replaced with the new covenant with Christians described in the New Testament.

The Old and New Testaments could also have been called the First Witness and the Second Witness. The First Witness—the Old Testament—is the story of the people of Israel, the Jews. For that reason, the Old Testament is sometimes called the Hebrew Scriptures. That section of our Bible represents the sacred Scriptures of the Jewish faith. The New Testament bears the same kind of witness for the origins of Christianity. Sometimes the testaments are also named as the Old and New Covenants—the covenant with the Jews came first, followed by the covenant with the Christians.

It is important to remember that it was never the intention of the biblical writers to replace the Old Testament with the New. When 2 Timothy 3:16 (in the NT) says, "All scripture is inspired by God and is useful for teaching, for reproof, for correction, and for training in righteousness," the only "Scripture" in existence was the Hebrew Bible. That passage is talking about the Old Testament.

In the mid-second century C.E., a bishop named Marcion of Sinope in Asia Minor, in what is now Turkey, decided that the entire Old Testament and anything in the early Christian writings that smacked of Judaism had become irrelevant. He believed that the God of the Old Testament was a different and inferior being to the God of Jesus Christ. He issued his own collection of Scriptures based on that premise and was excommunicated and deemed a heretic. His work was one of the things that spurred the official bodies within the church to define the authoritative writings of the Bible.

Christians often forget that Christianity began as a Jewish sect. Jesus and each of his twelve main disciples were Jews. Jesus was addressed as a rabbi and taught in synagogues. Jesus was born, lived, and died a Jew. That First Witness, the Old Testament, is critical to understanding the faith of Jesus, his disciples, and the world in which they lived. Those stories and histories, poems and songs, laws and proverbs were the writings that formed Jesus as a Jewish man.

The Second Witness, the New Testament, is not properly understood apart from the context of the First. That is why the Christian Scriptures include both the Old and the New Tes-

> ### The **Hebrew Bible**
>
> The Hebrew Bible (as used in Jewish worship) is also arranged by category, but that arrangement differs from the grouping in the Christian Old Testament. Because of that and other differences, this series will use "Old Testament" to refer to the Christian translation of these works and "Hebrew Bible" to refer to the text as used in Jewish worship and study.

taments. The Second Witness is an extension of, not a replacement for, the First. Apart from the Apocrypha (see p. 46), there are thirty-nine books in the Old Testament and twenty-seven books in the New for a total of sixty-six books in the Bible, written by a number of different authors in a wide variety of literary categories.

Within each of the Testaments, the books are arranged according to the type of literature they represent, or in some cases common authorship.

For our purposes here, I will refer to the Christian grouping as the Old Testament and the Jewish grouping as the Hebrew Bible. But first, a distinction to chew on as you read.

A Word about "Truth"

Before we dive in, we need to take a deep breath and remember the culture in which we now live. While we'll look at this issue again in Session 5, but along the way it will be helpful as you read to mull over the distinction between "truth" and "facts."

In the contemporary world, and especially in the contemporary Western world, we tend to think of "truth" as representing something that is factually accurate. Seems like a no-brainer, right? Here's one way that understanding has tripped me up.

When people ask about my birthday, I relate that I was born on Mother's Day. I once received a birthday greeting from a man in my congregation on May 10. I thanked him, while noting that his greeting was actually a day early—my birthday was May 11. He informed me that, no, my birthday was May 10. He had noted my age and researched when Mother's Day fell in the year I was born. He insisted that either my birthday was May 10 or I had misled the congregation by saying I was born on Mother's Day. **Mea culpa**, but let me explain.

My mother went into labor in the early evening of Mother's Day, which was indeed May 10. She did not sleep or cease her labor until I entered the world at about two in the morning on May 11. Those are the facts. To my mother, however, I was her Mother's Day gift and I was born on Mother's Day. The passing of the midnight hour and what they put on my birth certificate was immaterial to her. She well knew the facts and my birthday was correctly recorded on every form she ever filled out. But in our family narrative…in the meaning she found in my birth…the "truth" was that I was born on Mother's Day. For the man who challenged me, however, a thing had to be factual to be true and he felt misled.

From time to time in these sessions, you will be asked to reflect on what "truth" a passage might convey. When that happens (like it will in a page or two), try to put aside your twenty-first-century, post-enlightenment mindset that often equates truth only with science and verifiable fact. Try to remember that there is a very different kind of "truth" in stories and poetry and in the lived-out lives of human beings than there is in biology, physics, and the calendar in your phone.

Remember the fable Aesop told about the dog with the bone? The dog, yummy bone in mouth, sees his reflection in the water, and thinks it's another dog with another bone. Because the bone a dog has is never quite as good as the bone another dog has, Aesop's dog opens his mouth to grab the bone from the water dog. The real bone drops in the water and the dog ends up with no bone at all.

Now that story could be a factual story. It could, honestly, be a factual story about my dog, who would do something stupid like that before you can say "rawhide." However, the "truth" of that fable remains even if Aesop never saw such a dog or even if a dog were incapable of such an action. Because, of course, the story really isn't about dogs at all. It's about us.

As we delve into the stories of the Old and New Testaments, remember that looking to Scripture for factual truth is a relatively modern convention. For those writing the texts that came to be part of our Bible, it was the broader sense of "truth" that they sought to convey. There may well be facts in there, but that wasn't the point. It wasn't about how many calendar days passed from the creation of light to God's day of rest. It was about the "truth" that the God of Israel was the author of awesomeness and able to create order out of chaos.

You neither need nor want a fact-checker when you're reading the Bible. You want to sit at the feet of storytellers by the fire and see the truth of God and the world through their eyes. Then you are better equipped to judge whether what was "true" for them also rings "true" for you.

The Old Testament

The Old Testament contains thirty-nine books in four broad categories: The Pentateuch (pronounced pen-ta-tewk), History, Poetry and Wisdom Literature, and Prophets. The latter has a subdivision between the "major" and "minor" prophets. We'll look at each category in turn.

The Pentateuch: The Fab Five

It's impossible to overestimate the importance of these five books, both for Jewish and Christian faith. Tradition has it that Moses is responsible for producing these books and for that reason they are often called the

The **Pentateuch**

The word *pentateuch* is Greek, meaning "five books." So, if you open your Bible and count out the first five books listed, you have this group: Genesis, Exodus, Leviticus, Numbers, and Deuteronomy.

Five Books of Moses. In Jewish tradition, they are also called the Law or the Torah.

Both Christianity and Judaism would be unrecognizable if you took out these five books. Here you have the great stories of creation, Adam and Eve, Noah, Abraham, Jacob and his twelve sons who became the fathers of the twelve tribes of Israel, Moses and the Ten Commandments. You have the first directions for formal, communal worship, the foundation for all the kosher laws and the laws that would later comprise the Great Commandment of Jesus to love God with all your heart, soul, and strength, and to love your neighbor as yourself.

It is right that the Bible begin with these five books, since they are the foundation on which all the rest of it depends. Did Moses really write them? It depends whom you ask. Some insist he did, others insist he didn't, and you can get a sense of the reasoning from introductions and notes in your study Bible. But whatever camp you belong to, Moses is a major player in the texts themselves, from his appearance in the book of Exodus onward. More important than authorship are the stories these books tell, the laws they put forth, and the formation of a nation and a faith they describe.

> ***Read Genesis 1–3.*** What important truths do these stories teach? Would those truths change if the accounts were not factual? Have you encountered these stories outside of church? What do you like about them? What questions do they raise for you?

These five books underlie our culture, society, and politics in ways both subtle and profound. Debates about creationism vs. evolution, questions of where it might be appropriate to post the Ten Commandments, Blue Laws about keeping the Sabbath, dietary laws, claims of land ownership in the Middle East—it all starts here in the Pentateuch.

History

The next nine books of the Old Testament are considered history. It is in these books that we encounter stories set during a time period that archaeologists and historians can study, places that can be marked on a map, and at least some people who can be identified from non-biblical, historical sources.

That is not to say, however, that this section of the Old Testament reads like a history textbook. Within the books considered "history" are some of the best stories in the Bible. This is where you will find the inspiring story of David and Goliath as well as the lusty and murderous tale of David and Bathsheba. Here is the Battle of Jericho, Elijah facing off with the prophets of Baal and then with Jezebel, and the young Samuel hearing God's voice in the still of the night.

In the histories, women shine in their own right more than in any other part of the Old Testament. Deborah rises to be a judge over Israel—a military as well as a political position. There is the clever Rahab who secures safety for herself and her family through political shrewdness; Queen Jezebel, who makes Cruella deVille look saintly; and two women with entire books of their own: the faithful Ruth, a foreign-born woman who ends up being an ancestor of Jesus; and brave Queen Esther, who saves her people and whose story provides the backdrop for the Jewish festival of Purim.

But the histories are not just personal. Here is also the broad sweep of the history of a nation. Monarchies are established, land is apportioned; a country unites, then divides, then crumbles as its people are carried off into captivity by a foreign nation. There are good kings and bad kings and, ultimately, bold prophets, leaders, and craftsmen who return to rebuild Jerusalem and the Temple from ashes.

> *Read the story of David and Goliath in 1 Samuel 17. Then read 2 Samuel 21:19 and 1 Chronicles 20:5.* What are your thoughts? What truths might the David and Goliath story be trying to teach us? Would that change if someone else killed Goliath?

Several of these books are divided into two, with the Old Testament calling them 1 and 2 Samuel, for example. In the Hebrew Bible, however, all of the history books that the Old Testament divides are just one scroll and should be considered a unit.

Reading the **Name of God**

Many times in all Bible translations you will see the word LORD, all in capital letters. You will also see the word written in regular upper- and lower-case letters, as "Lord." In Exodus 3:14, Moses learns the name of God. However that name is considered by Jews as too sacred to speak aloud. While it was written (consonants only) in the scrolls as YHWH, those reading the scrolls aloud were in a bind. What to say when the name of God appears?

They settled on the word "Lord," which in Hebrew is Adonai. That worked for the reading of the text aloud, but translators still wanted the reader to be aware of when the word "Lord" was referring to the

Continued on next page

Reading the **Name of God** (Continued)

name of God and when it was a reference to the actual word Adonai in the text. So, the convention was adopted of putting LORD (in all capital letters), when the original had YHWH, and Lord (in a mix of capital and smaller letters), when the original word actually meant just the title, "Lord," which indicates a person of noble rank and authority.

> **Tetragrammaton**
>
> It means "word with four letters" and stands for the particular four consonants (YHWH) that represent the name of God given to Moses in Exodus 3:14. That's right. God is a four-letter word.

To confuse the matter further, remember the Masoretes? They were the Hebrew scholars at the end of the first millennium C.E. who went back and added the vowels to the Hebrew Bible. Well, they had an interesting conundrum. If they put the correct vowels into the name of God, someone would be able to pronounce it and might therefore speak God's name. That was to be avoided at all costs. So the Masoretes took the Hebrew word for Lord, Adonai, and put those vowels into God's name instead. That way if you did try to pronounce it, you would be respectful…but wrong. Thus you would avoid the sin of actually speaking God's name. When you put the vowels from Adonai together with the Hebrew consonants for the name of God (YHWH) you get, in English, "Jehovah."

Continued on next page

> Reading the **Name of God** (Continued)
>
> Most scholars today believe the original vowels would have resulted in the word "Yahweh," usually translated, "I am who I am." Since ancient Hebrew didn't distinguish between present and future tense, it could also mean, "I will be who I will be" or "I am who I will be" or "I will be who I am," or…you get the picture. Here's a question. If Moses asks God for a name and God answers, "I am who I am," is that really God's name or was it God's way of saying, "None of your business"?
>
> Christians in a public or interfaith setting today will generally follow the Jewish custom of not speaking the name Yahweh aloud, instead using "God," "Lord," or "Jehovah" to avoid causing offense.

Poetry and Wisdom Literature

This section—Job, Psalms, Proverbs, Ecclesiastes (sometimes called Qoheleth—pronounced koh-HEL-leth—which means "teacher"), and Song of Songs (sometimes called Song of Solomon)—is the closest the Old Testament gets to the Hebrew Bible category of the Writings. All of the Poetry and Wisdom Literature falls in that Hebrew Bible category, which also includes some of what the Old Testament considers history and prophets. In this section of the Old Testament, only the book of Job does not have a traditional connection to either King David or his son, King Solomon.

If you want to know where Pete Seeger got his inspiration for the song "Turn! Turn! Turn!" popularized in the 1960s by The Byrds, you need look no further than Ecclesiastes chapter 3. Thousands of funeral mourners have been comforted by King David's Psalm 23, which refers to God as his shepherd. Proverbs are what you would expect, and Song of Songs describes the delights of physical love, which the church has usually taken as a metaphor for God's love. And of course there is poor Job, beginning and ending with a narrative about a rich man who loses everything and an unsurpassed poetic middle filled with the advice of his friends and the response of God to Job's complaint.

The Prophets

In the Old Testament, the category of prophets has two subdivisions: Major Prophets and Minor Prophets. The Major Prophets consist of the books of Isaiah, Jeremiah, Lamentations, Ezekiel, and Daniel. The Minor Prophets are the remaining twelve books of the Old Testament. In fact, the Hebrew Bible places all of these latter prophets together in a category called the Twelve, which all fit on one scroll in Hebrew.

> **Read Ezekiel 37:1–14 and Isaiah 53.** What are your impressions and questions about these passages? Are any of them familiar to you? Many Christians believe that Isaiah 53 is a prediction about Jesus. Others believe this "servant" is a personification of the nation of Israel. What do you think?

The Old Testament and the Hebrew Bible differ somewhat in the identification of Major Prophets. They agree on Isaiah, Jeremiah, and Ezekiel, but the Hebrew Bible puts Lamentations and Daniel with the Writings rather than with the Major Prophets.

A word about prophecy. To contemporary ears, the word "prophecy" brings to mind Nostradamus and those who foretell the future. Biblical prophecy does include some future predictions, but that is not the prophet's primary role. A prophet in the Bible is one who speaks for God and delivers messages from God to God's people (and sometimes vice versa). Sometimes this was a message about what was coming down the pike, but more frequently it was a message from God either chastising or reassuring the people about their actions and the events happening around them.

> **Jeremiad**
>
> Jeremiah is the second longest book of the Bible. Jeremiah has so many miserable messages in that extended space that it has spawned the English word jeremiad. A jeremiad is what you call a long, literary work that seems all the longer because its tone is full of lament over the state of things, judgments about how things got that way, and the prediction that the morally decrepit state of affairs will result in society's downfall—sooner rather than later. The Puritans were especially good at this. If you have just been speaking and someone calls your words a "jeremiad," you will not be invited to many parties.

Being a prophet was not an enviable job. Poor Jeremiah always seemed to be stuck with delivering unpleasant messages to the King. Kings don't like unpleasant messages or those who bring them, and Jeremiah spent quite a bit of time at the bottom of a muddy cistern as a result (Jeremiah 38:6).

Quite frequently the prophets conveyed God's message through object lessons. Jeremiah, for example, creates a pot and then smashes it to bits (Jeremiah 19:10-11) and buys a plot of land just as the country has been taken over and its people marched into exile (Jeremiah 32:1-15). Isaiah walks around naked and barefoot for three years (Isaiah 20). Ezekiel creates a model of the city of Jerusalem in the middle of the street and then lies down beside it for almost a year. I don't even want to tell you how God wants Ezekiel to bake his bread (Ezekiel 4:1-17).

Often the messages from God come to the prophet in the form of visions. Parts of Isaiah and Daniel contain such visions, full of confusing symbols and metaphors. Perhaps the most famous visions came to the prophet Ezekiel and are popularized in song. "Zekiel saw de wheel, way up in de middle of de air…" Not only did this become a popular spiritual, but Ezekiel's vision of a giant wheel covered in eyes, guided by four strange creatures, is seen by some as the first recorded UFO sighting. It is also the genre of the Negro spiritual that popularized Ezekiel's vision of the Valley of Dry Bones that comes to life through the Spirit of God. "Dem bones, dem bones, dem dry bones…" A quick search on YouTube will turn up some wonderful renditions.

To label twelve books as Minor Prophets is more to speak of their length than their importance or content. This is where you find Jonah being swallowed by a whale while trying to run from God's command. In the book of the prophet Amos (5:24) are the stirring words we remember best coming from the lips of the Rev. Dr. Martin Luther King, Jr.: "Let justice roll down like waters and righteousness like a mighty stream." And if all the confusing visions and object lessons muddle your brain about what God does and doesn't want, you can count on the "minor" prophet Micah to sum it all up: "What does the LORD require of you but to do justice, and to love kindness, and to walk humbly with your God?" (Micah 6:8)

The Apocrypha or Deuterocanonical Books

To understand how this group of writings came to be set apart from the others in some traditions, we need to delve into some history and geography.

Your study Bible probably has a map that shows that while the landmass of Israel was (and still is) small, its location on the east side of the Mediterranean has always been strategic. Given the surrounding deserts, anybody who wanted to trade with the nations to the west needed access to the sea and, therefore, to the land Israel claimed for its own. Here come the invaders.

In 722 B.C.E. Assyria moved in and took the north part of the country. Then in 586 Jerusalem was sacked by the Babylonian Empire, the Temple was destroyed, and the people were taken into captivity. A good chunk of the Bible was written during this "Babylonian Captivity" or "Exile" as people reflected on what had happened to them and tried to make sense of it all. Fifty years later, under the leadership of Ezra and Nehemiah (who both have books of the Bible named for them), the Israelites were allowed to return and rebuild. The scrolls that became the Hebrew Bible were finished and solidified by Ezra during this time.

But Israel's location and strategic importance had not changed. As the power of Babylon faded, the power of Greece rose and the power of Greek culture made itself felt far and wide. Alexander wasn't called "the Great" for nothing, and his conquests around 330 B.C.E. ensured that both Greek culture and Greek language flourished wherever he went. In Israel, Hebrew began to be heard less and less and Greek flowed from Israelite lips more and more.

The Septuagint or LXX

Now religious leaders had a problem. People were less and less able to understand their own sacred texts, which were written primarily in Hebrew. This was especially true for Jews living outside of Palestine, where the Greek language reigned supreme. To address this need, some seventy or so scholars began work on a Greek translation of the Hebrew Bible in Alexandria sometime during the third century B.C.E. They produced the Septuagint.

The popularity—and the scope—of the Septuagint grew, however, and by 132 B.C.E. it included some additional writings that were not in the collection brought together by Ezra. These "extra" books were newer, Jewish writings from the Second Temple period (530 B.C.E. to 70 C.E.). These writings were of interest to Jews, but were not accepted as part of the canon of the Hebrew Bible. Because they were not in the Hebrew Bible, but only in the Septuagint, they became known as "hidden" books and in Greek that translates to "**apocrypha**." What to do with them? Christians had been using them as sacred texts from the beginning due to their inclusion in the Septuagint.

Many early Christian communities disputed the Jewish conclusion that these books were not to be considered part of the canon and continued to see and use the Apocrypha as part of Scripture. And why wouldn't they? They themselves were circulating "new" sacred texts. They had letters from Peter and Paul, all sorts of stories of the life of Jesus, and their own early history that provided nourishment for their souls and guidance for their lives.

> **Septuagint**
>
> The Greek translation of the Hebrew Scriptures. The translation was named the *Septuagint* (pronounced sep-TOO-a-jint), which means seventy in Greek, representing the approximate number of scholars who worked on the translation. Tradition has it that each of these scholars worked independently and that each one produced the exact same translation, thus confirming God's hand in the work and the reliability of the translation. Thus it is also often referred to with the Roman numerals for seventy, LXX.

A Solution

By 70 C.E. there was a new world super-power, Rome, and its official language, Latin. Eventually a Latin Bible translation was needed, and in the fourth and fifth centuries C.E., a Christian priest named Jerome provided it. His translation was known as the Vulgate (from the Latin for "language of the people") and included New Testament texts as well.

Jerome was later canonized for his efforts. Jerome did his Old Testament translation from the Hebrew Bible and not the Septuagint, so he had a decision to make. What to do with these "extra" books known as the Apocrypha?

Jerome took a middle road. He did not believe they should be considered part of the Bible, per se, but he did believe they were valuable. Other Christian leaders of the time thought they should be part of the Bible without reservation. So, he compromised. He included them in the Vulgate, but he separated them out in their own section. And so the Apocrypha sat in the Bibles of the church for the next thousand years, accepted by many as divinely inspired and questioned by others.

Those Pesky Protestants

When the Protestant reformers came along in the sixteenth century, however, the debate over these books was reignited. Believing the Hebrew

> ### In a **Nutshell**
>
> **Apocrypha**: (capital A) The word Protestants use for the contested books and stories of the Septuagint.
>
> **Deuterocanonical**: The word Catholic and Orthodox traditions use for the contested books and stories of the Septuagint.
>
> **Pseudepigrapha**: The word all Christian traditions use for ancient books about biblical people and events that are not formally accepted into the canon of any Christian tradition.
>
> **apocryphal**: (small a) A word that is interchangeable with pseudepigraphic.
>
> **Confused**: How most people who read these definitions feel.

Bible to be closer to the "original" than the Septuagint, the Protestants joined the Jews in refusing the authority of the contested books. Martin Luther kept them out of his German translation and eventually most Protestant translations took the Apocrypha out as well. Catholic and Orthodox churches, however, kept them (with a few small differences between the two traditions), and that is still the general rule. Roman Catholic and Orthodox churches refer to these books as **Deuterocanonical**, meaning "second canon." The original 1611 version of the King James included the Apocrypha, although it is difficult to find a later version of the KJV that has retained it.

In the late twentieth century there came to be more interest in the Apocrypha in Protestant circles. After all, the Septuagint was in broad use among Jews in first-century Palestine, so both Jesus and Paul would have known those stories and perhaps considered them sacred. Now you can find some Protestant translations that include the Apocrypha—as Jerome included it—in a separate section.

The Apocrypha includes some great stories, some additions to the books of Daniel and Esther, letters, prayers, and large swaths of history that give the reader a sense of what was happening in Israel during the two hundred years prior to the birth of Jesus. They are definitely worth reading. Did God inspire them? You'll have to decide that for yourself.

Still Other Writings: Pseudepigrapha

One last note. The books of the Apocrypha are not the only books that have been debated. There are other writings from both the Old Testament and New Testament periods that different sects, individuals, and traditions have claimed belong in the body of the Bible. In an uninspired moment, someone decided that these books should be dubbed "apocryphal," making an issue that was already confusing even more so.

Then, in an act of lexicographal one-upmanship, such additional books are sometimes also called pseudepigraphic or even the Pseudepigrapha (which means "false writing" in Greek). Pull that out at a party when you're eager to lose your current conversation partner.

The thing to remember is that the books and passages actually printed in some Bibles today comprise the Apocrypha (capital A). You will never find books that are simply "apocryphal" printed in the same bound volume as the rest of the Bible. But you will certainly find them printed separately and available online.

You can find them in collections with titles like <u>The Gnostic Gospels</u>, <u>The Other Bible</u>, and <u>The Nag Hammadi Scriptures</u>, or by their individual names. The Gospel of Thomas, the Gospel of Mary, Paul and Thecla, the Apocalypse of Peter, and the Shepherd of Hermas are all examples of writing in this category.

To declare such works "apocryphal" (small a) or "pseudepigraphic" is not to say that there is no truth in them. A number of them have considerable overlap with stories in the canonical books of the Bible. It is simply to say that no official Christian bodies have been convinced that they should be declared authoritative.

> **Read the book of Susanna.** If you have the Apocrypha in a separate section of your Bible (Protestant), you can find it there. If the Apocrypha is integrated into the text (Roman Catholic or Orthodox), this story is the thirteenth chapter of Daniel. If your Bible does not contain the Apocrypha at all, do an online search for "Susanna apocrypha." You can read the text there—it's only one chapter. If you were deciding, would you include that story in the Bible? Why or why not?

Please return this evaluation to:
*Massachusetts Bible Society, 199 Herrick Rd.,
Newton Centre, MA 02459
or e-mail to dsadmin@massbible.org.*

Student Evaluation

❗ Course (circle one):   I   II   III

Why did you take this course? Were your expectations met?

Did you do this study with a group or on your own?   ☐ Group   ☐ Alone

❗ Did you take this course for certification or CEUs?   ☐ Yes   ☐ No
If yes, please be sure that all of your written work is submitted to the Massachusetts Bible Society by either yourself or your group leader at the conclusion of the course.

Did your group have a mix of "Extra Mile" and informal students?   ☐ Yes   ☐ No

If "yes," did you find the mix helpful?   ☐ Yes   ☐ No

Why or why not?

Student Evaluation

Who was your group leader? _____

Scale: 1 - most negative, 10 - most positive

Please rate your leader on the following using a scale of 1-10.

- _____ Creating a welcoming and inclusive environment
- _____ Keeping the class sessions on track
- _____ Beginning and ending on time
- _____ Handling conflicting opinions with respect
- _____ Being prepared for class sessions

Scale: 1 - most negative, 10 - most positive

Please rate the physical setting for your group on the following using a scale of 1-10.

- _____ The space was free of distractions and interruptions
- _____ The space was physically comfortable and conductive to learning
- _____ The group could easily adjust to different configurations
- _____ It was easy to see instructional materials and group members
- _____ Restroom facilities were easily accessible
- _____ The space was accessible to those with disabilities

Do you have a particular faith tradition or spiritual orientation? If so, how would you name it?

```
┌─────────────────────────────────────────────────────────────────┐
│                                                                 │
│                                                                 │
└─────────────────────────────────────────────────────────────────┘
```

Did you feel that your opinions and perspective were respected in the following areas:

Course materials?   ☐ Yes   ☐ No
Class discussions?   ☐ Yes   ☐ No
By the group leader?   ☐ Yes   ☐ No

Student Evaluation

If you were an "informal student" (i.e., not a student seeking certification or CEUs), how much of the homework and reading did you complete? Please describe on a scale of 1-10, with 1 being virtually none and 10 being all of it. _____

Did you do any of the Extra Mile assignments?   ☐ Yes   ☐ No

Scale: 1 - most negative, 10 - most positive

Please rate the quality of the homework assignments using a scale of 1-10.

_____   It was easy to understand the assignment

_____   The work could reasonably be completed between sessions

_____   I learned important things from doing the homework

_____   I did not feel pushed to come to a particular conclusion

Please answer the following questions:

Did you visit the Exploring the Bible Facebook page or follow us on Twitter @ExploreBible? Do you find these tools useful in staying connected to the Exploring the Bible community? Are there other ways you would prefer to be connected? If you would like to be on the Exploring the Bible e-mail list, please include your e-mail address in the space below.

Did this study answer any questions you had at the beginning? What were some of the most important questions that were answered for you?

Student Evaluation

Did anything disappoint you in this study? Was there something you expected that was not provided? Questions you really wanted answered that were not?

What new questions do you have upon completion that you did not have at the beginning? Do you find those new questions exciting or frustrating?

Did you learn anything of interest to you from this study? If you studied with a group, indicate how much of that came from the material provided and how much from the group discussion.

Have your impressions/beliefs/thoughts about the Bible changed as a result of this study? In what way?

Student Evaluation

Would you recommend this study to a friend?

How would you rate this study using a scale of 1-10, with 1 being not at all helpful and 10 being exceptionally helpful.

Other thoughts, comments, or suggestions?

Please return this evaluation to:
Massachusetts Bible Society, 199 Herrick Rd.,
Newton Centre, MA 02459
or e-mail to dsadmin@massbible.org.

Appendix 3

Massachusetts Bible Society Statement on Scripture

The Massachusetts Bible Society is an ecumenical, Christian organization with a broad diversity of Scriptural approaches and interpretations among its members and supporters. The following statement on the nature of Scripture represents the guiding principle for our selection of programming and resources, but agreement with it is neither a pre-requisite for membership nor a litmus test for grant recipients.

> The Bible was written by many authors, all inspired by God. It is neither a simple collection of books written by human authors, nor is it the literal words of God dictated to human scribes. It is a source of religious truth, presented in a diversity of styles, genres, and languages and is not meant to serve as fact in science, history, or social structure.
>
> The Bible has authority for communities of faith who take time to study and prayerfully interpret its message, but it is also important for anyone who wants more fully to understand culture, religious thought, and the world in which we live.
>
> Biblical texts have been interpreted in diverse ways from generation to generation and are always filtered through the lens of the reader's faith and life experiences. This breadth and plurality, however, are what keep the Bible alive through the ages and enhance its ongoing, transformative power.

Appendix 4

A Covenant for Bible Study

We covenant together to deal with our differences in a spirit of mutual respect and to refrain from actions that may harm the emotional and physical well-being of others.

The following principles will guide our actions:

- We will treat others whose views may differ from our own with the same courtesy we would want to receive ourselves.
- We will listen with a sincere desire to understand the point of view being expressed by another person, especially if it is different from our own.
- We will respect each other's ideas, feelings, and experiences.
- We will refrain from blaming or judging in our attitude and behavior towards others.
- We will communicate directly with any person with whom we may disagree in a respectful and constructive way.
- We will seek feedback to ensure that we have truly understood each other in our communications.

Additional agreements for our particular group:

Appendix 5

Help! I Have Questions!

- If the question is specific to a particular Bible passage, look in the notes associated with that passage in your study Bible. Are there notes that address the question? Does someone else in your group have a different study Bible? Does it have any helpful notes?

- Google is your friend. It is quite likely that if you type your question into an Internet search engine verbatim, you will come up with more "answers" than you thought possible. Ditto for just putting in a Bible verse reference. These results, however, are unfiltered and will range from well-informed responses to the conclusions of the truly unbalanced or the simply ignorant. It is sometimes difficult to tell the difference if you don't have a biblical education yourself, so approach this option with caution. It will, however, give you a sense of the range of ideas out there.

- Submit the question to the Ask-a-Prof service of the Massachusetts Bible Society. This is a free service that takes your question to thirty-five professors from seminaries and universities across the US and the UK. Participating professors come from a variety of denominations and faith traditions and represent both liberal and conservative viewpoints. You can read more about them and ask your question at massbible.org/ask-a-prof.

- Register and use the Exploring the Bible Community forums on our website to discuss your questions with students in other groups and the Massachusetts Bible Society staff. You can find them at biblit.massbible.org.

- Ask your facilitator or a religious leader you trust for help.

- Remember that not all questions have "answers" per se. Sometimes a variety of opinions will be the best you can do.

Appendix 6

Dealing with Difficult Texts

Most people find at least some passages in the Bible problematic. A particular section might strike us as too violent, too naïve, too impractical, or incompatible with our understanding of the nature of God or the world.

There will not always be a way to resolve those issues, but looking at the passage in light of the following questions can sometimes help us at least to put the issue to one side and continue our study.

- What exactly do I have an issue with in this particular text?
- Does the larger context of the passage shed any light on the issue?
- Am I assuming an interpretation that isn't actually there?
- Does the Bible itself give an interpretation of the text in question?
- If I learned that this was a fable instead of a factual account, would that make a difference?
- Could my problem be lessened if there were mitigating historical circumstances?
- Is it possible that the biases/perception of the human author of the passage are coming through?
- Am I imposing a twenty-first-century, Western worldview on an ancient Middle Eastern culture?
- Is the text trying to make a point about human nature rather than something about God?
- Are there other portions of the Bible that present a different view?
- Does my issue reflect an underlying theological question about the nature of God, Jesus, or the Bible itself?
- What truths besides factual truths might this story/passage teach?
- Is there an experience or relationship from my own life that colors how I look at this passage?

Appendix 7

Glossary

A.D.
Abbreviation for the Latin *Anno Domini*, meaning "in the year of the Lord." A system of notating time, generally used with B.C.

Antichrist
With a small "a" it is one who denies or opposes Christ. With a capital "A" it refers to a great antagonist expected to fill the world with wickedness but to be conquered forever by Christ at his second coming.

Apocalypse (adj. apocalyptic)
One of the Jewish and Christian writings of 200 B.C.E. to 150 C.E. marked by pseudonymity, symbolic imagery, and the expectation of an imminent cosmic cataclysm in which God destroys the ruling powers of evil and raises the righteous to life in a messianic kingdom.

Apocrypha
Books included in the Septuagint and Vulgate but excluded from the Hebrew Scriptures and Protestant books of the Old Testament.

Ark
Something that affords protection and safety. Two different forms of this are prominent in the Bible. One is a boat—Noah's Ark—and the other is a sacred box—the Ark of the Covenant.

Babylonian Captivity (or Exile)
The period in Jewish history during which the Jews of the ancient Kingdom of Judah were captives in Babylon—conventionally 586–538 B.C.E. although some claim a date of 596 B.C.E.

B.C.
Abbreviation for "Before Christ." A system of notating time, generally used with A.D.

B.C.E.
Abbreviation for "Before the Christian Era" or "Before the Common Era." An academic and faith-neutral notation of time. Generally used with C.E.

Canon
An authoritative list of books accepted as Holy Scripture. The word is from the Latin meaning "rule" or "standard."

Catholic
With a small "c," the word means "universal." It is used this way in the Apostles' Creed. With a capital "C" the word denotes the Roman Catholic Church.

C.E.
Abbreviation for "Christian Era" or "Common Era." An academic and faith-neutral notation of time. Generally used with B.C.E.

Codex
A manuscript book especially of Scripture, classics, or ancient annals. A codex is bound like we are used to in a modern book instead of the more common scroll.

Codex Sinaiticus
A fourth-century, hand-written copy of the Greek Bible.

Concordance
An alphabetical index of all the words in a text or corpus of texts, showing every contextual occurrence of a word.

Conquest
The period of Jewish history described in the biblical book of Joshua. Many scholars believe the settlement of the Hebrews in Canaan took place over a much longer period of time and with less bloodshed than is depicted in Joshua. They would say that there was no actual "conquest" at all.

Covenant
A formal, solemn, and binding agreement.

Creationism
The doctrine or theory holding that matter, the various forms of life, and the world were created by God out of nothing in a way determined by a literal reading of Genesis.

Deuterocanonical
Of, relating to, or constituting the books of Scripture contained in the Septuagint but not in the Hebrew canon. Primarily Roman Catholic and Orthodox usage for the texts known to Jews and Protestants as the Apocrypha.

Diaspora
A scattered population originating from a single area. In this course the word refers specifically to Jews living outside of Israel.

Dispensationalism
A system of Christian belief, formalized in the nineteenth century, that divides human history into seven distinct ages or dispensations.

Evangelical
When used with a capital "E," this refers to those in Christian traditions that emphasize a high view of biblical authority, the need for personal relationship with God achieved through a conversion experience (being "born again"), and an emphasis on sharing the gospel that Jesus' death and resurrection save us from our sins. The tradition generally deemphasizes ritual and prioritizes personal experience.

Gilgamesh
A Sumerian king and hero of the *Epic of Gilgamesh*, which contains a story of a great flood during which a man is saved in a boat.

Hapax Legomenon (pl. Hapax Legomena)
A word or form of speech occurring only once in a document or body of work.

Hasmonean Dynasty
Those who ruled Judea in the late second century B.C.E. This represented a brief period of independence between the occupying forces of Greece and Rome and is described in the books of the Maccabees.

Hyksos
Of or relating to a Semitic dynasty that ruled Egypt from about the eighteenth to the sixteenth centuries B.C.E.

Inerrancy
Exemption from error. Infallibility.

Jerome
(ca. 347 C.E.–30 September 420 C.E.) A Roman Christian priest, confessor, theologian, and historian, and who became a Doctor of the Church. Best known for his translation of the Bible into Latin (the Vulgate). Recognized by the Roman Catholic and Eastern Orthodox churches as a saint.

LXX
See *Septuagint*.

Mainline
Certain Protestant churches in the United States that comprised a majority of Americans from the colonial era until the early twentieth century. The group is contrasted with evangelical and fundamentalist groups. They include Congregationalists, Episcopalians, Methodists, northern Baptists, most Lutherans, and most Presbyterians, as well as some smaller denominations.

Marcion (of Sinope)
(ca. 85–160 C.E.) An early Christian bishop who believed the God of the Hebrew Scriptures to be inferior or subjugated to the God of the New Testament and developed his own canon of Scripture accordingly. He was excommunicated for his belief.

Masoretes
Groups of Jewish scribes working between the seventh and eleventh centuries C.E. They added vowel notations to the Hebrew Scriptures.

Mordecai Nathan (Rabbi)
Philosopher rabbi of the fifteenth century C.E. who wrote the first concordance to the Hebrew Bible and added numbered verse notations to the Hebrew Bible for the first time.

Orthodox
With a capital "O" referring to the Eastern Orthodox Church (and its various geographic subdivisions), the Oriental Orthodox churches (and their subdivisions), and any Western Rite Orthodox congregations allied with the above.

Ossuary
A depository, most commonly a box, for the bones (as opposed to the entire corpse) of the dead.

Pharisee
A member of a segment of Judaism of the inter-testamental period noted for strict observance of rites and ceremonies of the written law and for insistence on the validity of their own oral traditions concerning the law.

Pentateuch
The first five books of the Bible: Genesis, Exodus, Leviticus, Numbers, and Deuteronomy.

Protestant
Used here in the broadest sense of any Christian not of a Catholic or Orthodox church.

Pseudepigrapha
In biblical studies, the Pseudepigrapha are Jewish religious works written ca. 200 B.C.E.–200 C.E., which are not part of the canon of any established Jewish or Christian tradition.

Rapture
The term "rapture" is used in at least two senses in modern traditions of Christian theology: in pre-tribulationist views, in which a group of people will be "left behind" and as a synonym for the final resurrection generally.

Robert Stephanus
Protestant book printer living in France in the sixteenth century who divided the chapters of the New Testament into the verses we have today.

Septuagint or LXX
An ancient Greek translation of the Hebrew Scriptures. Translation began in the third century B.C.E. with the Pentateuch and continued for several centuries.

Stephen Langton
Theology professor in Paris and archbishop of Canterbury in the thirteenth century who first added chapter divisions to the Bible.

Supersessionism
The idea that God's covenant with Christians supersedes and therefore displaces God's covenant with Israel.

Synoptic Gospels
From the Greek meaning to "see alike," the Synoptics are Matthew, Mark, and Luke.

Testament
With a capital "T" it means either of the two main divisions of the Bible: the Old Testament or the New Testament. With a small "t" the word simply means a covenant or agreement that is formalized in writing and witnessed.

Tetragrammaton
The four consonants in Exodus 3:14 (YHWH) that comprise God's name.

Vulgate
The late fourth-century Latin translation of the Bible done by St. Jerome.